THE COMPLETE BOOK
OF BOWHUNTING

The Complete Book of
BOWHUNTING

CHUCK ADAMS

Photography by the Author
Illustrations and Charts by Martha N. Nelson

WINCHESTER PRESS

Copyright © 1978 by Chuck Adams

Library of Congress Cataloging in Publication Data

Adams, Chuck.
The complete book of bowhunting.
Includes index.
1. Hunting with bow and arrow. I. Title.
SK36.A3   799.2'0285   78-6582
ISBN 0-87691-271-4

Published by Winchester Press
205 East 42nd Street
New York, N.Y. 10017

Winchester is a Trademark of Olin Corporation used by
Winchester Press, Inc. under authority and control of
the Trademark Proprietor.

Printed in the United States of America

9 8 7 6 5 4 3 2 1

To Annie Wolfe

CONTENTS

FOREWORD

I love to hunt and make no apology for it. My drive to stalk and kill game is every bit as natural as my drive to eat, a basic instinct bred into me by my hunting forefathers. In the dim, distant past, men who did not kill did not eat. The ones who survived and reproduced were vigorous hunters who passed this biological trait from one generation to the next.

I am the end product, an efficient machine programmed to hunt. My eyes are set in the front of my head to help me judge distance and help me hit where I aim. My hands are nimble so I can make and use a variety of hunting tools. My teeth, bones, muscles, and vital parts are designed to grind up, digest, and utilize the flesh of fish, birds, and animals. My pulse quickens as I move in for the kill, and adrenaline floods my body to sharpen my senses and reflexes. Like the wolf, I am a natural predator—a killer and eater of meat.

Before the filthy fingers of progress raped the land and castrated outdoorsmen by planting them in cities, hunting was a widespread and honorable lifestyle. Today, most men are out of touch with nature, living and dying in artificial worlds of concrete, steel, and plastic. Most still satisfy their hunger for meat by hiring professional butchers to raise and slaughter dumb domestic slave animals like sheep and cattle. But most no longer hunt. Their only contact with "wild" creatures consists of gazing at pitifully penned zoo animals on Sunday afternoons.

The dedicated hunter is a much luckier fellow. He starts with the biological instinct to hunt and nothing more. He learns the basics of woodsmanship and shooting from his father, friends, or magazines and books. He sharpens his skills through hours of enjoyable practice like a young bobcat chasing mice. If his instinct and determination are strong enough, he perfects his ability to hunt. In the process of learning his art, he develops an intimate knowledge of wildlife and a realistic view of his own limitations and abilities. His raw urge to hunt and kill turns to deep and abiding respect for wild things in general, respect which comes from being an active part of nature—not an outsider looking in.

Most active sportsmen learn to hunt with firearms first and graduate to bowhunting later on. Some go bowhunting to increase the challenge of bagging game. Some go bowhunting to take advantage of extra-long archery seasons offered by many states. Some go bowhunting to scout likely hunting areas for later gun seasons. But all go bowhunting because they appreciate the out-of-doors and the creatures which live there.

I enjoy all kinds of hunting, but bowhunting is my first love. I eat, drink, and sleep this wonderful sport. It has taught me more about the woods, more about wild animals, and more about myself than everything else combined. It is the cream of the hunting sports, demanding more knowledge, more skill, and more patience than any other. If this book helps you enjoy bowhunting half as much as I do, I'll be completely satisfied.

Chuck Adams

Part I—BASIC BOWHUNTING EQUIPMENT

Chapter 1—THE HUNTING BOW

Most experienced bowhunters remember the first bow they ever shot, but quite a few wish they could forget. Far too many would-be bowhunters select the wrong hunting bow, thus putting two strikes against them before they ever begin this satisfying sport. If your hunting bow doesn't match your physical build and the game you intend to hunt, you'll very likely wind up with sore muscles, bruised fingers, and an empty larder at the end of the season. There's no substitute for the right hunting equipment, and this is especially true with hunting bows.

I remember my first hunting bow—and it's a very painful memory. The sleek, well-finished recurve looked great in the discount-store window, and the price was right. At least I thought so as I shelled out $39.50 and wrapped my fist around the polished hardwood handle. I already had some ancient wooden arrows leaning in the closet and a moth-eaten finger glove someone had given me at a garage sale. That afternoon I stood in front of a pie plate tacked to a bale of alfalfa hay, ready for action.

The string on the 55-pounder came back easily for a few inches, and then my fingers stopped dead. I bit my lower lip, groaned, and really leaned into the bowstring. It came shuddering back to my face begrudgingly, and my whole body began quivering like a catfish gobbling a worm. I quickly pointed the bow in the general direction of the target, the bow twanged like a loose guitar string, and I yelped in pain as the bowstring sliced a neat furrow in my left forearm. I was also vaguely aware of a stabbing throb in my left palm and a biting numbness in my right fingers. I never did find the arrow.

Archery pro shops offer several advantages to beginners and experts alike. First, they stock an extremely wide selection of hunting bows and other gear. Second, their qualified sales help can make sensible equipment recommendations. And third, they normally have shooting range facilities to let a bowhunter try several bows before buying one.

I bought my second bow a week later after getting some advice from a member of the local archery club. I fell in love with that bow and hunted with it for over a decade, completely satisfied with its smooth, easy draw, quiet release, and total lack of handle recoil. Last time I checked, the hard-drawing, noisy mule I tried out first was still collecting dust in the basement.

Good hunting bows are available in a variety of places, but the rank beginner is best off going to one of the 8,000-plus archery pro shops across this country. These specialty stores offer a wide selection of hunting bows to suit every bowhunter's physical build and specialized needs. Most archery shops also provide shooting-range facilities so a customer can try out several bows on the spot to see which one he likes best. If a particular model doesn't fit his hand, feels uncomfortable as he draws the bowstring, or rattles like a cement mixer when he shoots, the buyer can set it aside before he plunks down his hard-earned money.

A neophyte can enter an archery store and leave with the proper bow, provided he knows what kind of game he wants to hunt. However, a beginner is best off learning a few things about selecting a bow before he shops around. If he learns enough, he can even buy a bow from a discount house, department store, general sporting-goods store, or private party without getting rooked. Good, reliable hunting bows are sold over the counter in many places, but the salesmen are sometimes less than expert on bowhunting gear, and sometimes recommend bows completely wrong for their customers.

RIGHT-HAND AND LEFT-HAND BOWS

The very first thing any bow buyer must determine is whether he should shoot a right-hand or a left-hand bow. Right-handed people usually shoot right-hand bows the best, but this is not always the case. The key to determining whether you need a right-hand or left-hand bow is your master, or dominant, eye. Almost everybody has one eye which is strongly dominant over the other, and this dominant eye is the eye a person subconsciously uses to aim with. The majority of right-handed people have right master eyes; as to left-handed people, the majority have left master eyes. However, quite a few right-handed people have left master eyes, and quite a few left-handed people have right master eyes. A person whose master eye is on the same side of his body as his dominant hand has very little aiming trouble, but a person with his master eye on one side and his dominant hand on the other must learn to use a bow that is held in his weaker, less coordinated hand. For instance, a right-handed man with a left master eye must learn to shoot a left-hand bow, even if a right-hand bow feels more natural at first.

If he mistakenly buys a right-hand bow he'll have all kinds of aiming problems because he'll be constantly crossfiring—trying to aim with his left eye, which is not directly behind the bowstring and the arrow. The farther away a target is, the farther to one side or the other a crossfiring person hits. It is virtually impossible to cure crossfiring problems without switching from a right-hand bow to a left-hand bow, or vice versa. A bowhunter's master eye should always be on the same side as the hand he pulls the bowstring with. This aligns his master eye directly behind the bowstring and the arrow, which leads to good accuracy.

A beginning bowhunter can eliminate the chance of crossfiring trouble by simply determining which eye is his master eye

A quick and easy method of checking your master eye is looking through a small hole formed by both hands, leaving both eyes open. Your dominant eye will automatically line up with the hole.

before he buys a bow. To determine your master eye, spread both your hands and then overlap them to form a small hole with the webs between your thumbs and forefingers. Pick out any small object (a doorknob, leaf on a tree, far-off car, etc.), stretch your arms straight out in front of you, and center this small object in the hole formed by your hands, *leaving both your eyes open*. Carefully close one eye, reopen it, and then close the other eye. Only one of your eyes will be viewing the object through the hole in your hands. This eye is your master eye. If you have a right master eye, buy a right-hand bow; if you have a left master eye, buy a left-hand bow.

RECURVE BOWS

There are two basic bow designs available these days—recurve bows and compound bows. Each design has certain advantages and certain disadvantages, and each has its fans.

Recurve bows are simple-looking tools made of solid fiberglass or fiberglass and wood. They all consist of a fairly short handle riser with long, curving limbs on either end, and all tend to look alike to a beginner. However, some are longer than others, some are heavier than others, some dismantle into two or three pieces for easy transport and storage, and some have laminated limbs. The only recurve bows a serious bowhunter should consider buying are those with laminated fiberglass-and-wood limbs. These shoot arrows much faster than solid bows, and tend to be a lot more accurate, too. A laminated-bow limb snaps back to its original position quicker than a solid limb, and does so more consistently.

Most recurve hunting bows measure somewhere between 50 and 64 inches from limb tip to limb tip when they're strung. The longer bows tend to shoot an arrow faster than the shorter bows, and also to pinch a bowhunter's bowstring fingers less. Longer bows are also smoother to draw because the limbs are longer and can bend more without running out of flex. Recurve bows shorter than 55 inches long are convenient to carry around, but most good bowmen prefer recurves at least 58 inches long. These bows are more accurate and more comfortable to shoot, especially for bowhunters with long arms.

The draw weight of a recurve bow is the amount of pressure the bowstring exerts on a bowhunter's fingers when he draws an arrow to full draw (all the way back). All recurve bows are marked with a 28-inch draw weight because the average bowhunter in days gone by shot a 28-inch-long hunting arrow. Modern bowhunters tend to be bigger and longer-armed than they were when bowhunting started becoming popular thirty or forty years ago, so the average arrow drawn today is probably closer

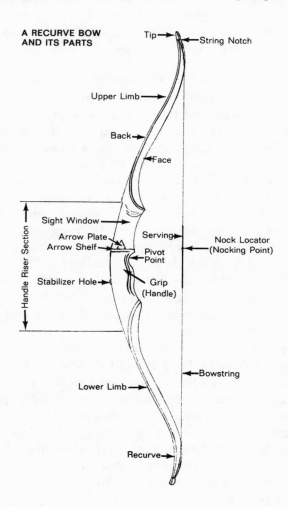

A RECURVE BOW
AND ITS PARTS

Tip → / String Notch

Upper Limb →

Back →

← Face

Sight Window →

Arrow Plate

Arrow Shelf →

Serving →

Nock Locator
(Nocking Point)

Pivot
Point

Stabilizer Hole →

Grip
(Handle)

Handle Riser Section

Bowstring

Lower Limb →

Recurve →

HOW TO MEASURE DRAW LENGTH
AND HUNTING ARROW LENGTH

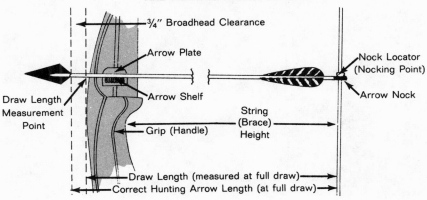

to 29 inches. However, the old 28-inch standard still determines what draw weights are marked on recurve bows.

After a bow buyer decides whether he needs a right-hand or left-hand recurve bow, he should determine his own personal draw length. A small woman might draw a 25-inch arrow; a big man might draw an arrow over 30 inches long. How long an arrow a person draws is determined by several things, but mainly by the length of his arms.

There are three standard ways you can determine your draw length. The most logical is to pick up a bow, nock an extra-long arrow, and draw it back to your anchor point (where you hold your bowstring hand just before you shoot). A friend with a lead pencil can mark the place on the arrow where the fully drawn arrow shaft and the front of the bow meet, and then you can measure the distance from the bottom of the nock slot (string groove) of the arrow to the pencil mark on the arrow shaft. This distance will be your approximate draw length.

However, a beginner usually knows very little about shooting a bow and almost never knows where his anchor point should be. Besides, his muscles are bound to be soft and he'll usually draw back shorter than he will after he gains experience and builds up his bow-shooting muscles. For these reasons, two other methods of determining draw length are far more practical

The yardstick-on-the-chest method of measuring draw length is quite reliable and requires no expertise with a bow and arrow . . . which makes it a dandy method for beginners.

and far more accurate. One is to place the end of a yardstick on the center of your chest and stretch the fingertips of both your hands as far out on the yardstick as possible. The distance from your chest to your fingertips will be very close to your draw length. Another reliable gauge of draw length is to stand facing at 90 degrees to a wall with the knuckles of your left fist (if you shoot a right-hand bow) against the wall. Swivel your head so you're looking at your fist and have a friend measure the distance from where the wall touches your knuckles to the right corner of your mouth (left corner for left-hand shooters). This distance will also be your draw length.

Once you know your draw length, you can determine the draw weight of any recurve bow at your particular draw length. If you luck out and have a draw length exactly 28 inches long, the draw weight marked on a recurve bow will be the bowstring weight you'll actually hold when you shoot that bow. If your draw length is longer or shorter than 28 inches, you can still determine how many pounds of pressure you'll be holding with your fingers when you shoot your bow. Simply add 3 pounds of pressure to the marked draw weight on the bow for every inch you draw over 28 inches, or subtract 3 pounds of pressure for

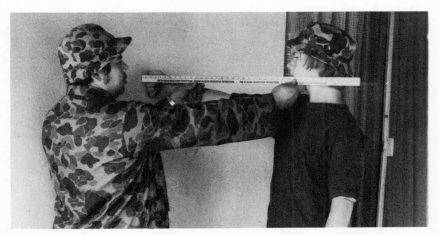

The knuckles-on-the-wall method of measuring draw length only takes a second if you have a friend to help you out. It duplicates the body position a person assumes when shooting a bow . . . without the muscle strain of holding back the bowstring.

every inch you draw under 28 inches. For example, if your draw length is 30 inches, you'll hold 6 pounds more than the draw weight marked on a bow. If your draw length is 25 inches, you'll hold 9 pounds less than the draw weight marked on a bow. A bow marked 50 pounds at 28 inches will be a 41-pound bow for a person who draws a 25-inch arrow, and a 56-pound bow for a person who draws a 30-inch arrow.

All this sounds complicated, but it's very important. Once you determine your draw length, you can select a recurve bow of the proper draw weight to match your physical strength and the kind of game you intend to hunt. A bowhunter should shoot a bow with the heaviest draw weight he can shoot comfortably and accurately. Almost any medium-sized man can shoot a 50-pound recurve bow accurately, and with regular practice the same man can pull a bow 5 to 10 pounds heavier. In contrast, a small woman may be able to handle only a 40-pound hunting bow. For recommended recurve draw weights, see the chart on the following page.

The heavier the draw weight of a hunting bow, the faster it shoots an arrow and the better it kills game. The size of an

RECOMMENDED RECURVE HUNTING BOW DRAW WEIGHTS

		Young Teenagers	Adult Women	Adult Men
AMOUNT OF PRACTICE	To Begin With	30-35	35-40	40-50
	With Regular Practice	35-40	40-45	50-55
	With Lots of Regular Practice	40-45	45-55	55-70

animal partially determines how heavy a bow should be used on that animal—a moose weighs eight to ten times as much as a whitetail deer and requires deeper arrow penetration for a quick, humane kill. A bowhunter who intends to hunt deer will get by very nicely with a 45- to 55-pound recurve bow, but for elk and moose he'll need heavier gear (see chart). The hunter who goes after moose and other big animals will have to practice hard for two or three months with a heavy-draw recurve bow to accustom his muscles and fingers to the extra draw weight required. Anybody can shoot a bow with a heavier draw weight than is normally recommended if he has the gumption to build up his muscles.

Another thing to consider when buying a recurve bow is its physical weight. Recurve bows vary a lot in weight, depending on how long they are and what materials their handle risers are made of. A bow with a massive Formica or metal handle riser will weigh considerably more than a bow with a streamlined rosewood handle riser. Some bowhunters prefer to shoot the lightest bows they can find because these are the easiest to lug around the woods. Others like heavy bows because they shoot a little smoother, kick back a little less when an arrow is released, and make steady aiming simpler. A lightweight hunting bow is easier to carry in the field, and a heavyweight hunting bow is usually easier to shoot accurately because it has more mass. Most bowmen compromise with a medium-weight bow that has other options they need.

Different recurve bows offer different options. Some take

down (dismantle) for easy transport and storage—an appealing feature for traveling bowhunters. Others have special threaded holes in their handle risers to accept accessories like bow stabilizers, bow quivers, and bowsights. After you zero in on several recurve bows you like, your final decision may very well be made on the basis of the options these various bows offer.

To sum up: When choosing the proper recurve hunting bow, you must determine your master eye, figure out your draw length, and then select a bow of the proper draw weight (at your draw length) to take the game you want to take without wrecking your muscles and destroying your accuracy. This bow should be at least 55 inches long so it shoots hard and smooth, and should have fiberglass-and-wood laminated limbs for the best accuracy and arrow speed. Chances are an archery shop has several recurve bows that fill all these requirements, and you should make your final selection based on how comfortable a bow's handle feels, how attractive it is to your eye, how quiet it is when shot, how it feels to you when shot, and what options it offers. These are all subjective determinations an archery pro can help you with. Generally speaking, however, you get what you pay for in bows, and the more expensive recurves are quieter, better-designed tools than the cheaper models.

RECOMMENDED BOW WEIGHTS FOR VARIOUS ANIMALS

DRAW WEIGHTS	Rabbits, Squirrels	Foxes, Bobcats	Deer, Black Bear	Elk, Caribou	Moose, Brown Bear
30-40	X				
40-50	X	X			
50-60	X	X	X		
60-70		X	X	X	
70-80			X	X	X

COMPOUND BOWS

Compound bows became popular in the late 1960s when several manufacturers began offering them to the public at reasonable prices. These bizarre-looking bows are available in a wide variety of designs, but they all utilize a network of cables and wheels which gives a bowhunter two major mechanical advantages over conventional recurve bows.

First, compound bows relax in draw weight when pulled all the way back to full draw. For example, one 70-pound compound bow I own puts 70 pounds of pressure on my fingers

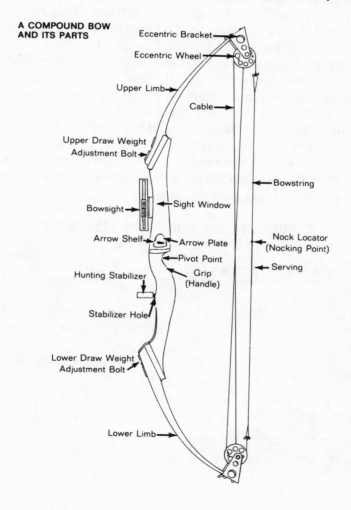

A COMPOUND BOW
AND ITS PARTS

Eccentric Bracket

Eccentric Wheel

Upper Limb

Cable

Upper Draw Weight
Adjustment Bolt

Bowstring

Bowsight — Sight Window

Arrow Shelf — Arrow Plate

Nock Locator
(Nocking Point)

Pivot Point

Serving

Hunting Stabilizer

Grip
(Handle)

Stabilizer Hole

Lower Draw Weight
Adjustment Bolt

Lower Limb

One of a compound bow's primary advantages is bowstring let-off. A bowhunter exerts the most effort at ½ to ¾ draw— this peak weight subsides as much as 50 percent when a bowhunter pulls on back to full draw.

when I draw it back halfway, but this 70-pound peak weight eases off 50 percent as I draw on back to full draw. In other words, I'm only holding 35 pounds of bowstring pressure on my fingers at full draw. This pressure relaxation, sometimes called bowstring let-off, makes a compound bow easier to shoot than a recurve bow because there's a lot less pressure on a shooter's bowstring fingers and shoulder muscles as he shoots. He can aim longer at a target or an animal without quivering from muscle strain or getting bruised fingers, which means he'll shoot more accurately.

The second advantage a compound bow offers is faster arrow flight than produced by a recurve bow. How much faster depends on many factors, but the average compound bow shoots an arrow at least 8 to 10 percent faster than the average recurve bow. I own several compound bows that shoot medium-weight hunting arrows at 210 to 220 feet per second. My fastest-shooting recurve with the same arrows shoots around 190 feet per second. The increased arrow speed delivered by a compound bow is very important to a bowhunter because it gives him better penetration on game and flatter arrow trajectory to minimize misses at unknown distances. It also helps prevent big-game animals from "jumping string"—dodging or ducking arrows.

There are many compound designs available these days, and God only knows what will appear in the years to come. However, these mechanical bows are held and shot the same as recurve bows, so the only significant differences between the two designs are the unconventional appearance of compound bows, the fact that compounds are easier to shoot accurately with a minimum of practice, and the fact that compounds shoot arrows a little faster.

Modern compound bows are every bit as reliable as recurve bows, something which could not be said a few years ago. Some of the first compounds were prone to fly apart when cables separated, limbs exploded, and handle risers broke in two. These bugs have been smoothed out over the years, and most of the compounds available now are dependable lifetime investments. The moving parts on a compound bow must be lubricated from time to time, but maintenance requirements are minimal.

Most modern bowhunters shoot compound bows because of their superior performance. Compounds vary a lot in price, but almost all shoot reasonably well. The more expensive bows are generally a little faster-shooting than the cheaper bows and offer special features like draw-weight adjustment bolts, draw-length adjustment screws, special ramps for mounting bow-sights, and other options. When you pay more for a compound bow, you're generally paying for more versatility and a little more arrow speed, not for a vastly superior hunting tool. Obviously, though, the bigger, more reputable companies have a better handle on compound technology and put out sturdier, better-shooting, more reliable products.

Every compound bow lets off or relaxes at one particular draw length, and if you try to shoot a compound bow set at the wrong draw length for you, you'll end up having all sorts of problems. With some compound-bow designs, you can't draw past the bow's preset draw length at all—you hit a solid wall of weight if you try. For instance, a long-armed man with a 30-inch draw length might not be able to draw a compound bow set for 28 inches all the way back. At 28 inches the bow would stop drawing—period. Some compound bows *can* be overdrawn, but only at the risk of breaking the bow limbs. If you decide to try out compound bows at the local archery store, be sure to use the yardstick-on-the-chest method or the knuckles-on-the-wall method before shopping around so you know your exact draw length. Otherwise, drawing some compound bows will be uncomfortable or downright impossible.

The draw weight marked on a compound bow is usually the peak weight of that bow (the pressure you feel on your bowstring fingers before the bow relaxes or lets off in draw weight at full draw). Modern compound bows let off in draw weight anywhere from 18 to 50 percent, depending upon the design and the configuration of the wheels on the bow limbs. The average compound bow lets off 30 to 50 percent, which means a bowhunter is holding substantially less weight on his bowstring fingers at full draw. As a result, bowhunters can usually shoot compound bows with peak weights 5 to 10 pounds heavier than recommended recurve-bow draw weights. A medium-sized man may only be able to shoot a 50-pound recurve bow, but he can probably shoot a 60-pound compound bow with ease. This is because he's only holding 30 or 40 pounds of pressure on his fingers after he brings his compound bow to full draw. Obviously, the more a particular compound bow lets off at full draw, the easier it is to hold back for extended periods of time. A 60-pound bow that

RECOMMENDED COMPOUND HUNTING BOW DRAW WEIGHTS

		Young Teenagers	Adult Women	Adult Men
AMOUNT OF PRACTICE	To Begin With	35-40	40-45	45-55
	With Regular Practice	40-45	45-50	55-65
	With Lots of Regular Practice	45-50	50-60	65-80

lets off 50 percent exerts only 30 pounds of pressure on your bowstring fingers as you aim; a 60-pound bow that lets off only 20 percent exerts 48 pounds on your fingers.

Generally speaking, the less a compound bow lets off in draw weight, the faster it shoots an arrow. However, many bowhunters prefer compound bows with 40 to 50 percent let-offs because these bows are so easy to hold at full draw. The best way to compare the feels of various compound bows is to try out a few at an archery store.

No matter what kind of hunting bow you decide to buy, choosing the proper bow will be fairly easy if you take it step by step. First, determine which eye is your master eye so you know whether to buy a right-hand or a left-hand bow. Second, find out what your draw length is. Third, study the draw-weight charts in this chapter to determine how much draw weight a person of your age and sex can normally shoot comfortably. Fourth, zero in on the specific draw weight you think would be best for the animals you intend to hunt, using the chart in this chapter. And fifth, look at a variety of hunting bows that fit your specifications and make your final choice based on what options a bow offers, how heavy it is to pack around the woods, how quiet it is to shoot, how comfortable its handle feels, and how much it costs. There are dozens of excellent hunting bows available today, and finding the right one should be fun and easy if you take the time to do some intelligent shopping.

Chapter 2—THE HUNTING ARROW

The arrow is the single most important part of any bowhunter's equipment. The proper arrow will fly well from a variety of bows, including some that are less than perfectly suited to a particular bowhunter. The wrong arrow won't fly worth a darn from any bow, regardless of how expensive or how finely made that bow happens to be. A bowhunter can compromise on most of his equipment if money is a problem, but he should never compromise on his arrows. An arrow must be made from top-notch materials and must be of the right stiffness, weight, and length to match a hunter's bow and his shooting style. Other-wise, it will probably miss the mark and cancel out all the other careful planning a bowhunter has done before a hunting trip.

An arrow consists of a central shaft with an arrowhead on the front end and a nock on the back. Just ahead of the nock are anywhere from three to six turkey feathers or plastic vanes, called fletching. Shafts, arrowheads, nocks, and fletching are available in a variety of sizes, shapes, materials, and weights to perform well in a variety of situations. For example, a standard big-game hunting arrow sold in an archery store usually consists of a fairly large, fairly stiff shaft made of tubular aluminum, a sharp multi-bladed arrowhead called a broadhead, a plastic snap-on nock that fits snugly on the bowstring, and three plastic, parabola-shaped fletches about 5 inches long and ½ inch high. Most experts feel that such an arrow is best suited for taking big-game animals like deer, bear, elk, and moose. In contrast, a bird-hunting arrow often has a shaft made of wood, an arrow-head made of four large piano-wire loops, a loose-fitting plastic nock, and six feather fletches 6 inches long and 1½ inches high. Different arrows are designed to do different things.

A HUNTING ARROW AND ITS PARTS

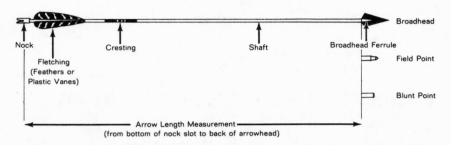

Some experienced bowhunters buy the various components of arrows separately and assemble different combinations they feel best suit their needs. However, the beginner is best off buying assembled arrows in an archery store. He'll have his hands full buying his basic gear and learning to use it; he should postpone starting from scratch with some loose arrow shafts, a bag of nocks, a box of arrowheads, a bundle of feathers, and the tools and glue needed to assemble these items into usable arrows.

A wide variety of arrows can be bought at archery stores for a wide variety of prices. This large selection often boggles a beginner's mind. Here's how to choose the right arrow for you and the bow you hunt with.

SHAFTS

Most arrow shafts are made of wood, fiberglass, or aluminum. Each shaft material has its good points and each has its bad, but they are not of equal quality—not by a long shot!

Wooden arrow shafts are generally made of straight cedar logged near Port Orford, Ore. Wood is the cheapest arrow-shaft material because it's the easiest to turn into usable shafts. Its two main advantages are cheapness and light weight. A light arrow flies fast and flat, making game easier to hit. However, wood shafts are never very uniform in straightness, stiffness (called "spine"), and weight—the three factors that determine how accurately arrows will fly. Wood shafts also break on impact with solid objects like rocks and trees, and tend to warp in wet weather. Thousands of game animals have been shot with wooden arrow shafts because these were all bowhunters had to use for decades. However, cedar shafts are not used much for serious hunting these days because there are much better shaft materials available.

Most fiberglass arrow shafts are made by wrapping glue-soaked fiberglass cloth around a straight steel mandrel. This process produces tubular shafts of solid fiberglass which are much stronger than wood, reasonably straight, and reasonably uniform in weight and stiffness. Fiberglass arrow shafts are fairly accurate, never bend, and seldom break. They are also totally waterproof. The one drawback fiberglass has as a shaft material is its excessive weight—a fiberglass arrow shaft is heavier than any other kind. This means such a shaft flies with a slow, looping trajectory, making targets and animals more difficult to hit. A heavy arrow retains its energy better than a light one, so if you do hit an animal with a fiberglass shaft, it will penetrate better than a lighter cedar shaft shot out of the same bow. Some bowhunters who hunt deer from tree stands and seldom take long shots prefer fiberglass because it penetrates so well; the looping trajectory of fiberglass doesn't handicap their hitting ability in close-range situations.

Almost three-quarters of the bowhunters in this country use tubular aluminum arrow shafts, and there are definite reasons for this. Quality aluminum shafts are extremely straight, extremely uniform in weight and stiffness, and extremely rugged and durable. Aluminum shafts sometimes bend when they hit hard objects, but can be restraightened as good as new at any archery shop for a small fee. The best aluminum shafts are amazingly uniform in diameter and wall thickness, factors which determine exactly how stiff an arrow is and how accurately it will fly compared to others of the same kind. Over the past three decades, *all* major national and international archery tournaments have been won with aluminum arrows, proof that they're the most accurate choice.

Aluminum shafts are also available in the widest variety of diameters and wall thicknesses, giving a bowhunter some flexibility to choose an arrow that flies well and has the weight

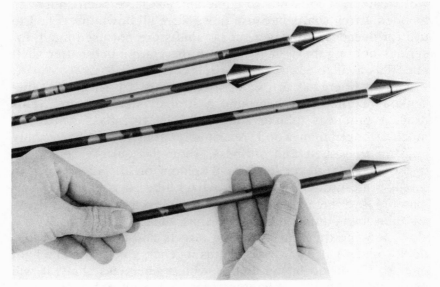

.Dull-anodized, nonglare aluminum arrow shafts are ideal for bowhunting. One company offers popular two-tone camouflage shafts which blend remarkably well with a variety of backgrounds.

characteristics he desires. Aluminum hunting shafts are now sold with camouflaged, nonglare finishes, too. The colors of popular anodized-aluminum hunting shafts vary from a bright orange to a camouflaged two-tone pattern of green or brown. All blend with the woods when viewed through the eyes of color-blind game animals, so all work very well. Aluminum arrow shafts are the most expensive shafts commonly sold in this country, but the beginning bowhunter should try to scrape up enough dough to use them, even if he has to skimp on other things.

Less frequently used arrow-shaft materials include graphite for special-purpose target shooting, solid fiberglass for bowfishing, tubular steel for bowfishing, and heavy compressed cedar for close-range big-game hunting. After you become proficient with conventional gear, you might want to experiment with some of these special-purpose shafts.

A bowhunter must match the size of his arrow shaft to his draw length and the draw weight of his bow. An arrow shaft of a particular length and spine (stiffness) flies best from a bow of a particular draw weight. Arrow-shaft manufacturers have formulated complex charts to determine which shaft size or sizes will fly the straightest from a particular bow drawn back a particular distance. Aluminum arrow shafts give a bowhunter the most versatility when choosing a shaft—there are usually two or three aluminum shafts of different weights which will all fly well from the same bow. This lets a bowhunter decide whether he wants to shoot a lightweight shaft for maximum arrow speed, a heavy shaft for maximum penetration, or a middleweight shaft which compromises between speed and penetration.

Complex arrow-shaft selection charts may be obtained from archery dealers. These help a bowhunter match his shaft to his bow and his personal hunting style.

EASTON ALUMINUM HUNTING SHAFT SELECTION CHART
(Most popular size selection is shown in the unshaded area of each box)

CORRECT HUNTING ARROW LENGTH (Your Draw Length Plus ¾ Inch Clearance)

RECURVE BOW WEIGHT (At Your Draw Length)	26½-27½ 27" Shaft Size	Arrow Weight	27½-28½ 28" Shaft Size	Arrow Weight	28½-29½ 29" Shaft Size	Arrow Weight	29½-30½ 30" Shaft Size	Arrow Weight	30½-31½ 31" Shaft Size	Arrow Weight	31½-32½ 32" Shaft Size	Arrow Weight	COMPOUND BOW PEAK WEIGHT 30% Let-off	50% Let-off
35-39	1913* 1816 1718	(415) (438) (457)	1913* 1816 1916	(422) (447) (467)	2013* 1916 1818	(451) (477) (497)	2013* 1916 1820**	(460) (487) (552)	2114 2016 1918	(493) (513) (544)	2114 2016 2018	(503) (523) (578)	41-46	47-52
40-44	2013* 1916 1818	(433) (459) (476)	2013* 1916 1918 1820**	(442) (467) (511) (529)	2013* 2016 1918 1820**	(451) (493) (522) (540)	2114 2016 1918	(483) (503) (533)	2114 2016 2018	(493) (513) (566)	2213* 2117 2018	(503) (571) (578)	47-52	53-59
45-49	2013* 2016 1918	(433) (472) (499)	2114 2016 1918	(463) (483) (511)	2114 2016 1920**	(473) (493) (559)	2114 2016 2018 1920**	(483) (503) (554) (569)	2213* 2117 2018	(493) (559) (566)	2117 2018	(571) (578)	53-58	60-66
50-54	2114 2016 1918 1920**	(453) (472) (499) (533)	2114 2016 2018	(463) (483) (530)	2213* 2117 2018 2020	(473) (535) (542) (576)	2213* 2117 2020	(483) (547) (589)	2117 2020	(559) (602)	2117 2216	(571) (575)	59-64	67-72
55-59	2114 2018 1920**	(453) (517) (533)	2117 2018 2020	(523) (530) (563)	2213* 2117 2018 2020	(473) (535) (542) (576)	2117 2216 2020	(547) (551) (589)	2117 2216	(559) (563)	2216 2219	(575) (627)	65-70	73-79
60-64	2213* 2117 2018 2020	(455) (511) (517) (550)	2117 2216 2020	(523) (527) (563)	2117 2216 2020	(535) (539) (576)	2117 2216 2219	(547) (551) (599)	2216 2219	(563) (613)	2219	(627)	71-76	80-86
65-69	2117 2020	(511) (550)	2117 2216	(523) (527)	2217 2216 2219	(535) (539) (585)	2216 2219	(551) (599)	2219	(613)	2219	(627)	77-82	87-93
70-80	2216 2020	(515) (550)	2216 2219	(527) (571)	2216 2219	(539) (585)	2219	(599)	2219	(613)			83-95	94-107

*Available in dull-anodized Autumn Orange XX75 shafts only.
**Available in dull-anodized green GAME GETTER shafts only.
†NOTE: The shaft sizes 1718 through 2219 are contractions of actual physical dimensions of the tubes. Example: 2016 has a 20/64" outside diameter and a .016" wall thickness.
††NOTE: The arrow weight in grains (437.5 grains per ounce) includes a 125-grain broadhead, 30-grain point insert, and 35 grains (average between plastic vanes and feathers) for nock and fletching.

An arrow which does not match a bow will usually wobble badly when shot from that bow, ruining accuracy and slowing the arrow down drastically. Every arrow flexes when a bowstring slams it in the rear end, causing it to bend around a bow's arrow plate and oscillate back and forth several times in front of the bow before it straightens out. This bending phenomenon is called "archer's paradox." An arrow of the proper stiffness for a particular bow straightens out almost immediately instead of continuing to wobble as it flies toward the target. It is vital that a bowhunter choose the correct arrow-shaft size for his bow—otherwise he'll reduce his chances of scoring on game.

Arrow shafts must be cut off to match your own personal draw length. They should be about ¾ inch longer than your draw length so a big broadhead doesn't bump the front of your bow when you draw it back. Arrows that hang out more than ¾ inch are too long—the extra length simply adds extra weight to your arrows and slows them down. An archery shop will cut your arrows to the proper length, or you can do it yourself (see Chapter 9).

NOCKS

An arrow nock is the grooved, oblong piece of plastic on the back end of an arrow shaft. Several nock styles are available to hunters, the most common one being the teardrop-shaped, snap-on Bjorn nock. This nock grips the bowstring firmly and stays on the string even when a bowhunter isn't holding the arrow there with his fingers. Other less expensive nocks are also available, but most don't grip the bowstring. This can be remedied by dipping them briefly in boiling water and then quickly squeezing both ears of these nocks together slightly. Any nocks sold at archery shops will give good accuracy, but most experienced bowhunters prefer nocks which grip the bowstring.

FLETCHING

Arrow fletching is a hotly debated subject among veteran bowhunters, a subject surrounded by dozens of myths and old wives' tales. Some bowhunters like four-fletched hunting ar-

The popular Bjorn arrow nock is precision-made for accuracy and hugs a bowstring firmly so a bowhunter doesn't accidentally drop his arrow. This kind of nock also has a raised index to let an archer nock his arrow properly by feel.

rows, some like three-fletched arrows. Some swear by plastic vanes, and some snarl at anything but good ol' turkey feathers. Some like their vanes 4 inches long, some 5 inches long. A few also use old-style shield-cut fletching instead of the more popular parabolic-shaped fletching.

The fletching on an arrow does two things. It puts a slight drag on the back end of the arrow so the arrow doesn't tumble end over end, and it makes the arrow spin as it flies to prevent wobble and prevent big arrowheads from planing (flying erratically because of uneven air friction on the surfaces of these arrowheads). Generally speaking, the bigger and more heavily spiraled the fletching on an arrow is, the more it drags through the air and the better it stabilizes and promotes accuracy. Fletching glued on an arrow shaft at a 5-degree angle stabilizes an arrow better than 3-degree fletching does; 5-inch vanes or feathers stabilize a hunting arrow much better than 3 or 4 inch.

Most bowhunters use arrows fletched with three feathers or plastic vanes, but a few prefer four-fletched arrows because four smaller fletches stabilize an arrow just as well as three bigger ones and give much better clearance around the cables on some compound bows, which results in better arrow flight. A three-fletched arrow should be nocked on the bowstring so the cock feather points straight out from the bow—if the arrow is nocked the other way, the cock feather points into the bow and hits the bow when an arrow is released, causing poor arrow flight. Nocking a three-fletched arrow with the cock feather out is more critical with stiff plastic vanes than with feathers because plastic vanes do not flatten out as they pass by a bow. Four-fletched arrows can be nocked either way because two fletches stick out symmetrically on either side of the arrow nock. Some modern nocks have raised indexes on one side so a bowhunter can nock his arrow properly by feel instead of looking down at the cock feather, a definite advantage when he has his eye on game. The cock feather on a three-fletched arrow is traditionally a different color from the other two fletches, but doesn't really have to be if indexed nocks are used. Three-fletched arrows must be nocked with the cock feather out, but this nocking procedure is automatic with experienced bowhunters. Therefore, the only real advantage four-fletched arrows offer is better cable clearance when shot from some kinds of compound bows.

The bigger and more spiraled the fletching is on an arrow, the faster that arrow slows down after it leaves the bow. The reason is simple enough: Bigger, more sharply angled fletching creates more air friction, which puts the brakes on an arrow as it flies along. As a result, many archers, target archers in particular, try to get by with the smallest, least-spiraled fletching they can attain good accuracy with. Small fletching is fine for target archers because they use slender target arrowheads and always shoot over open ground from a relaxed, standing position. However, stable arrow flight is harder for a bowhunter to achieve consistently. For one thing, a big hunting arrowhead tends to steer an arrow off course like the rudder on a ship unless the arrow has proper drag on the tail end. For another, bowhunters often have to shoot through heavy woods, where an arrow is sometimes deflected by branches and begins to wobble badly unless the fletching on the back end is big enough to straighten it out again.

Bowhunters sometimes find themselves in awkward shooting positions, too. I remember one time when I made a sneak on a nice whitetail buck in central Montana. The wind was right, the ground was damp from a light rain the night before, and the buck was facing away, feeding peacefully. An hour and a half later I had closed the gap to less than 30 yards, but a big quaking aspen stood directly between me and the buck. The only way I could move enough sideways to get off the shot was by climbing a deadfall log to my right. The problem was, the log was 3½ feet in diameter. I gritted my teeth and shuffled sideways, rolling my eyeballs to watch the deer. I carefully slipped my right leg over the log and put a little weight on it experimentally. The loose bark on top groaned like a boxer belted in the gut, and my beautiful buck snapped up his head to look.

It was now or never, so I canted the bow sharply to clear the log, drew the arrow back, and tried to aim. My right leg was nearly as high as my head, and my body was twisted like a pretzel. I let go of the string as best I could, but the release was anything but smooth. The lower limb on my old recurve bow swatted the log as the arrow zoomed away, and I could see it wobble badly right in front of the bow. However, the three heavily spiraled 5-inch feathers on the back straightened it out, and a split instant later it sank deep in the buck's lungs with a watermelon "plunk." An arrow with smaller fletching would never have stabilized under those adverse conditions, and I might have missed the buck entirely or, worse yet, might have scored a poor hit with poor arrow penetration to boot.

An arrow that porpoises (wobbles up and down) or fishtails (wobbles sideways) is bad news in bowhunting for two reasons. First, a wobbly arrow is not accurate, and sometimes planes off in weird directions if the arrowhead is big enough. Second, a wobbly arrow sheds energy faster than a good-flying arrow, which means it doesn't penetrate as deeply even if it does hit an animal. It's ironic that some well-intentioned bowhunters go afield with small, barely spiraled fletching so they can pick up a little more arrow speed, and then hit a branch or release their arrow poorly and completely miss their animal or lose more arrow speed because of arrow wobble than they originally gained with the marginal fletching. A bowhunter is best off using feathers or plastic vanes that are 5 inches long, ½ inch high, and heavily spiraled around the shaft. If he uses four fletches instead of three, he can shoot slightly smaller fletching and accomplish the same purpose. However, he should place a premium on stable arrow flight instead of any minute gains in arrow speed he can pick up by skimping on the size and spiral angle of his fletching.

Which are better for bowhunting—plastic vanes or traditional turkey feathers? More manufacturers sell arrows with plastic vanes these days because they're cheaper to produce and easier to glue to shafts. But they're also better for most bowhunters, provided they're 5 inches long and glued on with a fairly sharp spiral. Plastic vanes are totally waterproof, for one thing, and give good accuracy even in a downpour. By comparison, feathers get soggy and eventually mat down in wet conditions, even when sprayed with good commercial waterproofer.

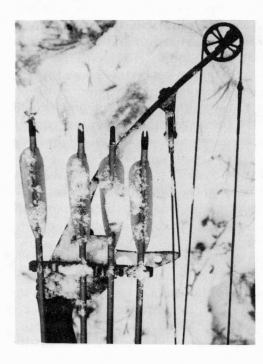

Plastic vanes are unaffected by moisture—a definite advantage over feather fletching. A feather wilts when coated with rainwater or wet snow, destroying its ability to stabilize an arrow properly.

Some bowhunters slip a plastic bag over feathers when it's rainy, but doing this can be a nuisance. Plastic vanes also last longer than feathers when shot repeatedly into bales of hay and target butts. They weigh slightly more than feathers, but not enough to slow an arrow down significantly.

Although plastic vanes are superior in most situations, they don't create as much drag on the back of an arrow as feathers do because they have slick surfaces. They don't flatten as they fly out of a bow, either, which sometimes causes wobbly arrow flight when a bowhunter gets a less-than-perfect bowstring release. If a bowhunter cannot get vane-fletched arrows to fly consistently well from his bow, feathers might be the solution. They drag the rear end of an arrow more and flatten out when leaving a bow. Feather-fletched arrows slow down faster than vane-fletched arrows but are the most forgiving when a bowhunter makes a sloppy arrow release, hits a limb with an arrow, or simply cannot get plastic vanes to fly right.

Fletching shape makes little difference in arrow flight. Old-fashioned shield-cut fletching has a pointed shoulder on the back, which tends to make a little more noise as it sizzles through the air than more modern parabolic-shaped fletching. However, both fletching shapes have been successfully used by bowhunters for years.

The only other kind of fletching worth mentioning here is flu-flu fletching, which is used to slow arrows down fast when they're shot up in the air at flying birds, tree squirrels, and other overhead targets. There are two kinds of flu-flu fletching—oversized six-fletch, and corkscrew fletching. The oversized six-fletch is much more accurate than the corkscrew fletching and is preferred by most good archers. The corkscrew fletching is simply a big gob of feathers spiraled around the back end of an arrow shaft, and provides a lot of drag. The oversized six-fletch consists of six big feathers glued lengthwise on a shaft, and provides the arrow with some guidance as well as drag.

Some commercial bowfishing arrows come equipped with flexible rubber fletching, but this is strictly a cosmetic touch which has no practical value at all. Fish are usually shot at very close range, and bowfishing arrow shafts are very heavy. The

Different kinds of fletching are designed to do different things (left to right): heavily spiraled plastic vanes meant to stabilize big hunting arrowheads; mildly spiraled feather fletching to be used with small, streamlined arrowheads; corkscrew flu-flu fletching for extremely close shots at flying game; oversized six-fletch for maximum accuracy combined with rapid arrow slow-down.

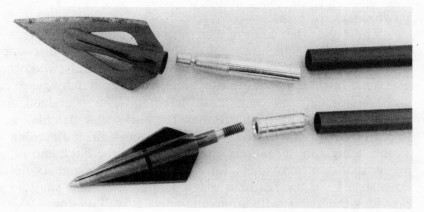

A hunting broadhead can be attached to an arrow shaft by means of a tapered, glue-on point adapter (top) or a handy screw-in point adapter (bottom). Both tapered and screw-in point adapters are glued into the ends of hollow arrow shafts with hot-melt ferrule cement.

small rubber fletching on bowfishing shafts cannot steer these heavy shafts, and steering is not a problem at close range anyway.

Fletching color is largely a matter of personal choice, but a bowhunter who expects to sneak close to game should always use dark to medium-colored fletching to prevent an animal from spotting a cluster of light-colored fletches in his arrow quiver. Some bowhunters, especially tree-stand hunters, prefer white fletching so they can track the flight of their arrows in low-light conditions (see Chapter 20 for more on fletching colors and their uses).

ARROWHEADS

Most hunting arrowheads weigh somewhere between 100 and 150 grains. They are available in a wide variety of configurations to do a wide variety of jobs. A bowhunter should be familiar with the more common types of arrowheads so he can use the right ones when he goes hunting.

Broadheads are used to hunt big game, medium-sized varmints, and some large species of birds. All broadheads consist of a center section called a ferrule surrounded by two to six cutting blades. A broadhead and any other kind of arrowhead can be attached to an arrow shaft in one of two ways—either by gluing it onto the 5-degree taper on the front end of an arrow shaft with hot-melt ferrule cement similar to that used on fishing-rod ferrules, or by screwing it into one of the fairly new screw-in point adapters, which cement to the end of an arrow shaft.

A screw-in point adapter allows a bowhunter to quickly replace a dull broadhead with a sharp one while in the field, and also lets him interchange different kinds of arrowheads in seconds. For example, if he's on a big-game hunt and decides to do a little grouse hunting, he can screw out a few broadheads and replace them with special bird-hunting arrowheads. However, a bowhunter should be careful when using such an interchangeable point system. Every arrowhead has its own flight characteristics, so a broadhead may not shoot the same place as a bird-hunting head or some other kind of arrowhead screwed into the same arrow and shot from the same bow.

Another problem is sometimes created by screw-in point adapter systems. A bowhunter may shoot field points (discussed later in this chapter) for several months, get his arrows flying extremely well and his bow sighted in exactly, and then head for the woods without trying out his broadheads to see how *they* fly. He figures he can quickly screw in broadheads the night before his hunt and shoot them well. The trouble is, these broadheads may not hit the same place as his field points, as previously mentioned, and even worse, they may not fly well at all because he has insufficient fletching on his arrows to stabilize his broadheads and keep them from planing off in different directions. Field points and other slender arrowheads often stabilize well with small, slightly spiraled fletching, giving a bowhunter with screw-in point adapters false confidence in his untried, easily attached broadheads. A bowhunter who practices with screw-in field points should attach broadheads well before his hunt to make sure they hit the same place and fly accurately. This precaution can prevent a lot of frustration.

Tapered point adapters have been used for years to install arrowheads, and are still used by many big-game bowhunters who shoot broadheads the year round and can see no big advantage in quickly screwing out one kind of arrowhead and screwing in another. The bond between a glue-on arrowhead and a tapered point adapter is also a little stronger than the bond between a screw-in point adapter and a screw-in type arrowhead, which means that a glue-on arrowhead can take a little more abuse before breaking off or bending to the side.

Both screw-in and glue-on mounting systems offer advantages, and a bowhunter must decide whether quick point interchangeability or a little greater sturdiness is most important in his type of bowhunting.

There are dozens of good big-game broadheads on today's market, and most of these do a fine job on game if they're sharp enough to shave with. Most broadheads must be sharpened by hand, which takes considerable talent and experience (see Chapter 14 for sharpening details). However, several presharpened broadheads are now available which do a very good job on game. Most of these feature replaceable blades so that a bowhunter can keep his arrowheads sharp at all times, and most conveniently screw into arrow shafts instead of requiring a bowhunter to glue them on over a hot stove, which is the way most conventional unsharpened broadheads are usually attached.

Most medium- to high-priced hunting broadheads *with three or more blades* will kill big-game animals quickly and humanely, provided they are razor-sharp. However, some are better than others. The subject of broadheads is even more hotly debated among bowhunters than that of arrow fletching, but a beginning bowhunter can tell a lot about broadheads simply by looking at them. The best designs have heavy steel blades that won't easily bend or break upon impact with an animal's heavy bones. Some broadheads have thin blades about the thickness of razor blades, and the blades in others actually *are* razor blades. Such blades look deadly and sometimes take game, but just as often break up on impact when they hit heavy bones—which can result in poor cutting action and lost animals. A good broadhead is also made of top-quality steel that takes and holds an edge well. Steel quality is difficult to check out until you actually use a broadhead, but the higher-priced, better-known brands all feature reasonably good steel in the 43 to 45 Rockwell hardness range.

The best big-game broadheads cut a hole at least an inch wide, and preferably $1^1/_{16}$ to $1\frac{1}{4}$ inch wide. Such broadheads do a better job of killing game than smaller ones, and fly accurately when used with heavily spiraled 5-inch feathers or plastic vanes. Big arrowheads are often badmouthed by bowhunters who use small fletching on their arrows, but any accuracy problems these complainers have are caused by their poor choice of fletching, not by the broadheads.

Field points are slender, pointed steel arrowheads used on hunting arrows during target-practice sessions and target matches between bowhunters. They are very accurate to shoot, even with small fletching, and don't tear up grass mats, styrofoam flocks, excelsior bales, and other fragile target butts. Field points are also great for hunting ground squirrels, rats, and other animals under 2 pounds. They are inexpensive, rugged, and accurate.

Blunts of various kinds can be used to hunt animals under

5 pounds and most species of birds. These arrowheads are made of rubber, hard plastic, or steel, and have wide, flat noses designed to shock instead of penetrate. Rubber blunts can be used inside buildings to shoot pigeons, rats, and other pests because they won't easily penetrate walls and corrugated steel roofs. Steel blunts are the number-one choice for shooting at hard natural targets like logs and stumps because they do not wedge tightly in wood as broadheads and field points do. They smash squarely into wood, penetrating shallowly with no wedging action at all. As a result, they are easily pulled from the hardest stumps and logs.

Bowfishing arrowheads are long, slender steel contraptions with one or more fixed or spring-loaded barbs which prevent these arrowheads from backing out of fish once they penetrate. Most bowfishing arrowheads have holes drilled through their ferrules to accept the heavy fishing line with which a bowman

Replaceable point adapters allow the quick replacement of one kind of arrowhead with another. This lets a bowhunter match different arrowheads to different situations. Shown here are (left to right): a heavy-duty presharpened broadhead, screw-in field point, and simple steel blunt.

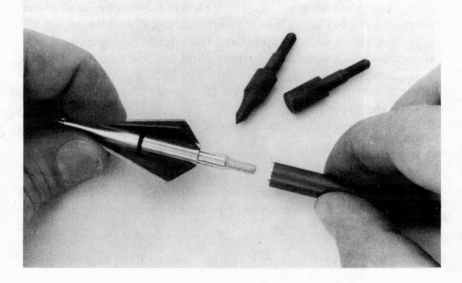

plays his fish after it is hit. The better models also feature removable nose sections so a bowfisherman can unscrew the
barbed portion of his arrowhead after he lands a fish and then
easily back the shaft out of that fish.

Bird-hunting arrowheads provide oversized "contact
zones" to minimize near misses on flying pheasants, ducks, and
other game birds. The biggest bird head available consists of
four big piano-wire loops attached to a small blunt ferrule. This
head is a full 6 inches wide, and flies with reasonable accuracy.
Other bird-hunting heads are available in a variety of configurations, and all knock birds for a loop when they connect.

Choosing the proper arrow to hunt with requires some careful planning. First, you must decide which shaft material to use
and then consult manufacturers' charts to find out which shaft
size or sizes will shoot best from your bow. Second, you should
consider what varieties of game you intend to hunt so you can

No, these aren't rocket ships! They're bowfishing arrowheads,
complete with heavy-duty barbs and holes to accept stout fishing
line.

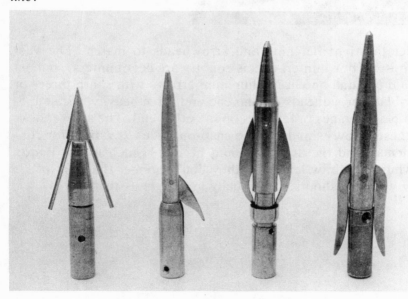

A proper hunting arrow flies accurately and stops game efficiently. The author shot this tiny Wyoming prairie dog at 45 yards with a flat-shooting aluminum arrow tipped by a steel blunt— an ideal choice for these small, open-country varmints.

select the right fletching and arrowheads to match. The vast majority of bowhunters in this country are deer hunters, so most should use dull-anodized aluminum arrows with sharp three- or four-blade broadheads on one end and three heavily spiraled, 5-inch plastic vanes or feathers on the other end. The arrow nocks on these arrows should be the snap-on, indexed variety for convenience, and the arrows should be cut ¾ inch longer than a bowhunter's draw length so they don't clobber the front of his bow when he shoots. It's usually as simple as that.

Chapter 3—OTHER SHOOTING GEAR

Selecting a suitable hunting bow and top-quality arrows to match are the two most important decisions a beginning bowhunter must make. But he'll need some other basic equipment before he can start shooting his bow, and this equipment should also be selected carefully to prevent headaches later on.

ARROW RESTS

An arrow rest is the little gizmo on a bow that the arrow rides across when a bowhunter draws back and releases a shot. An arrow rest consists of a shelf, which the bottom of the arrow rests upon, and a plate, which the side of the arrow rests against. There are dozens of well-designed arrow rests on the market, and many of them are fine for hunting. Most arrow rests attach to a bow with some sort of adhesive, letting a bowman experiment with a variety of rests without marring the finish on his bow when he removes one and installs another. Many hunting bows are sold complete with a suitable hunting arrow rest, but some are not, and in any case a bowhunter should know something about what makes an arrow rest a good hunting rest.

The two key words when talking about hunting rests are "rugged" and "quiet." A hunting rest should attach solidly to a bow and stay put, even when exposed to heat, cold, and moisture. It should be simply constructed to prevent a malfunction in the woods, and should be heavy-duty to prevent breakage at the wrong time—like when the biggest buck you've ever seen comes prancing by 10 feet away. Many target-shooting arrow rests are fragile little things full of tiny springs, moving wires, and other parts likely to break whenever the breezes blow too hard. Most good bowhunting arrow rests are one- or two-piece affairs made of durable nylon, plastic, or hard rubber. Some sturdy models have separate shelves and plates made of two different materials. One popular hunting rest consists of a stiff bristle shelf and a horizontally adjustable nylon plate that screws in and out. It's a good one. A few reliable bowhunting arrow rests have adjustable plates to "fine-tune" arrow flight and spring-loaded shelves and/or plates that fold or flatten out of the way when an arrow comes zipping past.

Most arrow rests are carefully designed and shoot arrows well. However, not all of them are quiet enough to hunt with. The slightest clank or scrape made as an arrow slides across an arrow rest can spook an alert animal like a deer, so the bow hunter should take pains to make certain his arrow rest is perfectly quiet. Rests made of nylon, teflon, rubber, stiff feathers, plastic bristles, and leather are usually very quiet. Hard plastic and bare metal can be real culprits, though, causing unwanted squeaks, squawks, clatters, and clanks when an arrow is drawn back and shot. Any metal parts on a good-quality arrow rest are usually covered with felt, teflon, or some other quiet substance to dampen noise. If you like a particular arrow rest that makes noise, you might try lubricating the parts that touch your arrow with a little powdered graphite, baby powder, or another dry lubricant. If noise persists, get another rest.

BOWSTRINGS

A bowhunter should own at least two extra bowstrings of the proper size and length to fit his bow. Hunting bowstrings are usually made with twelve to sixteen strands of strong Dacron fiber, and come in an unbelievable number of lengths. You should carefully read the literature that came with your hunting bow or contact your local archery shop to find out how many strands your bowstrings should have and how long they should be. A bowstring of the proper length "braces" a bow to the right "brace height" (the distance from the back of a bow's grip to the bowstring when that bow is strung). The correct brace height ensures maximum performance from a bow with a minimum of shooting noise.

Bowstrings sometimes break or become frayed after lots of

shooting, and sometimes get cut inadvertently on sharp objects. If you have a couple of extras on hand, you can quickly replace a damaged bowstring and continue shooting or hunting. Most bowhunters carry an extra bowstring at all times in case they accidentally cut the one on their bow with a sharp broadhead or fray it on a rock, tree limb, or pickup bumper.

Both the string on your bow and your extra strings should be installed with some sort of nocking point (nock locator) so you can nock your arrow the same place every time (see Chapter 8 for details). Your extra bowstrings should also have the same kind of silencers and other string accessories on them that your original bowstring has. Otherwise, they'll probably shoot arrows differently than the original.

Commercial bowstrings are inexpensive and very well made, eliminating the need for a modern bowhunter to fool around with making his own. The most durable bowstrings have a central serving section made of hard monofilament, which wears like iron even when shot repeatedly with a grimy shooting glove or tab. Nylon bowstring serving is also fairly common; it wears reasonably well but abrades faster than mono and tends to fray with heavy use.

A bowman should also own a bowstringer designed for his particular bow. A bowstringer should always be used to string and unstring a recurve bow to prevent the bow limbs from becoming twisted. It makes replacing a frayed string on a compound bow a lot quicker and easier than totally dismantling the bow. There are many kinds of bowstringers available. Select one that works on your bow and one you can easily carry and use in the woods.

BOWSIGHTS

Bowsights are fairly standard equipment among bowhunters these days because they greatly improve accuracy on targets and game. There are many kinds of bowsights available, including some models with built-in range-finding devices. Most bowsights are attached to bows with screws or tape, and most modern bows have flat ramps on their handle risers designed to accept a variety of commercial bowsights. Basically, a bowsight

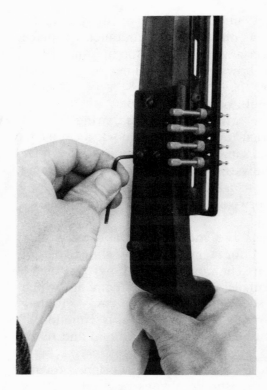

*Most good bowsights
have multiple sight pins
which adjust along a
metal slide. They usually
bolt directly to sight
platforms that are
provided on most modern
hunting bows.*

consists of one or more movable or stationary sight pins that
can be set for distances at which a bowhunter is likely to shoot.
The bowsights I hunt with have five separate sight pins set for
20, 30, 40, 50, and 60 yards. When I get within range of an
animal, I quickly estimate the distance of the shot, draw my
bow, put the appropriate sight pin in the appropriate spot, and
release the arrow. Most bowhunters shoot best with a bowsight
if they have the ability to accurately estimate range. The various
range-finding devices that can be attached to bowsights are of
questionable value because they're seldom very accurate and
seldom very fast to use. The best bowhunters usually practice
hard at range estimation so they can make split-second judg-
ments in the field and get off shots before animals vamoose.

Unless you know for a fact that you're a good instinctive
bowshot (good at shooting without a sight), you're best off in-

vesting in one of the simple, medium-priced bowsights available at archery stores. The most popular, most reliable sights consist of a metal (usually aluminum) sight ramp with four adjustable sight pins attached. Such sights are uncomplicated, dependable, and fairly inexpensive.

QUIVERS

Every bowhunter needs a quiver to carry his arrows in. There are several basic kinds of arrow quivers, and each has its own peculiar traits. Which quiver you choose will depend upon what kind of hunting you intend to do.

The shoulder quiver is the simplest and oldest kind of hunting quiver, the kind Robin Hood supposedly used in Sherwood Forest. A shoulder quiver is carried high on a bowhunter's back and really has very little going for it. A lot of arrows can be

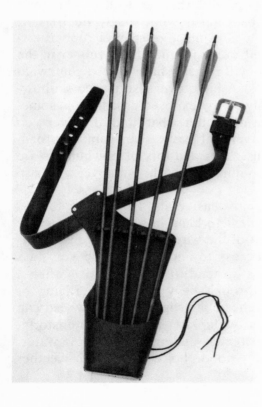

A sturdy hip quiver is practical in open country and dry weather. The eight-arrow model shown here features a deep, protective broadhead cup and vise-like rubber arrow clamps. It also flares arrows slightly to prevent fletches from rattling together and spooking game.

carried in a shoulder quiver, and it's fairly inexpensive. However, arrows in a shoulder quiver tend to rattle and grate together badly when a bowhunter walks, which scares animals out of their hides and quickly dulls sharp hunting broadheads. A bowhunter has to reach over his shoulder to pull an arrow from this type of quiver, creating a lot of game-spooking arm movement. A shoulder quiver is also a pain to carry in heavy brush and trees because the arrows ride high in the air and hang up on everything in sight. This rumples your arrow fletching (if you use feathers), makes lots of noise, and generally makes moving along a darn nuisance. My first quiver was a shoulder quiver, and I'll never own another. Between the unnecessary arm movement, ungodly racket, irritating tangles, ruined arrow fletching, and dull broadheads this little number causes, it's a solid loser. I understand Robin Hood is a myth, anyway.

The hip quiver, which usually attaches to a bowhunter's belt, is much better. The best hip quivers snugly hold six or eight arrows in special arrow clips made of steel or rubber. Arrowheads are usually tucked safely in thick foam rubber in the cup of the quiver, where they'll remain sharp and be somewhat protected from the elements. A hip quiver also protects a bowhunter from getting seriously cut by exposed broadheads, something of utmost importance no matter what kind of quiver you decide to use. An arrow quiver that leaves sharp hunting broadheads exposed is dangerous. Lots and lots of bowhunters are injured each year by cheapo quivers that do not cover up sharp arrowheads.

Hip quivers are fairly inexpensive and fairly quick to use. They are especially convenient to hang in a tree beside a tree stand, providing a good out-of-the-way place to store extra arrows and ensuring quick access to another arrow if you miss your first shot. Hip quivers do tend to be a bit noisy when a bowhunter sneaks along through heavy woods, scraping or hanging up on nearby branches and twigs. The arrowhead cap on a hip quiver also fills up with water in a heavy rainstorm, exposing sharp broadheads to edge-dulling, rust-forming water. A hip quiver is a reasonably good choice for the fair-weather bowman who plans to hunt on foot in open country or sit in a tree stand.

Back quivers (not to be confused with shoulder quivers) were originally designed to carry a lot of arrows in an out-of-the-way place. A back quiver rides low on a bowhunter's back, right between his shoulder blades. It is attached to his body with a network of straps, and is not uncomfortable to wear if these straps are properly adjusted. Most back quivers carry at least a dozen arrows, and are practical for bowhunters who intend to be afield a long time and expect to take a lot of shots. Back quivers hold arrows firmly and quietly and protect them from wet weather with a rooflike hood on top. They also require a minimum of game-spooking arm movement to reach a second arrow—a bowhunter simply slips his hand around behind him and plucks another arrow from the quiver. Back quivers are not commonly used by bowhunters, and are not normally stocked in archery stores. If you're going on a long backpack bowhunt and need to carry a lot of arrows, this quiver might appeal to you. Otherwise, another design will suit you better.

The bow quiver is far and away the most popular hunting quiver on the market. There are many designs available these days, but all attach directly to a hunting bow instead of attaching to a bowhunter's body. These quivers are popular because they're the most convenient to use and provide the fastest access to arrows. A bowhunter can easily maneuver his arrows through the heaviest trees and brush when they're in a bow quiver, which prevents noise and irritating tangles. If he misses a shot at an animal, another arrow is waiting within inches of his hand. A few bowhunters claim that bow quivers unbalance their bows and make them "shoot funny," but the vast majority of bowhunters have no trouble shooting well with quivers attached to their bows. A bow quiver is easy to use in practically any situation, whether a hunter is on the ground or in a tree. It's a nifty design.

A good bow quiver always has a roomy, protective cap that completely covers sharp broadheads. This cap should be made of heavy plastic, metal, or some other material that cannot

be easily punctured. The arrowhead cap on a bow quiver does
three things—it protects arrowheads from limbs, rocks, and
other objects that might come in contact with exposed broadheads and dull them; it protects arrowheads from rust-causing
moisture; and it protects you from accidentally cutting yourself
on exposed, razor-sharp broadheads.

A bow quiver should also hold enough arrows to last you
a whole day. Most bow quivers hold from four to eight arrows,
which is plenty for most kinds of hunting. I personally like to
carry at least six arrows on my bow, just in case I get goofy and
miss an extraordinary number of shots at an extra-dumb deer.

Good bow quivers hold arrows securely in nonslip rubber
clips so they don't rattle around when a bow is shot. They also
attach solidly to a bow with bolts, tape, or spring-steel clips so

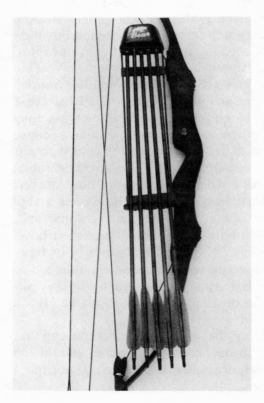

*A bow quiver attaches
directly to a hunting bow,
greatly simplifying arrow
transport and access.*

they don't clatter against a bow, rattle loose, or actually fall off a bow when it's shot repeatedly. A bow vibrates violently when shot, and anything but the most solidly designed, solidly mounted bow quiver will make hideous noises when a bowhunter releases an arrow—noises that scare the daylights out of any sort of game.

The best thing to do when choosing an arrow quiver is browsing around the local archery shop to see what's available, having a salesman demonstrate several designs, and then pondering the whole complicated deal for awhile. Most bowhunters use either hip quivers or bow quivers, and the vast majority use bow quivers. Which you choose depends on your finances and your individual druthers, but it's hard to beat a well-made bow quiver for general use.

In addition to his regular hunting quiver, a bowhunter should invest in a cheap, tube-type target-style hip quiver. It's a pain to continually snap arrows in and out of a hunting hip quiver or bow quiver when you're target practicing, and eventually wears out the arrow clips on these quivers. A target-style hip quiver rattles arrows around a bit, but who cares unless there's a nervous game animal around?

FINGER PROTECTION AND ARMGUARDS

A bowhunter needs two other pieces of bow-shooting equipment—a finger glove or tab to protect his bowstring fingers when he shoots, and an armguard to protect his forearm from painful string slap after he releases an arrow. These items are inexpensive, but they are vitally important to accurate, comfortable shooting. Far too many beginners head for the archery range with a brand-new bow, a dozen arrows, and most of the other essential shooting gear—and head home again an hour later with rosy-red, blistered fingers and a black-and-blue forearm. There's no reason to punish yourself that way.

Some bowhunters use a finger glove to protect their bowstring fingers; some prefer a tab. A glove is a little easier for a beginner to use, but a tab gives most bowhunters a smoother, slicker string release, which means a little better accuracy. A glove tends to develop grooves where the string crosses a bow-

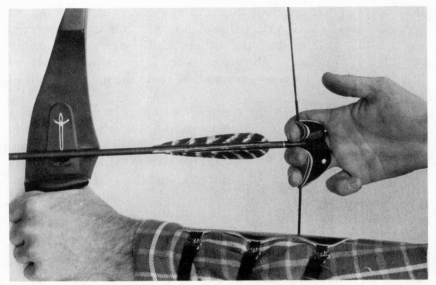

A finger tab takes some getting used to, but provides an ultra-slick bowstring release and complete finger protection.

hunter's fingers, grooves that hang up the bowstring when a shooter tries to release it smoothly. However, the difference between a glove and tab is small, and only the best bowhunters make an issue out of it. If possible, a beginner should try both kinds of finger protection and then select the one he likes best. Most beginners choose finger gloves because they take less getting used to. A few bowhunters with extra-tender fingers use a tab and glove together, something to consider if the bowstring hurts your fingers with a glove or tab alone. For double protection, put a glove on first, then slip a tab over it. It works!

Most alternate forms of finger protection are total flops. One company offers thick rubber sleeves that slip over the bowstring in the area where a bowhunter holds the string. These heavy sleeves slow down arrow flight because they slow down the bowstring, and they provide marginal finger protection at best. Better use a finger glove or tab.

An armguard is an oblong piece of leather or plastic which attaches to a bowhunter's forearm with straps of one sort or

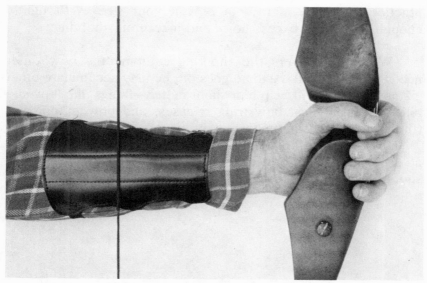

A bowstring normally slaps a hunter's forearm six to eight inches behind the wrist. A hunting armguard should be positioned to completely cover this vulnerable area.

another. Most armguards are about 6 inches long and 3 inches wide, but some are at least twice as long and cover the entire inside of the arm from the wrist to the middle of the biceps. A bowhunter should use a shorter armguard unless he has an unorthodox shooting style that causes the bowstring to strike his arm above the elbow.

An armguard performs two functions—it protects a bowhunter's arm from string slap, which can be excruciatingly painful, and it mats down a baggy shirtsleeve to prevent the bowstring from hitting it. When a bowstring hits a baggy sleeve, it makes noise and sometimes makes a shot go wild. No bowhunter can afford to bruise his arm, make a lot of noise, or miss easy shots, so he should always wear an armguard when he shoots his bow. A few bowmen prefer to wear their armguards *under* tight-fitting shirts or jackets on the theory that the bowstring makes less noise when it slaps a tight wool or cotton garment than when it slaps a leather or plastic armguard. This practice has some merit, but only if your sleeves fit tightly enough to prevent excess noise and inaccurate shooting.

Well, that covers the shooting equipment a bowhunter needs to get started. As time goes on, he may accumulate other gizmos he feels will help him shoot better—things like bow stabilizers, mechanical bowstring releases, and powder pouches (these and other shooting accessories are discussed in Chapter 7). However, the basic shooting equipment mentioned so far is all a bowhunter really needs, and may be all he'll *ever* need to shoot well on targets and game.

Chapter 4—TARGET-RANGE EQUIPMENT

A bowhunter doesn't need much equipment to set up a target range, and the equipment he does need is fairly inexpensive and easy to find. Serious target archery requires special targets, special target butts, and other standardized gear, but all a bowhunter really needs is something to shoot into that safely stops his arrows without damaging them, and something he can aim at to test his accuracy.

TARGET BUTTS

There are several kinds of commercial target butts offered by archery companies, but most are less than ideal when shot at repeatedly with hunting bows. Most butts made of corrugated paper, styrofoam, Indian rope grass, and other standard target-butt materials are simply not tough enough to withstand the repeated hammering of arrows shot from a 60- or 70-pound hunting bow. These butts endure for a little while, and then simply fall apart.

Most commercial target butts were not designed to be shot with hunting broadheads, either. A broadhead cuts up Indian rope grass, burlap, and other target-butt materials like a hot knife slicing through soft Parkay. However, since most broadheads hit a different place than other kinds of arrowheads, bowhunters like to shoot them all year long or at least for a few weeks prior to hunting season. This tends to create target-butt problems.

One of the most practical commercial target butts for the bowhunter who shoots field points a lot is a small Indian rope grass mat. Grass mats are available from any archery store, and most archery mail-order houses, too. These target butts are round and come in sizes from 48 inches in diameter down to 16 inches. They do a fairly decent job of stopping field points shot from hunting bows with draw weights up to 55 or 60 pounds, provided the cords that hold the grass together are tightened periodically and the matts are soaked in water once in a while to swell the grass. A 16-inch or 24-inch grass mat is handy to lug around on a hunting trip (a 16-inch mat weighs only 10 or 12 pounds) and can be set up on a commercial mat easel or simply leaned against a tree. However, mats can only be shot at with field points, which limits their usefulness.

A bowhunter who wants to investigate the possibility of buying a commercial target butt should go to an archery store to see what's available. New butt materials are being introduced all the time—from cardboard to cotton to various kinds of styrofoam—and most will last at least a little while when shot at with bows with draw weights under 60 pounds.

The old standby butt for most bowhunters is a bale made

A 24-inch Indian rope grass mat is big enough to shoot at safely and small enough to lug around. Such a target butt will effectively stop field-point-tipped arrows shot from bows under 60 pounds.

of straw or hay. Bales made of excelsior, cedar shavings, and other materials are also available in some areas, but hay and straw can be found almost anywhere. Excelsior and cedar make good target butts for the heaviest hunting bows when tightly baled, but can only be shot with field points. On the other hand, hay and straw bales can take a fair amount of broadhead shooting if they're tight and dry, even from bows in the 70-pound class. They're incredibly inexpensive, too, so when they give out you can haul 'em to the dump without sobbing over the capital loss.

Straw bales usually hold up better than hay bales because straw is tougher and more resilient. Alfalfa hay bales stop arrows well for a while, but once they get crumbly the jig is up. Different kinds of straw perform differently as target-butt material, too. By far the best is wheat straw, which tends to be fibrous and seldom crumbles, even when shot into repeatedly. Most other kinds of straw, like barley straw and oat straw, still work better than hay, but wheat is the undisputed target-butt champ. A big, tightly baled, three-wire wheat-straw bale will take several hundred hours of broadhead shooting before giving up the ghost, and still costs less than five bucks at most feed stores. That's a lot less than a big hay bale costs, and considerably less than a commercial target butt costs. A straw bale is admittedly a bit messy when it starts to crumble, but that's just about its only drawback. It's difficult or impossible to pull some thin-bladed broadheads backward out of straw bales without bending or breaking the blades, another drawback if you use such broadheads. Thin-bladed broadheads have to be pushed on through straw bales, which weakens these bales and eventually damages feather fletching. Many bowhunters I know, including myself, don't use such fragile broadheads anyway because they sometimes break up when they hit heavy bones in big-game animals. However, if you decide to shoot thin-bladed broadheads into straw, beware of the consequences.

The perfect target butt stops all kinds of arrows no matter how fast they're going, never wears out, is easy to attach targets to, and doesn't damage arrows or arrowheads. Very few things are perfect in this imperfect world, but I'm happy to report that

A sand-trap butt stops arrows within inches, and causes no damage to hunting broadheads or arrow shafts. The bowman pictured here is David Feil, well-known bowhunter and target champion. Like many experts, Dave prefers a sand trap butt over all others.

the perfect target butt *does* exist. It's called a sand-trap butt, costs quite a bit to build, and takes several hours to put up. However, it works like a charm with the heaviest hunting bows and the biggest, meanest broadheads.

Sand-trap butts vary in size and basic configuration, but all consist of a heavily built open-topped plywood box with the back a lot higher than the front and sides that angle straight down from the back to the front. Most I've seen have a floor about 3 feet square, a back about 5 feet high, and a front about 3 feet high. This open-topped box is filled with some sort of fine sand, usually the superfine casting sand available at most lumberyards. This sand is carefully sloped down from the high back of the box to the low front, providing a target surface of sand at least 2 feet deep to shoot into. Sand is amazing stuff, and seldom slides to a level position even when shot into repeatedly. Once in a great while you have to reslope the sand in a sand-trap butt so it's high in the back and at least a couple of feet lower in the front, but not very often. This kind of butt is fairly expensive to build, especially if you must pay for the sand, but it more than pays for itself in the long run. Sand stops arrows cold within a few inches, allows them to be pulled free with almost no friction, never wears out, and doesn't significantly abrade arrowheads or arrow shafts if it's extremely fine. A sand-trap butt is too heavy to move once it's built and filled with sand, but that's just about its only fault. It is not a beginner's butt, however—if a bowhunter cannot consistently hit a target area 2 feet square, he'll end up missing a sand-trap butt entirely or worse yet, burying arrows in its plywood walls, which is not good for either the arrows or the sandtrap butt.

Other fairly good target butts include sandbanks and soft dirt banks, but these are seldom conveniently located in the backyard and are usually slightly damp anyway. Wet sand or dirt clings to arrows and arrowheads, requiring a minor cleanup job after every round of shooting. Some bowhunting clubs lay out broadhead-shooting ranges in hilly country, placing targets against soft sand or dirt hillsides. However, if the soil is even slightly rocky, bent and broken arrows will result from such a setup.

I remember one time years ago when I was bowhunting by myself miles from the nearest road. My bowsight rattled loose from my bow one day because of a defective mounting system, but I luckily had some plastic tape in my backpack to cinch it back down. Next came sighting in the bow all over again. I looked around for a soft dirt bank, and eventually found a likely looking mound of silt along a mountain stream. I put a big yellow leaf in the middle to aim at, backed off 20 yards, and let an arrow fly. It sailed toward the leaf, a touch low, smacked the dirt—and then cracked like a cherry bomb exploding in an alley. I gritted my teeth, trotted to the target, and nervously pulled the arrow. The heavy steel broadhead had snapped in two like a breadstick, and the aluminum shaft was severely bent. A little pawing through the dirt uncovered half a dozen fist-sized rocks—not exactly the perfect things to hit with a fast-flying arrow. Needless to say, I inspected the next pile of dirt I found *before* shooting into it.

TARGETS

The kind of target a beginning bowhunter learns to shoot at is not too important as long as it provides him with something fairly small to aim at. There are many kinds of commercial bull's-eye targets available at archery stores, including standard black-and-white Field Round targets and big, multi-colored American Round targets. A beginning shooter should learn right away to aim at a particular spot on a target, so bull's-eye targets are best to start out with. A bull's-eye over 6 inches in diameter encourages sloppy shooting—most bowhunters using bowsights should quickly become able to hit a 6-inch bull almost every time at 15 or 20 yards.

Commercial bull's-eye targets are fairly expensive, and most serious bowhunters prefer to make their own simple targets to save money and frequent trips to the archery store. Broadheads are especially bad about chewing up targets, and an ac-

The author's favorite homemade bow-shooting target consists of a nine-inch pie plate with a three-inch bull's-eye. A pop can and a black felt pen are the only tools needed to make this inexpensive, durable target.

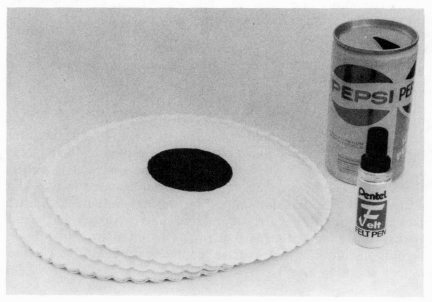

curate shot who uses broadheads will destroy several bull's-eyes during an hour or two of shooting. If you're really serious about becoming a good shot, you'll go through hundreds of targets the first few months you practice, which almost requires you to make your own targets to protect your monthly paycheck.

My favorite bow-shooting target is simple and cheap. All you need to make it is a white 9-inch paper plate, a black felt-tipped pen, and a soft-drink or beer can. First, mark a black circle on the center of the plate, using the bottom of the can as a guide. After drawing this circle, simply blacken in the circle. The result is a white target with a black 3-inch bull's-eye in the middle—all you need to practice on. Such a target costs a couple of cents to make and lasts just as long as a commercial target which costs a dollar or more.

Other good, cheap targets include small pieces of cardboard and bits of paper. Unless a bowhunter is concerned about competing with others under standard target-range conditions, all he has to worry about is learning to hit a small object regularly at distances out to 30 yards or so. A paper cup is just as easy to aim at as the fancy yellow bull's-eye on a commercial target.

After a bowhunter masters the art of hitting a standard bull's-eye or some other small, easily aimed-at object, he should begin shooting at animal-sized targets *without* definite aiming spots. This will get him accustomed to picking a particular spot to aim at on a deer, bear, or similar animal. Animals don't have bull's-eyes on their hides, and it takes special skills to put an arrow in a big animal's vital zone without having a small, round spot to aim at. Far too many bowhunters become deadly shots on paper, head for the hills, and completely blow shots at close ranges because they aren't used to putting an arrow in one particular part of a big gray or brown object like a deer.

A wide variety of animal targets are available at archery stores, and every bowhunter should try his luck on these before going afield. Most of these commercial targets do not have bull's-eyes, although many have large circles indicating the general area where a vital shot should go. Bowhunters must be aware of animal targets and use them periodically to sharpen up for actual hunting situations.

If you have an artistic bent, you might try drawing your own animal targets on large pieces of construction paper or cardboard. Some bowhunters simply cut out chunks of brown cardboard roughly resembling the body shape of a deer and practice aiming at particular areas on these crude targets. No matter what kind of animal target you use, the key is learning to hit the area you want to hit even if there's no visible spot to aim at.

Moving targets are fun to shoot at with a bow, especially if several bowhunters participate. However, they have limited practical value for a serious bowhunter. Very, very few bowhunters can accurately place an arrow in a running big-game animal, so most bowhunters should never shoot at one. To do so invites total misses or worse yet, poor hits and wounded game. A few talented, instinctive bowshots can consistently kill moving game (see Chapter 18), but the man who uses a bowsight is making a mistake when he draws on fast-moving animals.

Archery clubs sometimes sponsor running-animal tournaments, in which archers shoot at styrofoam or cardboard animal targets rolling along railroad rails or sliding down long, slanting wires. Bowhunters sometimes put circular bull's-eye targets inside big rubber tires and have helpers roll these tires down hillsides, shooting at the bouncing, fast-moving targets as they come zipping past. All this activity is exciting sport, and a good way to kill an afternoon. However, it is not the way to kill an *animal* with a bow unless you have rare instinctive shooting abilities.

A few forms of moving-target practice *are* beneficial for a bowhunter. A bowhunter who wants to shoot birds on the wing must practice diligently on flying targets to sharpen his reflexes and shooting eye. Special targets are available for this kind of practice, including small disks made of styrofoam and cardboard. These are usually hand-thrown by a strong-armed friend. Likewise, a bowman who plans to do some bowfishing should practice on moving objects to increase his chances of success. The best way I know to practice is actually going bowfishing; the second-best way is taking your bowfishing equipment to the bank of a fairly deep, fast-flowing stream and practicing shots at wood chips, leaves, and other natural targets in the water.

Commercial bow racks come in many shapes and sizes. This upright four-bow model features rubber-coated arms which completely protect the finish on a bow.

If a bowhunter is so inclined, he can hammer a few nails in convenient trees beside his target range to hang his bow on while he walks up to retrieve his arrows. Or he can go whole hog and buy a commercial bow rack, or several, for his target range. Packing a bow back and forth with you when you go to get your arrows is only a minor nuisance, but a little preplanning can prevent this little range problem.

A bowhunter doesn't need much target-range equipment—just a suitable target butt made of straw bales or sand, a selection of commercial or homemade bull's-eye and animal targets, and perhaps a place to hang or lay his bow while he retrieves his arrows. These simple props are relatively inexpensive and easy to find or make, letting a bowhunter concentrate on shooting well instead of maintaining an elaborate shooting facility.

Chapter 5—CLOTHING FOR THE BOWHUNTER

The best bowhunters are terribly fussy about the clothes they wear. They know the wrong duds can completely ruin a hunt, even if everything else is perfect. Every bowhunter should take pains to make sure he's properly dressed when he heads out for the woods.

First of all, everything a bowhunter wears should be quiet and camouflaged. Game animals like deer, bear, elk, and antelope have exceptionally good ears and eyes—these senses help to keep them alive. A garment with a hard, scratchy surface makes loud, unnatural noises when it touches brush, tree limbs, and other obstacles a bowhunter is likely to encounter in the woods. A soft garment can scrape against the same things without so much as a whisper, allowing a hunter to sneak along or sit or stand without alerting the big cupped ears of the animals he's after. Similarly, a bowhunter who moseys through a dark-green forest with light-brown trousers on will stand out like a neon sign on Park Avenue. If he sees any game at all he'll be lucky, and what animals he does see will probably be hotfooting it to safety. The same bowhunter with dark, multi-colored pants would have a much better chance for success.

There are a few special times when a bowhunter's clothes need not be quiet or hard to see, such as when he's jumpshooting pheasants over a good dog or shooting carp with a bow. However, in the vast majority of cases, a bowhunter without quiet, camouflaged clothes is handicapping himself severely.

Bowhunting clothes should not interfere with shooting a bow, either. They should fit a bowhunter's body snugly so the bowstring doesn't collide with an extra fold of cloth and send an arrow rocketing into space, but they should also fit loosely enough to allow a hunter to draw his bow easily without feeling pinched or cramped.

Finally, bowhunting clothes must match the weather conditions a hunter plans to encounter so he can hunt comfortably instead of being distracted by a shivering body, numb fingers, and chattering teeth.

A properly camouflaged hunter blends with a variety of backgrounds. This bowman is decked out in traditional cotton leaf-print coveralls and a lightweight cotton headnet—good concealment from sharp-eyed animals like deer.

HATS AND OTHER HEADGEAR

Bowhunters wear many kinds of headgear, depending on the weather they expect to encounter, the terrain they're in, how they shoot a bow, and their own preferences. The best hats for general big-game hunting are close-fitting stocking caps or bowl-shaped Jones-style hats. Wool stocking caps of medium to dark colors are extremely quiet and blend into the woods extremely well. Soft cotton Jones-style hats and other close-fitting hat styles also work well, provided they are plaid or marked with a traditional leaf-print pattern. One of my favorite bowhunting hats is an old red-and-black-plaid bill cap with the bill cut off. It's quiet, camouflaged, and comfortable to wear.

All game animals and most game birds are totally color-blind, something a bowhunter should keep in mind when selecting his hat and his other bowhunting clothes. Traditional green-and-brown leaf-print garments blend in well with most backgrounds, but so do colorful plaids. The key to camouflage is wearing *multi-hued* garments, all of which tend to blend well with a variety of backgrounds. If you're unsure how particular bright-colored garments will look to a color-blind animal, a simple way to tell is taking a black-and-white photo of these garments against a natural background.

Medium hues work well in average situations, but a bowhunter should try to match his hat and other clothes to the terrain he intends to hunt. For example, a bowhunter in the light-gray desert country of southern Arizona should wear much lighter duds than a bowhunter in the cool green forests of northern Pennsylvania. Regardless of the basic hue of the clothes you wear, you should never wear large solid-colored garments. Solid-colored hats are okay if they aren't too big, but solid shirts, jackets, and pants generally stand out like sore thumbs against most backgrounds. Multi-colored clothes work 100 percent better. I'll occasionally bowhunt open-country animals like mule deer and antelope in a multi-colored jacket and plain old blue jeans, but for close-in situations on sharp-eyed animals like whitetail deer, wearing solid jeans can be a bad mistake.

Back to bowhunting hats. It's usually a mistake to wear a wide-brimmed hat when bowhunting, for a couple of reasons.

A bowhunter normally draws his bowstring within two inches of his forehead, which means a hat must be small to avoid a collision with the string. This man is wearing a narrow-brimmed Jones-style hat— a fine choice for most hunting situations.

For one thing, such a hat tends to collide with every bush, limb, and tree trunk within 3 feet. A bowhunter who's sneaking through heavy woods or sitting in the crotch of a leafy tree cannot afford to bump his hat repeatedly into head-high objects, and he cannot afford to bob his head around like a turkey gobbler to avoid them, either. The extra noise and extra movement caused by a wide-brimmed hat can catch a deer's attention and send it packing.

The second reason a wide hat can be bad news is best illustrated by a bowhunting trip a buddy of mine took a while back. He practiced shooting until he could knock off a gnat at 20 yards, bought quiet, warm, camouflaged clothes, and then practiced some more to make sure his clothes felt comfortable when he shot his bow. The day before he went hunting it started to drizzle, so he rushed out to a nearby sporting-goods store and bought a big, wide-brimmed "safari hat" to keep the water off his face and neck. The next morning he climbed into his tree stand well before daylight and settled down in the rain to wait. The morning woods slowly came alive, and about nine o'clock a nice little eight-point whitetail came tiptoeing by, 15 yards away. My buddy stood up, drew back slowly—and knocked his hat plumb off his head with the bowstring! The buck heard the commotion overhead and dove into the brush like a turpentined tomcat.

Some bowhunters can wear big hats and still shoot their bows, but most hunters hit excessively wide brims with their bowstrings as they come to full draw. If you can shoot your bow while wearing a wide-brimmed hat, such a hat can come in handy to prevent sunburn in open country and a wet head in a rainstorm. However, big hats are a detriment in most bowhunting situations.

Some bowhunters like to wear camouflage headnets when they hunt because these prevent animals from spotting their light, shiny complexions. Most of the headnets sold at archery stores are made of cool cotton netting, and most work very well. A bowhunter with light complexion *must* camouflage his face with something to keep from spooking animals, and wearing a headnet is the easiest way to accomplish this. A bowhunter can cover his face with camouflage makeup, charcoal, or mud and be just as well off, but it's faster to slip a headnet on and go hunting. You don't have to wash off a headnet, either.

Some manufacturers offer camouflage headnets without eyeholes, something that makes me wonder if some bowhunting manufacturers have ever gone bowhunting. A bowhunter needs clear vision to spot game and shoot accurately, and the fuzzy images seen through fine cotton mesh simply do not qualify as "clear." A headnet must have two big eyeholes in it, and preferably one wide slot for both eyes. I use a headnet alot when hunting alert animals like whitetail and blacktail deer, and always cut a small nose hole in mine so the rough cotton mesh doesn't rub my snozzle raw. One other tip: A bowhunter should practice shooting with his headnet on to find out if he can shoot well this way. Quite a few bowhunters have trouble anchoring their bowstring hands to their faces with a headnet in the way.

SHIRTS, JACKETS, AND TROUSERS

As I've said, shirts, jackets, trousers, and anything else a bowhunter wears should be super-soft to prevent unnecessary noise. The two quietest fabrics available are wool and soft cotton, both of which are offered by many clothing companies in a wide variety of garments. Wool is a bit quieter than cotton and has the unique trait of staying warm even when it's wet. However, wool tends to be excessively warm in hot weather, making cotton a better choice during midsummer bow seasons. Several outfits sell camouflaged cotton flannel shirts that are very, very quiet, and conventional plaid flannel shirts work every bit as well. Soft bowhunting pants are harder to come by than shirts and jackets, but wool pants can be found at some stores and a few brands of fairly soft cotton bowhunting trousers are also sold at archery shops and general sporting-goods outlets. Corduroy pants are great for bowhunting in warm weather because they're lightweight, soft, and inexpensive. The resourceful hunter can tie-dye corduroys in several colors with clothing dye and end up with some dandy bowhunting pants.

Fabrics to stay away from when shopping for bowhunting clothes include rip-stop nylon, hard-weave cloths like "60/40 cloth," and slick-finished cotton. It's surprising how many so-called "bowhunting" suits are totally unsuited for bowhunting because they're made of hard-surfaced materials. *If you can scrape your fingernails across a particular kind of fabric and hear noise, it isn't a good bowhunting fabric.* It may be great for gun hunting—rip-stop nylon, 60/40 cloth, and a few other noisy fabrics are almost standard equipment among gun hunters—but it's far too noisy for close-range bowhunting.

As mentioned before, good bowhunting clothes can be either traditional leaf-print garments or more common plaids. The important thing is that a shirt, jacket, or pair of pants have several colors in it so it blends with several backgrounds. One of my favorite cold-weather bowhunting outfits is a red-and-black-checkered wool shirt and matching pants. I've sneaked up on hundreds of animals in this clothing combo, and it works extremely well. I remember one occasion in particular.

Plaid clothes are every bit as camouflaged as more traditional leaf-print outfits. One of the author's favorite bowhunting garments is a red-and-black wool coat. He shot this big Montana muley at 55 yards as it stared blankly at his colorful getup, proof positive that big-game animals are totally color-blind.

I was pussyfooting through the soggy Colorado woods, eyeballs peeled for elk. Suddenly a bull bugled up the mountain a quarter-mile away, sending involuntary shivers up and down my spine. The animal hit five distinct notes, and the last one was the gravel-voiced grunt that only an old granddad can muster up. I hustled toward the sound, putting on the brakes when I suddenly heard bark crunching and branches popping 100 yards away. The big brute was slowly moving toward me like a D-8 Caterpillar clearing a fire trail. I backed into a little green spruce to wait, nervously fingering my bow. I'd just bought my red-and-black outfit, and I was worried the elk might see the color and run. I knew elk were supposed to be color-blind, but I got jittery almost to the point of panic every time I glanced down at my bright new getup.

Suddenly a cow slipped from behind a pile of deadfalls 15 feet away, walking straight at me. A steady breeze was blowing crossways between us—perfect! She stared at me blankly and tiptoed by, actually brushing the little tree I was leaning against. Next came a tiny spike bull, another cow, and then a runty four-point. The damp ground squished softly as they shuffled past barely 3 feet away, and the pungent, cowlike odor of their damp bodies filled my nostrils. Then I saw antler points moving above the deadfalls—long, heavy, ivory-tipped antler points. I took a deep breath and drew my 65-pound compound bow. A split-instant later the old veteran's head, neck, and chest rolled into view barely five yards away. I aimed hastily, released the arrow with a dull plunk, and listened to it plunk again as it buried to the feathers in his chest. The big five-point wheeled, stumbled 30 yards, then folded like a heart-shot pheasant. I decided that colorful plaids just might work in bowhunting situations!

Baggy bowhunting pants can't really hurt anything, but a baggy shirt or jacket can. It depends on your bow-shooting style. Most bowhunters draw their bowstrings close to their bodies when they shoot, and a few actually rest their bowstrings on their chests. A baggy shirt or jacket can catch a bowstring when an arrow is released, making noise and ruining the accuracy of the shot. Baggy sleeves are usually no problem if a bowhunter uses a big armguard to flatten out his bow-arm sleeve, but shirts and jackets should fit fairly snugly for best results.

Shirts, jackets, and pants should obviously match the weather conditions a bowhunter intends to hunt in. Most rubber raingear is noisy, glary stuff totally ill-suited for bowhunting. A fellow can get away with wearing rubber clothes if he plans to sit in a tree stand, but even then he's running a calculated risk. A deer close to a tree stand can usually hear cold rubber "crinkle" when a bowhunter draws to shoot, diminishing that hunter's chances of scoring a hit. A much better bet for wet weather is wool, which remains quiet and fairly warm even when totally drenched. Unless you have a health problem or happen to be unusually cold-blooded, wool is the way to go in the rain.

Cotton is best in very warm weather, especially the thin cotton-mesh parkas sold by several outdoor firms. When it gets really hot, these cool, camouflaged uppers can be worn over a T-shirt or bare skin with good results.

For middle-of-the-road weather, a bowhunter should dress in layers so he can be comfortable in the chilly early-morning hours and shed clothes as the day warms up. I often start the day wearing a light cotton shirt, a down vest, and a heavy wool coat on top, stashing the coat and vest at midday and putting them on again toward evening. Incidentally, a noisy-surfaced nylon vest can be successfully worn *under* wool or cotton—used this way, it is totally quiet.

FOOTWEAR

A bowhunter should choose his footwear carefully to match weather conditions he intends to encounter and the kind of hunting he intends to do. Generally speaking, bowhunting shoes should be reasonably well camouflaged, have soft, quiet soles, and be well constructed to withstand the normal wear and tear any hunting shoe is likely to get. A lot of bowhunters go first class on the rest of their clothes and then slap on the same boots they gun-hunt in. This is usually a mistake.

Leather boots and shoes turn dirty brown after a few miles in the woods, and since dirty brown is a nice, camouflaged color, leather footwear is seldom spotted by sharp-eyed game animals. The same cannot be said for white tennis shoes, light-colored deck shoes, and similar forms of footwear worn by uninformed bowhunters all over this continent. It never ceases to amaze me when I'm moseying along through the pines and suddenly find myself staring at a couple of oversized white tennis shoes dangling over the edge of a tree stand at eye level. Such a sight shocks whitetail deer into soiling their drawers, and scares the living pee out of most other animals, too. A bowhunter walking along in light-colored shoes is also easy to spot from quite a distance—his feet are moving more than any other part of his body, flashing danger signals to every alert animal in sight. A bowhunter should always wear medium-colored boots or shoes when hunting wild animals.

A bowman who intends to do any walking to speak of should wear boots or shoes with soles made of neoprene or another soft substance. Vibram-type lug soles are extremely popular among sportsmen because they wear like iron and grip like flypaper. However, Vibram-type soles are also the noisiest darn soles in the world, and should *never* be worn by a bowhunter who intends to sneak along through the woods or stalk far-off animals. A soft sole like neoprene allows a bowhunter to feel his way along over sticks, branches, loose rocks, and other noisy objects. A soft sole also gives a little when a bowhunter accidentally steps on a crackly leaf or twig, wrapping around this potentially noisy object without snapping or crunching it loudly. A hard, Vibram-type sole crumples everything in sight because it has no give. A Vibram-type sole *is* valuable to a tree-stand hunter because it grips a tree as he climbs and gives him nonslip protection as he hovers far above the ground. However, Vibram should never be worn by a bowhunter who plans to hunt on foot.

Neoprene-soled boots are the quietest footwear for a serious bowhunter, letting him feel branches and twigs underfoot before he steps down with full force.

In fairly wet weather, a bowhunter can oil or wax his leather boots and get by nicely. In sopping wet weather, he's better off wearing rubber boots. Most quality rubber boots come in medium to dark colors and have soft, quiet soles, so they're no handicap to bowhunt in unless they glare excessively. A little fine sandpaper will cut the glare on any rubber boot and make it a usable bowhunting shoe.

GLOVES AND MITTENS

Some bowhunters wear gloves; other prefer not to. In extremely close-range situations an animal might spot the movement of a hunter's light-colored hand, but it isn't likely. Camouflaged cotton gloves are available at archery stores for the perfectionists who want to make sure nothing goes wrong, and any medium-colored leather glove works just as well. Some bowhunters have trouble shooting with gloves on because a regular glove interferes with their tab or finger glove. These hunters usually rub a little mud, charcoal, or camouflage makeup on their hands prior to a critical stalk. In extremely cold weather, a bowhunter sometimes has to protect his hands, and regular gloves may be the answer for some. A better answer, in my opinion, is a pair of oversized down mittens which can be shed fast just before a shot is taken. A hunter can wear his shooting tab or finger glove under one mitten and a light cotton glove under the other to protect his hand from the cold handle of his bow. In any case, a bowhunter should experiment with gloves before heading for the hills; otherwise, he might discover much too late that all that junk on his hands is worse than worthless.

As a bowhunter becomes more and more experienced, he gradually accumulates a closetful of clothes and shoes that match his own personal hunting style. No two bowhunters hit on exactly the same magic clothing combination, but all *good* bowhunters make sure the duds they own are quiet, hard to see, easy to shoot in, and comfortable to wear. That's one reason they're good bowhunters.

Chapter 6—TREE STANDS AND BLINDS

Waiting quietly for game is sometimes the easiest, most effective way to score with a bow and arrow. Some species, like whitetail deer, are very predictable and live in small territories, allowing a bowhunter to study their movements and ambush them from a well-placed tree stand or blind. During extremely dry weather, taking a stand may be the *only* way a bowhunter can be successful if the forest floor is littered with crunchy leaves and other noisy debris. In dense cover, a tree stand or some other kind of elevated blind lets a bowhunter see a lot farther than he could if he were eyeball-deep in brush or trees, and also puts him high above game where he can't be easily seen or smelled.

Before a person thinks seriously about trying a tree stand, however, he should find out if there are legal restrictions on the use of tree stands in his hunting area. Some states ban the use of tree stands entirely, and some allow only certain types of tree-stand equipment to be used. A bowhunter should know the laws governing tree-stand hunting in his area so he can choose legal equipment and use it in a legal manner.

PORTABLE TREE STANDS

Many types of portable tree stands are offered by sporting-goods stores and mail-order houses. Most of these were designed specifically for bowhunters, and most have at least limited value when properly used. Some are large, bulky affairs meant to be put up and left awhile; others are fairly light and work great as temporary fixtures which can be backpacked in and out of a hunting area in a single day. Some are so-called "climbers," which allow a bowhunter to inch up a smooth, limbless tree trunk for 20 or 30 feet without bruising his arms, tearing off his fingernails, or breaking both legs. Others are nonclimbers, meant to be hand-carried or hoisted into a tree that has lots of convenient climbing limbs or steps attached. Some stands have tiny platforms that give a big-footed man a lot of trouble; others have large platforms with more than enough room for a stool to sit on, a lunch pail, and any other small pieces of gear a bowhunter wants to carry aloft. The large tree-stand selection these days can be mind-boggling for a novice, but he can make an intelligent choice if he knows what kind of country he'll be hunting in and a few basic facts about tree-stand design.

Climbing tree stands are just the ticket in areas with tall, smooth-trunked trees like pines, hickories, and aspens. About the only other ways a bowhunter can install a tree stand in a tall, limbless tree are using a set of climbing spikes and a safety belt, or installing commercial tree-stand steps all the way up the trunk. Climbing spikes tear the heck out of trees, and are dangerous for all but the most skillful climbers to use. They are also illegal in some areas because they do serious damage to some kinds of trees. Most types of commercial tree-stand steps take quite a bit of time to install, but if you intend to sit in the same tree over and over again, they save the body strain of using a climbing tree stand to get up where you want to go. Regular old wooden tree-house steps work great when nailed between two trees, but tend to twist and pull out when nailed to a tree trunk.

Climbing tree stands vary a lot in design, but most do not damage tree bark and most are reasonably safe to use if a hunter follows directions. The best climbing-stand setups have two parts—a hand-climbing tool held in both hands above the head, and a platform section, held by the feet. Both sections grip a tree firmly when pulled downward, and slide upward easily when pushed in that direction. The general climbing procedure is sliding the hand-climbing tool as high on the trunk of a tree as possible, pulling the tree-stand platform up a little ways with your feet by bending your knees, straightening your knees to put all your weight on the platform section, pushing the hand-climbing tool up a little farther on the tree, pulling the platform up some more with your feet, and so on. Climbing tree stands without hand-climbing tools require a bowhunter to "hug" a

Using a hand-climbing tool with a climbing tree stand makes short work of ascending a limbless tree (left). Climbing without a hand-climbing tool is not nearly as easy, requiring a hunter to hug the tree and expose his chest and face to abrasive bark (right). (Photographs courtesy of Baker Manufacturing Co.)

tree all the way up with his arms. This can cause painful chest, arm, and face abrasions on all but the smoothest-barked trees, and puts a lot of strain on arm muscles too. If you buy a climbing tree stand without a hand-climbing tool, it's a good idea to buy such a tool separately to prevent problems.

Inchworming up a tree with a climbing tree stand requires that a bowhunter be in good physical condition—otherwise, dangerous falls can result. Most climbing tree stands are fairly small in size and light in weight to facilitate moving up a tree—an advantage if you have to pack your stand a ways, and a disadvantage if you want a roomy platform to sit on once you've climbed high above the ground.

Nonclimbing tree stands must be used in areas with trees that have low-growing limbs. These are bigger on the average than climbing models, providing a more roomy platform once you're aloft. They vary a lot in weight, configuration, and the way they're strapped to a tree, but most are light enough to be lugged in and out of a hunting area without busting a gut.

The kinds of trees that grow in your hunting area will determine whether you need a climbing stand or a nonclimbing stand, but no matter what kind of commercial tree stand you buy, be sure it fastens to a tree securely and has a platform big enough to let you be comfortable as you wait for game. Most tree stands are roped or chained to a tree at the back of the platform and supported at the front by arms that extend upward or downward on the tree. The tree stands with support arms that attach to a tree *above* the platform are usually sturdier, safer units than those with support arms underneath. However, every design is different and a bowhunter must use his noodle to determine what seems to be safe and what doesn't. It's quite a feeling to be sitting in your tree stand one second and dropping like a baked potato the next—especially if you're dropping from 25 or 30 feet above the ground.

Portable tree-stand platforms vary in size all the way from about 1 square foot up to 6 square feet. The smallest ones require a bowhunter to stand up, which can be terribly tiring after several hours. The bigger ones are better as long as they don't weigh a ton, allowing a bowhunter to sit comfortably on a stool or at least kneel and change positions from time to time to prevent cramped muscles. A 24-by-18-inch platform is plenty big enough for most bowhunting needs. Anything much bigger is awkward to put up and easy to spot from the ground; anything much smaller is uncomfortable or downright dangerous to perch on for extended periods of time. The best portable tree stands have platforms a little longer than they are wide so a bowhunter isn't jammed up against a tree trunk. A tree trunk is great to lean against, but can clobber your elbow when you draw back to take a shot.

A handyman can study a variety of portable commercial tree stands and then design his own. Lots of bowhunters make their own portable tree stands and have a lot of fun doing it, but commercial tree stands are not overly expensive, and the man who makes his own will not save money. He'll merely experience the satisfaction a do-it-yourselfer always feels after creating something on his own.

PERMANENT TREE STANDS

If a bowhunter has permanent access to a particular hunting area, he can increase his chances of scoring considerably by erecting one or more permanent stands in suitable locations. A permanent tree stand can be as large or as small as the trees in an area allow, but a small, roomy platform of 9 square feet or so (3 feet square) is plenty big enough. Anything larger can be an eyesore.

You have to use your imagination when building a permanent tree stand, taking advantage of existing limbs and tree trunks to support a fairly level platform of sturdy lumber. The most common permanent tree stands are attached to three near-vertical limbs or separate tree trunks. Good-quality 2×4s are nailed around these three solid supports, forming a triangular base that can be covered with 1-inch lumber, ¾-inch plywood, or something similar. A permanent tree stand of this sort lets a bowhunter watch and shoot in all directions, something a portable stand does not allow.

How high a permanent tree stand should be built depends on many things, including the surrounding terrain, the prevailing breezes, the configuration of the trees it's attached to, and any state or local regulations governing legal heights. Most tree stands, both portable and permanent, are set up somewhere between 10 feet and 30 feet. The key is to place a stand where game can't see or smell you, where you have maximum visibility, and where you have reasonably good shooting flexibility (see Chapter 18 for details on the proper use of tree stands).

It's sometimes a good idea to build a wooden ladder or wooden steps leading to a permanent tree stand, but these can invite other bowhunters in a heavily hunted area to appropriate your stand. For this reason, it might be better to rough it and use available limbs to reach your stand instead. Regardless of whether or not you install permanent steps, your tree stand should be sprayed with automotive primer or similar paint so it isn't easily seen by animals and other hunters. Bare wood stands out against green leaves or pine needles, letting the whole world know where your best bowhunting spot is located.

TREE-STAND ACCESSORIES

The bowhunter who decides to use a tree stand should invest in several inexpensive accessories. First, he should own some sort of safety belt so he can tie himself to the tree he's sitting in. A good safety belt allows a hunter to lean out over the edge of his stand to take shots at animals directly beneath him, and also protects him in case he slips.

A few years back a close friend of mine decided to try bowhunting from a tree stand, but neglected to invest in a safety belt. He didn't figure this little precaution was really that important. He was wrong.

He sat 35 feet above the ground for five full days without seeing one deer, climbing up well before daylight and heading back home well after dark. His stand's platform was one of the biggest available at the time, measuring almost 2 by 3 feet. He was a bit nervous about the altitude at first, but soon got used to feeling like a bird.

Shortly before sunrise on the sixth morning, Bob heard the leaves rustle 30 yards to his left and rolled his eyes to look. A big fat whitetail doe was walking along the trail that ran past his stand, sniffing the ground here and there as she went. Bob stood up, waited patiently for her to walk past, then put an arrow just behind her shoulders at less than 15 yards. She leaped in the air and took off like a scalded cat, disappearing in the brush 50 yards away. Bob watched her leave, listened a minute to track her movement through the heavy trees . . . and then took a big step forward into thin air! When he came to he somehow managed to crawl to the highway a quarter-mile away, and spent the next six months in bed recuperating from severe internal injuries and two broken legs.

A safety belt is the most important tree-stand accessory you can buy, and it should be of excellent quality to give you complete protection. The best safety belts hold several thousand pounds of pressure without breaking, and won't cinch up on your midsection like a hangman's noose if you fall.

A tree-stand hunter also needs some sort of rope to haul up his bow, arrow quiver, and other equipment after he reaches his stand. A bow and other objects are awkward to hang onto as a hunter climbs, making falls more likely. A long fall to hard ground is dangerous enough, but falling on the sharp broadheads in your bow quiver or hip quiver can be fatal. A bowhunter should always use a rope to raise and lower his shooting gear from a tree stand—otherwise he's increasing the chances of seriously hurting himself.

One other necessary bit of equipment for long waits high above the ground is a can or pail to be used as a toilet. A tree-stander who answers nature's call over the side of his platform is marking his location every bit as well as a dog marks its territory. Animals like deer can smell human urine and other body wastes extremely well, and shy away from these odors with complete disgust.

Other tree-stand accessories a bowhunter might need include a small stool for him to sit on, a rope ladder to help him

A safety belt lets a bowhunter bend at the waist to take shots directly below him. It also prevents nasty falls from high above the ground. (Photograph courtesy of Baker Manufacturing Co.)

Natural elevated blinds put bowhunters above an animal's line of sight and give them a much better view of the countryside. Haystacks are top choices if bowhunters keep low and stack a bale or two in front of them to break their outline against the sky.

climb to his stand, and a nail or hook to hang his bow on while he waits for game. Once he gets his basic tree-stand gear, he'll discover soon enough what other things he needs to make his aerial life easier.

TOWER STANDS

Bowhunters sometimes use other sorts of elevated stands to get above an animal's line of sight. Permanent bowhunting "towers" are commonplace in the Texas brush country, giving a bowhunter the same advantages a tree stand offers—without the tree. Such fixtures are fairly expensive and time-consuming to erect, but work well in country with heavy brush and no trees big enough to support a regular tree stand. I know of one fellow who bowhunts from a tall wooden stepladder. He shoots his deer every year, and claims the ladder puts him far enough in the air to let him see better and prevent animals from seeing him. It's something to consider. A bowhunter can also use more natural elevated blinds if they're handy. Haystacks, big tree crotches, and rock ledges can work well at times if they're high enough to give good visibility and happen to be located near regularly used game areas.

BLINDS

Ground blinds of various sorts are popular with riflemen, but are of very limited value to a bowhunter. A properly dressed bowhunter is already a ground blind of sorts—he's camouflaged and blends right in with things. An artificial "pen" made of camouflaged cotton netting, cardboard, or something similar won't make a bowhunter any tougher to see, and will definitely handicap his ability to move about and draw his bow. However, a ground blind of some sort does let a fidgety bowhunter move around inside without scaring game, and if a hunter simply cannot sit still, he may be best off planted behind something fairly solid with little holes he can peek through.

Several manufacturers sell blinds and blind components made of wood, cardboard, cotton netting, and other materials, and as long as these are multi-colored and closely match the foliage they're set up against, they probably won't spook animals. I say "probably" because animals like whitetail deer

Ground blinds have little value in bowhunting. A properly dressed bowhunter with a camo headnet or face makeup is a self-contained ground blind, blending well with many backgrounds.

know their stomping grounds by heart and usually detect any change that takes place at eye level. A bowhunter who wants to hunt whitetail deer, blacktail deer, pronghorn antelope, and other alert creatures from a blind is best advised to put it up several weeks ahead of schedule so animals in the area have time to get used to it.

Shooting a bow from a blind creates other problems. A bowhunter either has to step to one side or rise up quite a ways to take a shot, sometimes causing noise and always creating enough movement to spook some animals right out of their skins. A well-dressed bowhunter is better advised to use natural cover when sitting or standing at ground level—he'll blend in better than a big blind, and he'll be able to shoot his bow with a minimum of movement.

The woods are full of natural objects a bowhunter can use to help him ambush game, including logs, stumps, tree trunks, low-growing trees, and bushes. The trick is sitting or standing *in front of* these natural objects—*not behind*. A bowhunter behind a bush or stump must continually raise and lower his head to watch the country in front of him, causing far too much body movement. To repeat a point, the well-dressed bowhunter is a walking ground blind—all he has to do to be well concealed is back up against some natural object which breaks the outline of his body. His quiet, camouflaged clothes will do the rest.

I'll never forget the first pronghorn antelope I shot at with a bow. I watched the medium-sized buck for three days before figuring out where he watered every evening. The fourth day I was crouched behind a big clump of sagebrush when he tiptoed down to drink. My heart was pounding like a triphammer by the time the gorgeous white-and-orange animal finally dropped his head and began gulping water, barely 30 yards away. I rose above the clump, drawing the bow as I eased into sight. I hadn't reckoned on the superb side vision these spooky animals have. By the time my arrow was all the way back the buck had wheeled around, muscles bunched like bedsprings. I let the arrow go, the buck popped sideways like a cork, and my arrow sliced harmlessly into the pond. If I'd been kneeling *in front of* that sage clump, the outcome might have been entirely different.

A smart bowhunter makes a point of finding out about tree stands, other elevated stands, and ground blinds. He learns what's available, what he can make for himself, and which equipment works best in which situations. Once he knows these things, he doesn't try to sneak around when the woods are especially dry, the brush especially thick, or the animals especially spooky. He simply takes an elevated stand or plants himself on the ground . . . and waits.

Chapter 7—MISCELLANEOUS BOWHUNTING GEAR

A beginning bowhunter should concern himself first with the basic gear he has to have—a proper hunting bow, the right arrows to match, a sturdy arrow quiver, a bowsight, a shooting glove or tab and an armguard, practical target-range equipment, adequate clothing and footwear, and a well-built tree stand or elevated blind. However, there are several other important bowhunting items he may also need. These must be classified as "miscellaneous gear" because some bowhunters use them and others do not. However, all these things are widely used and regarded by many bowhunters as standard bowhunting equipment.

SHOOTING STABILIZERS

Bowsights and bow quivers are so widely used that they hardly qualify as miscellaneous bowhunting gear, but several other common bow accessories do. For example, many bowhunters attach one or more short, heavy shooting stabilizers to their bows on the theory that these gizmos will improve their accuracy. Stabilizers have been used for years in tournament archery to help shooters better their scores, and they definitely help some bowhunters, too. A stabilizer is a heavy, elongated bar that attaches to the front of a bow's handle, usually about 3 inches below the grip (see bow diagrams in Chapter 1). A stabilizer adds weight to a bow and helps prevent a shooter from torquing or jerking his bow off target as he releases an arrow. A heavy rifle is easier to shoot well than a light one because it's harder to pull off target with quivering, jumpy muscles, and the same is true with a bow. Many bowhunters with less than perfect shooting form tend to "grab" their bows as they release arrows, sending those arrows somewhere other than the middle of the bull's-eye. A stabilizer can help a bowhunter who has this problem. A shooting stabilizer also absorbs some of the vibration that travels through a bow when it is shot, making some bows more comfortable to shoot and slightly quieter, too.

The best bowhunting stabilizers are fat, stubby affairs weighing anywhere from 3 to 10 ounces. They are generally made of steel, brass, or some other heavy metal, and screw directly into the stabilizer hole provided on most good hunting bows. A target stabilizer often consists of a long, slender rod with a heavy weight on the end, and can measure up to 4 feet in length. However, a hunting stabilizer should never measure over 6 inches long—a hunting bow with a longer stabilizer is a nuisance to carry in the woods and is more likely to clobber limbs, tree trunks, tree-stand supports, and other noisy objects.

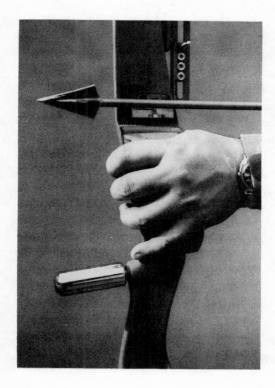

A shooting stabilizer hangs out front below a bow's grip, dampening bow noise and improving accuracy. Many commercial hunting stabilizers are shiny, chrome-plated affairs which need to be camouflaged prior to hunting season.

WRIST SLINGS AND FINGER STRAPS

Some bowhunters who have trouble with grabbing their bows when they shoot can also improve their accuracy by physically tying their hands to their bows. A wide variety of wrist slings, finger straps, and other leather, nylon, or metal devices have been designed to let a bowhunter keep his bow hand open when he shoots without worrying about the bow falling to the ground. A bowhunter who learns to keep his bow hand open cannot grab his bow and send an arrow wild, and wrist slings and similar devices allow him to do this without dropping and damaging his bow.

MECHANICAL RELEASES

A few bowhunters use mechanical bowstring releases instead of holding the bowstring with their fingers. This practice may not be legal in your area, so check your bowhunting laws before you try it. Mechanical bowstring releases of various designs have been standard target-archery aids for several years, and in some cases they can improve a bowhunter's shooting tremendously if a bowstring bruises his hand or he cannot seem to master the art of releasing the bowstring with his fingers. However, using a mechanical bowstring release generally handicaps a bowhunter's ability to shoot quickly and get off a fast second or third shot if the need arises. Using a mechanical release requires a fairly slow, deliberate shooting style, and many animals will not stand still long enough to get shot slowly and deliberately. A mechanical release is totally useless for shooting at flying birds, running rabbits, and fast-swimming fish—it is simply too slow to operate. A mechanical bowstring release is a very accurate tool in experienced hands, but not something most good bowhunters bother with unless they have serious trouble releasing a bowstring smoothly and comfortably with their fingers.

RANGEFINDERS

Rangefinding devices of one sort or another have become increasingly popular with bowhunters during the past two decades, mainly because bowsights have also become popular. A hunter who uses bowsights must accurately estimate the yardage between him and his target or he'll hit high or low. The very best way to estimate yardage is with your eyes. If you can become good at this by practicing a lot, you'll be able to take shots quickly with a minimum of extra hand and body movement. Fumbling around with a rangefinding device often wastes precious seconds you cannot afford to waste, even if you don't mind carrying a rangefinder with you at all times. It takes two hands to operate most rangefinders, which leaves you *no* hands to hold your bow and arrow. Your bow must be set down, hugged between your legs, or tucked under your arm while you turn the dial or dials on your rangefinder to determine the right yardage—a hassle at best.

Rangefinders do have their uses. A bowhunter sitting in a tree stand can hang his bow on a peg or nail beside him, leaving both hands free to operate a rangefinder. He can use this tool on animals that stroll slowly by, and he can also use it beforehand to determine the exact distance to rocks, trees, stumps, and other landmarks within bow range of his stand. Then if a deer comes by and he doesn't have time to use the rangefinder on the animal itself, he can still closely gauge the distance of the shot by using landmarks at known distance that are close to his target. Rangefinders are also the cat's meow for bowhunters with depth-perception problems. If you can't learn to judge distance because of some eye disorder, by all means buy a bowhunting rangefinder and learn to use it.

Some rangefinders are accurate enough for bowhunting use, and others are not. One model I tried a while back gave readings which varied up to 10 yards when used repeatedly at 60 yards. A bowhunter must know the distance within 2 or 3 yards for 40- to 60-yard shots with average bows and arrows—if he's 4 or 5 yards off at these distances, he'll miss a deer clean. If you can, test a rangefinder at several known distances before you buy it. This precaution could save some bitter disappointment later on.

POWDER POUCHES

Another shooting aid worth mentioning is a powder pouch, a small, flat container with a porous front that clips or straps to a bowhunter's belt. This little shooting accessory is filled with talcum powder and should be tapped lightly from time to time with a shooting glove or tab, releasing a little bit of powder onto the glove or tab through the screenlike front. The powder makes a glove or tab slippery, which gives a bowhunter a smoother bowstring release. Tiny clouds of excess powder also drift away, indicating the exact wind direction. I always carry a powder pouch when bowhunting to keep my tab slick and show me which way the breezes are blowing.

BOWFISHING REELS

One other important bow accessory is a bowfishing reel, which attaches to the front of a bow and holds the heavy fishing line that is tied to a fishing arrow. There are several kinds of bowfishing reels available, but most are simple drums that bowfishing line can be loosely wrapped around. When a bowfishing arrow is shot, fishing line spins off the outside of a drum-type reel freely and evenly. Most drum-type bowfishing reels are either taped to a bow or screwed into the threaded stabilizer hole on the front of a bow's handle. Some bowhunters simply tape pushbutton baitcasting reels to their bows instead, and these work well with fairly light monofilament line suitable for landing fish up to 20 or 30 pounds. However, serious bowfishermen who go after gar, sharks, and other magnum-sized fish need drum reels loaded with braided, heavy-test line. A bowfisherman should always be sure that his fishing line is evenly wrapped on his reel, and that he has more line on the reel than he intends to shoot away. If heavy-test line snags up on a bowfishing reel, or if an arrow reaches the end of its rope while still zipping along, it can turn around and come zipping right back at your head—an interesting experience, even if it misses!

BOW CASES

A darn good investment for every bowhunter is some sort of protective case for his bow. Most riflemen I know wouldn't think of storing or transporting their pet firearms without some kind of protection, but an amazingly large percentage of bowhunters throw their expensive equipment around like so much

Glenn Helgeland, well-known bowhunter, scored this rare double on carp by using a tape-on, drum-type bowfishing reel. Such a reel is just the ticket for shooting fish at fairly close range. (Photograph courtesy of Glenn Helgeland)

garbage. I've seen bowhunters spend several thousand dollars on an out-of-state big-game hunt, then toss their bow in the back of a pickup bed and let it bounce around for several hours. A good bow is a fine piece of equipment, and most bows are also fairly fragile. Even the simplest recurve bow usually has a bow-sight attached, and any bowsight can be easily knocked out of alignment with rough-and-tumble use. A recurve's bowstring can also become frayed or broken when the bow is knocked around. And if recurve bows are fragile, compound bows are downright delicate. They have cables to snag, wheels to break, bowstrings to fray, bowsights to bust, and adjustment screws and bolts to break off or rattle out of kilter. The bowhunter who doesn't case his prize hunting bow is not very wise.

A foam-rubber-lined case protects a valuable hunting bow from rough-and-tumble transport in hunting vehicles. A quiver full of arrows can be laid between the handle riser and bowstring in a roomy case.

A good selection of soft bow cases is offered by most archery stores. Some of these have fairly thin walls; others are heavily padded to protect a bow even when it is knocked around severely. Especially good are soft cases that are roomy enough to accept a bow with a bow quiver full of arrows attached. These let a hunter carry his shooting gear to and from the woods without scarring it up.

Bowhunters who travel a lot on airplanes need heavily padded soft cases for their bows and arrows, or the hard plastic or aluminum transport cases offered by several outfits. If you've ever seen airline baggage "gorillas" toss stuff around, you know why. Once I checked a bow as baggage in a fairly well-padded soft case, and when I opened the case at the other end of the line, all five sight pins were bent almost double. I had to drive 90 miles to find an archery shop, buy a new set of sight pins, and completely resight my bow before I could begin my hunt.

The best hard transport cases available are fairly stream-lined, but still have room inside for one or two bows, a couple dozen arrows, a bow quiver, and some other bowhunting equipment. Almost as handy are specially made cases designed to carry bows and arrows separately. Such cases are worthwhile investments even if a bowhunter never flies airplanes—they completely protect his gear when it's bouncing around in the back of a jeep or jammed under a mountain of other duffel.

BINOCULARS

One of the most important pieces of equipment for most bowhunters is a first-quality set of binoculars. A pair of binoculars is not too important to the man who bowhunts from a tree stand in the forests of the Deep South—he seldom sees deer past 15 or 20 yards. However, any bowhunter who hunts in open terrain is operating under a handicap without binoculars.

Binoculars are essential when a bowhunter needs to look for game past 50 yards. The author loves to sit on high ground, glass for animals, and then go after them as they feed or rest.

Far-off animals are sometimes difficult or impossible to locate
without good glasses—and you certainly can't go after an animal
you can't see. Binoculars are most useful to a trophy bowhunter
because he has to size up an animal's horns or antlers before he
can decide whether or not to go after that particular animal. But
every bowhunter who expects to see animals beyond 100 yards
should carry binoculars. They let him find animals, size them
up, and simply enjoy watching them under high magnification.

There seems to be a contest going on among some bowhunting groups to see who can carry the tiniest pair of binoculars. If you can hide them in your clenched fist, so much the
better! Why some bowhunters gravitate toward little binoculars
puzzles me considerably. Tiny glasses are okay in their place,
but their *only* redeeming features are their compact size and
inconsequential weight. They all have fairly narrow fields of
view, most have poor light-gathering qualities, and none are

Deer lure like doe-in-heat
scent should be squirted
on trees and bushes near
a hunter's stand, and also
applied liberally to his
clothing. A pant leg is a
good place to squirt this
potent concoction—the
farther away from your
nose the better!

easy to hold steady in a breeze. Ultra-compact binoculars may be all right for the old, the sick, and the crippled. However, a good-quality medium-sized glass has it all over the itty-bitty models.

Most of the best bowhunting binoculars weigh somewhere between 15 and 30 ounces, and magnify from 7 to 10 power. They are best carried on a neck strap to allow quick use, unless a bowhunter's bowstring collides with them when he shoots. This neck strap should be fairly short to prevent them from swinging like a pendulum at belt-buckle level and continually clobbering your bow and every tree in sight. They should be fairly dull-finished to prevent game-spooking shine, and they should be easy to operate with one hand so you don't always have to lay your bow down to use them.

The very best bowhunting binoculars, in my opinion, are the so-called armored binoculars offered by several well-known optical companies. These binoculars are almost completely covered with soft, nonglare rubber, making them totally camouflaged and totally quiet. They're good!

CAMOUFLAGE MAKEUP

Camouflage makeup is used by a lot of bowhunters in lieu of a headnet or charcoal smeared on their faces. Camo makeup is available in several shades. Most kinds wash off with soap and water, and some kinds are impregnated with insect repellent to make exposed flesh unappealing to the mosquitoes, gnats, and flies that buzz around the woods. Camo makeup is usually smeared liberally on the face, and some bowhunters use it on their hands, too. It is a bit of a nuisance to apply and remove, and makes a person look a little bizarre when he enters a restaurant to eat lunch between morning and afternoon hunts. However, it successfully covers a light, shiny complexion and helps a bowhunter get his game.

BUCK SCENTS

How much good so-called "buck scents" really are is highly debatable. Some bowhunters swear by these strong-smelling concoctions; others swear *at* them. Every bowhunter should try the various kinds available and then decide whether they work on the variety of game he hunts. There are two basic kinds of commercial scents available—odor-masking scents and animal lures.

Odor-masking scents are strong-smelling potions designed to partially or completely cover up a bowhunter's body odor. Some common odor-masking scents include apple scent, wild-grape scent, and skunk scent. These and other "fragrances" are usually sold in plastic squeeze bottles, and are meant to be squirted liberally on a bowhunter's clothes immediately before he starts hunting. They can also be squirted on bushes and trees near a tree stand or ground blind to cover the BO a bowhunter leaves behind as he approaches his stand.

Animal lures are designed to attract various kinds of game. The most common one is doe-in-heat scent, which is meant to lure in rutting whitetail bucks. Bowhunters squirt this foul-smelling concoction along the trails leading past their tree stands, the theory being that lovesick bucks will come gallivanting in to find whatever left that heavenly odor. Some bowhunters also cut the tarsal glands out of the hocks of deer they kill, store these in zip-lock bags, and carry them each time they go hunting. Again, the theory is that other deer will be attracted to this familiar smell, or at least won't smell the human odor mixed with it.

Odor-masking scents and animal lures work at least part of the time, depending on the animals involved, how long it's been since a bowhunter has had a bath, and which way the breezes are blowing. You owe it to yourself to give 'em a try and decide just how valuable they are for you.

PACKS

Fanny packs and small frameless backpacks are very popular with bowhunters because bowhunters usually have to carry quite a bit of gear with them when they hunt—a lot more than gun hunters have to carry. Included in a bowhunter's field kit should be the normal outdoor aids all hunters carry: a sharp knife, matches, toilet paper, a compass, a small meat saw, a canteen, and other standard items. However, a bowhunter needs to carry other things, too—things unique to the sport of

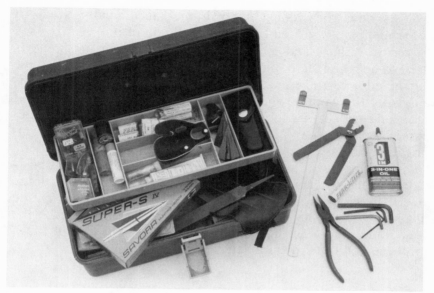

A bowhunter collects a variety of tools and gizmos as he goes along. A fisherman's tackle box is a first-rate place to store important gear needed on extended hunting trips.

bowhunting. For instance, he should carry either a few sharp replacement broadheads in case the ones on his arrows get dull, or a file and whetstone to resharpen his arrowheads after he shoots and misses. He should carry an extra bowstring in case the one in his bow becomes frayed, and a bowstringer so he can easily replace the damaged string. He may also decide to carry things like a small rangefinding device, camouflaged gloves to be slipped on for close sneaks on animals, several kinds of odor-masking scent or deer lure, and a roll of fluorescent plastic tape to hang from trees along a hard-to-follow trail.

These and other items must be carried somewhere, and a small fanny pack or frameless backpack is just the ticket. Such a pack should be as small as possible to prevent unnecessary tangles and noise in the heavy trees or brush, and should be camouflaged to blend in with the countryside. Many kinds are available at sporting-goods stores, some designed specifically for bowhunters. Take your pick.

As time goes along, a bowhunter accumulates scads of other equipment related to his sport. Some of this gear is used to repair, adjust, and maintain his basic equipment. Some is used to help him shoot his bow better. And some is used to give him an edge when he's actually out hunting. As a matter of fact, a dyed-in-the-wool bowhunter usually owns a whole closetful of tools and gadgets he feels will improve his odds of being successful—things like Allen wrenches, screwdrivers, cans of lubricating oil, bowstring wax, bow squares, nocking-point pliers, shaft-cutting tools, fletching glue, hot-melt ferrule cement, bowstring silencers, camouflage bow socks, files, whetstones, knife steels, fletching jigs, cans of dull spray paint, and dozens and dozens more. Some of these items are vitally important to the sport, and others are just fun to experiment with. We'll touch on these and other gizmos later in this book.

Part II—USING THE EQUIPMENT

Chapter 8—PREPARING THE BOW
TO SHOOT

A brand-new hunting bow won't be ready to shoot the instant you buy it. Not by a long shot. It will probably have a bowstring and some sort of arrow rest attached, but nothing more. Before you can begin practicing sensibly with your bow, you'll need to install a suitable arrow rest unless the bow already has one, put a nock locator of some sort on the bowstring to ensure accuracy, adjust the arrow plate so your arrows will fly reasonably well, install a bowsight solidly on the handle riser of the bow, and attach a bow quiver if you decide to use one. Some archery shops normally do these things before they give a customer his bow, and almost all will do them if you ask politely. However, a self-sufficient bowhunter would rather prepare his bow himself, giving him extra insights into how bow-shooting equipment works and letting him set up his bow just right for his own kind of hunting.

ARROW RESTS

Most hunting bows have an arrow rest when they leave the factory, and some factory-installed rests are fine for hunting. The key is how quiet and durable they are (see Chapter 3 for details on arrow-rest design). If your bow has a soft, sturdy arrow rest, fine and dandy. If not, you'll have to browse around and select one that will serve the purpose.

The arrow rest on a bow is usually attached directly above the handle, near the bottom of the sight window. It may simply consist of an adhesive-backed "rug" on a shelf that is actually part of the bow's handle riser, and a simple leather or plastic arrow plate glued to the bottom of the sight window. However, most better hunting bows have separate one- or two-piece arrow rests that are attached somewhere near the bottom of a bow's sight window. Every bow is designed to operate most efficiently with the arrow rest in one particular spot. If a rest is placed elsewhere on the bow—even ½ inch above, below, or to the side of the recommended spot—the bow may be noisier to shoot than normal, and may shoot arrows slower and/or more erratically than it should. Hunting-bow manufacturers sometimes provide information on where rests should be installed on their bows, but if not, a replacement rest should be placed as close as possible to where the original one was located. Many modern bows have threaded holes in their sight windows to accept a separate adjustable arrow plate that is either solid or spring-loaded to "cushion" an arrow as it leaves the bow. If your bow is drilled and tapped for a separate arrow plate, an adhesive-backed arrow shelf should be placed directly beneath this hole.

A one-piece arrow rest or separate shelf usually has an adhesive back designed to stick securely to a bow's sight window. A few rests and shelves are attached to bows with wood or metal screws. The screw-on types are simple to install because they fit predrilled holes in a bow, eliminating the need to worry about putting them in the right place or attaching them securely. A few twists of a screwdriver and they are in place. Installing an adhesive-backed arrow rest or separate shelf is also easy, but requires a few simple precautions. First of all, the area the rest is attached to must be clean and dry. It's a good idea to scrub a bow's sight window thoroughly with a cloth soaked in rubbing alcohol or another mild cleaner before attaching an arrow rest or shelf—this ensures a good bond with the bow. After a bow's sight window is clean and dry, the arrow rest or shelf should be pressed in the proper place *with the shelf at right angles to the bowstring*. The whole cleaning and installation procedure will only take a couple of minutes.

POSITIONING THE NOCK LOCATOR

The next step is to put a nock locator of some sort on your bowstring. A nock locator, sometimes called a nocking point, allows a bowhunter to nock his arrow on the bowstring in ex-

actly the same place every time, which is a must for accurate
shooting. Arrows that are nocked in slightly different places on
the bowstring fly different places. Usually, the higher an arrow
is nocked on the bowstring, the lower it will shoot. A nock
locator of some sort provides a slightly raised area on a bowstring that the nock of an arrow can be slipped *under*. Some
bowhunters install two nocking points on their bowstrings, one
above and one below where the nock slips onto the serving of
the string. However, most hunters find that one nocking point
above the nock is all that's necessary for consistent shooting.

Several kinds of commercial nock locators are sold at archery stores. One common type of nocking point consists of a
circular, open-ended band of metal with a circular rubber cushion inside. This small rubber-and-metal band is slipped over the
bowstring, positioned in the correct spot, and then clamped
tightly around the bowstring with a pair of nocking-point
pliers. The rubber cushion protects the bowstring from the edges
of the metal ring, and also prevents the nocking point from moving from its proper position on the bowstring serving. A rubber-
and-metal nocking point can be loosened and moved slightly if
a bowhunter wants to experiment with its location to improve
the flight of his arrows, a definite advantage in some cases.

Another widely used commercial nocking point is the heat-
shrink type. This kind of nock locator is slipped over a bowstring, moved into position, and then carefully heated up with
a match or cigarette lighter. The heat causes it to constrict
tightly around the bowstring, making it a permanent fixture.

Some bowhunters prefer to make their own nocking points
by wrapping a little dental floss or nylon thread around the bowstring in the right spot. A slightly raised bead of floss or thread
makes a good, solid nocking point as long as the ends of the
floss or thread are tied off securely and dabbed with a little
fingernail polish or some durable cement.

A beginning bowhunter should start out with a movable
nocking point like the rubber-and-metal clamp-on design. This
will let him experiment with different nocking-point locations to
achieve perfect arrow flight (see Chapter 12 for details). The
proper location of a nocking point on a bowstring is usually

WHERE TO INSTALL YOUR NOCKING POINT

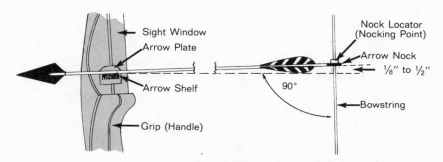

somewhere between ⅛ inch and ½ inch above *a line drawn at right angles to the bowstring from the shelf of the bow's arrow rest to the bowstring* (see diagram). Most bow manufacturers recommend that an arrow be nocked about ⅜ inch above 90 degrees to the arrow shelf—this will usually result in good arrow flight. The exact location of a nocking point on a bowstring is not usually too critical, but with a few bow-and-arrow combinations a nocking point must be placed in exactly the right spot on the bowstring to prevent arrows from porpoising (wobbling up and down in the rear end). Unless the literature that comes with your bow says otherwise, put the *bottom* of your nocking point about ⅜ inch above 90 degrees to the arrow shelf. This placement should give you good, consistent arrow flight.

Putting the nocking point in the right location on the bowstring requires the use of some sort of square, either a large carpenter's square or a regular bow square sold at archery stores. A bow square clips to the bowstring and slides up and down the string to give quick, easy alignment with the arrow rest. Most bow squares are also calibrated in fractions of an inch to allow easy placement of a nocking point. A bow square is a handy, inexpensive tool every serious bowhunter should have. It lets him install nocking points on his bowstrings, and lets him check their location periodically to make sure they haven't slipped out of place. A more conventional square will serve the purpose, but is awkward to line up exactly with the bowstring and the arrow shelf.

A bowhunter should install nocking points on at least two

spare bowstrings by detaching his original bowstring and temporarily attaching each spare string to his bow. He should shoot a dozen arrows or so to stretch out each spare string, and then attach a nocking point to each in the same location as the nocking point on the original string. Once this is done, he can quickly replace his old bowstring with an identical new one when the old one becomes frayed or broken.

A bowhunter should also wax his bowstring heavily before starting to practice. A tube of bowstring wax costs just a few pennies, lasts years, and greatly prolongs the life of a string. Bowstring wax lubricates the synthetic strands in modern bowstrings to prevent wear as these strands rub against one another when a bow is drawn and shot over and over again. Waxing a bowstring is simple—just rub wax all over the exposed strands on the string (not on the center serving section that a bowhunter holds in his fingers, and not on the wrapped ends of the bow-

A bow square makes nocking-point installation a breeze, and lets a hunter check nocking-point placement periodically with a minimum of fuss.

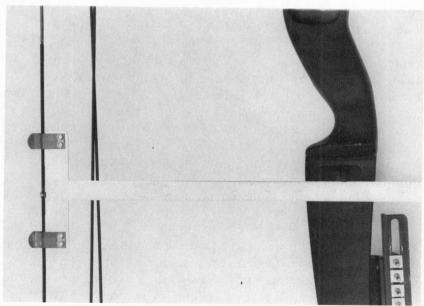

string). When a bowhunter is shooting regularly, his bowstring should be waxed once a month or so to keep it in tip-top shape.

ADJUSTING THE ARROW-REST PLATE

The next step in preparing your bow to shoot is adjusting the plate on your arrow rest to ensure good arrow flight. The fastest, most stable arrow flight is usually achieved when the centerline of an arrow lines up perfectly with a line drawn down the middle of both limbs on the bow (see illustrations). A bow-and-arrow setup of this kind is said to be "centershot," and puts every bit of energy from the bow limbs and the bowstring directly behind an arrow when that arrow is shot. In other words, in a centershot setup the arrow leaves the bow in exactly the same direction as the bowstring is traveling—all the energy from the bowstring is aimed right down the centerline of the arrow, not off to one side.

The best way to line up an arrow with the centerline of your bow's limbs and the bowstring is by gently clamping your bow upright by its lower limb in a small vise, and then nocking an arrow in the bow with it resting on the arrow shelf and resting against the arrow plate (the way it would be before you shot it). Then stand a few feet behind the bow, shut one eye, and line up the bowstring with the centerline of both bow limbs. If the centerline of the arrow *also* lines up with the bowstring (if the string splits the arrow in two visually along the whole length of the arrow) then your bow is centershot. If the tip of the arrow juts to the left or right of the bowstring when the bowstring is lined up with the centerline of the bow's limbs, you must move the plate of your arrow rest in (if the arrow tip is to the left) or out (if the tip is to the right) until the arrow is centershot in the bow (reverse this procedure for left-hand bows).

Moving an adjustable arrow plate is easy, which is why many bowhunters prefer adjustable arrow rests. You simply screw or slip the plate in or out (to the right or left) until the arrow point lines up with the bowstring and the centerline of the bow limbs. Nonadjustable arrow rests present special problems. Most bow manufacturers try to design their hunting bows so the average nonadjustable rest will put an arrow pretty close to cen-

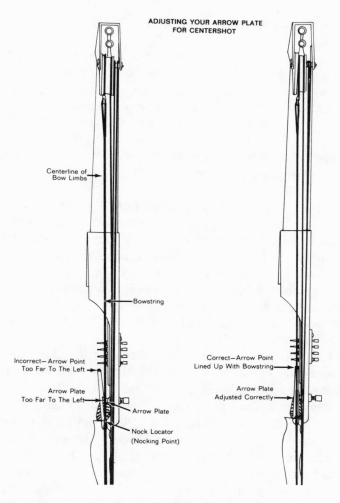

ADJUSTING YOUR ARROW PLATE
FOR CENTERSHOT

Centerline of
Bow Limbs

Bowstring

Incorrect—Arrow Point
Too Far To The Left

Correct—Arrow Point
Lined Up With Bowstring

Arrow Plate
Too Far To The Left

Arrow Plate
Adjusted Correctly

Arrow Plate

Nock Locator
(Nocking Point)

tershot; however, sometimes a bowhunter has to move the plate on his rest quite a distance to achieve centershot. The best way to move adhesive-backed, nonadjustable arrow plates out (to the left on right-hand bows) is to shim them with thin layers of paper, cardboard, or wood. The only way to move a nonadjustable arrow plate in (to the right) is to cut away part of the arrow plate with a knife or file, something that is sometimes possible and sometimes impossible to do. It depends on the kind of arrow rest involved. If you simply cannot adjust a particular arrow rest to centershot, you'll have to find another rest you *can* adjust.

Chances are your bow and arrow will be close to centershot to begin with, making any adjustments easy and quick to make. You may have to make some more minor arrow-plate adjustments later on to achieve perfect, completely non-wobbly arrow flight with the particular type of arrows you are shooting (see Chapter 12). However, your arrows should fly reasonably well once you make the adjustments just described—well enough to practice with and learn the basics of good shooting.

INSTALLING THE BOWSIGHT

A bowsight must be firmly attached to a bow's handle riser so it doesn't slop around and destroy accuracy. Some bowsights are designed to fit particular bows and simply screw or tape to these bows in particular places. Other sights are designed to fit a wide variety of bows with a wide variety of handle-riser shapes. Where and how a bowhunter mounts a bowsight on his bow depends on the sight and bow involved and the bowhunter's personal tastes.

Many bowsights can be mounted at either the front or the back of a bow's sight window. Each sight-mounting location has advantages and disadvantages. A sight mounted in front of the sight window instead of in back is several inches farther away from a shooter's eye, giving him a little better sight definition (the sight pins are in a little sharper focus). Better sight definition can result in slightly better shooting, all else being equal. However, a bowsight that hangs out on the front of a bow is more apt to get clobbered and knocked out of alignment than a sight mounted on the side of the bow closest to the shooter. Bowhunters who expect to bat their bows around like football training dummies are probably better off with sights mounted at the back side of the sight window.

Unless a hunter's bow is drilled and tapped to accept a particular kind of bowsight in a particular location, he's best off attaching his sight to his bow with a few wraps of masking tape to begin with. This way, he can experiment with several mounting locations before permanently anchoring the sight to his bow.

Otherwise, he might discover that his arrow or arrow fletching hits the sight when he shoots, or that part of the sight touches his bow hand and causes painful abrasions, or that the sight would be a little easier to see when mounted in a slightly different place. A bowsight that is lightly attached with masking tape is a lot easier to move around than one that is soldily anchored with wood screws or several dozen wraps of heavy plastic tape.

ATTACHING A BOW QUIVER

If a bowhunter decides to use a bow quiver, he should attach it to his bow before he starts shooting, and also fill it with arrows. Almost all bow quivers are quickly attached to a bow with tape, spring-steel arms, screws, or bolts. This quick-attachment feature allows a hunter to remove his bow quiver when he's traveling, and put it on again within seconds after he reaches his hunting area.

Because bow quivers are so easily attached and detached, many bowhunters practice without them on their bows and install them just prior to a hunt. This can be a mistake. A bow quiver is a fairly heavy piece of equipment, especially when it's filled with six or eight hunting arrows. Such a quiver can alter the way a bow "feels" when a hunter shoots, and it can also change the way a bow recoils and vibrates. Major recoil and vibration changes can drastically alter the way arrows fly from a bow—enough to shift point of impact as much as 2 or 3 feet at 30 yards. A bowhunter who practices shooting for several months without a bow quiver, sights in his bow without a bow quiver, and then attaches a quiver to his bow is asking for trouble. His arrows may hit about the same place they did before, and then again they may not. In any case, the change in the weight and balance of a bow and arrow caused by attaching a bow quiver full of arrows is often enough to make a bowhunter's gear feel "funny" to him, causing him to shoot poorly on game. A bowhunter should practice with the exact equipment setup he intends to use in the field.

Some bow quivers can be attached either with the arrowhead cap up or with it down. The standard, preferred way to attach a bow quiver to a bow is with the cap up, mainly because this protects sharp broadheads from edge-rusting moisture and various kinds of debris that can also dull them. A bow quiver installed with the cap down tends to accumulate all sorts of natural junk like leaves, dirt, and twigs, and also tends to fill up like a municipal swimming pool when it rains.

If a bowhunter draws an exceptionally long arrow, say 31 or 32 inches, he may decide to mount his bow quiver with the arrowhead cap down so the nock ends of his arrows don't stick out past the lower tip of his bow. This way he can rest his lower limb tip on the ground or the toe of his shoe without driving his arrow nocks in the dirt. It's disconcerting to say the least when you miss your first shot, grab another arrow, and suddenly realize the nock slot is packed completely full of terra firma. More than one buck has been lost this way.

A bowhunter should also attach any other gear to his bow that he knows for a fact he'll be using in the woods—a hunting stabilizer, for example. Other accessories like bowstring silencers can sometimes affect the way a bow shoots, but until a bowhunter shoots awhile he won't know for sure which silencers will work best with his particular bow and arrow, or for that matter, whether or not he needs silencers at all. Things of this nature he can experiment with after he shoots a month or two.

Hunting-bow preparation doesn't take much time, really, but it's vitally important. Unless a bowhunter sets up his gear correctly before he begins to practice, practice will do him little or no good. A bowhunter can only shoot as well as his bow—if his bow doesn't shoot worth a darn because of improper setup, neither will he.

Chapter 9—PREPARING THE ARROW TO SHOOT

Many bowhunters buy their hunting arrows ready-made at archery stores, then have these shops cut their arrows to the proper length and install either field points or broadheads. Most archery shops will cut arrows to length and attach arrowheads for a small fee, making these services worthwhile for the bowhunter who doesn't want to be bothered with the mechanics of getting his arrows ready to shoot. However, a bowhunter who learns to assemble his own arrows from scratch can save money, learn a lot in the process that will help him repair and maintain his arrows, and most important, experiment with various kinds of nocks, shafts, fletching, and arrowheads to find a combination that gives him extra-flat trajectory, superior accuracy, and/or exceptional penetration on game. Factory-assembled arrows are usually very well made, but no factory can stop to produce a dozen arrows custom-made for you and your bow. Only you can do that.

All the components and tools needed to make quality hunting arrows are sold at archery stores. This includes unadorned full-length arrow shafts made of cedar, fiberglass, and aluminum; nocks of various kinds; feather and plastic fletching in a variety of shapes, sizes, and colors; tapered nock inserts for fiberglass shafts; tapered and threaded point inserts of various sizes and shapes for fiberglass and aluminum shafts; tapering tools for wooden shafts; dipping tubes and lacquer for wooden shafts; various glues to attach nocks, inserts, and fletching to shafts; fletching jigs to fletch arrows with; and dozens of other arrow-making accessories.

The bowhunter who wants to shoot three-fletched aluminum arrows, for example, will need a dozen shafts of the proper size to match his bow; a dozen hunting nocks of the proper size to fit his shafts; a fletching jig of some sort and three dozen feathers or plastic vanes; glue to attach nocks and fletching; some field points, broadheads, and/or other kinds of arrowheads to attach to the finished arrows; either screw-in point adapters for screw-in-type arrowheads or tapered point adapters for glue-on-type arrowheads; and a tube of hot-melt ferrule cement to install the point adapters and possibly the arrowheads. This list of arrow-making gear looks as long as your leg, but won't cost much money and will give you total versatility in making your own custom aluminum arrows. The list of materials and tools for making wood and fiberglass arrows is a little longer, but not by a great deal.

ATTACHING THE NOCK

The first thing that is usually attached to an arrow shaft is the nock, mainly because arrows cannot be fletched without nocks, and cannot be easily cut to length without nocks. There are several ways to attach nocks to arrow shafts, depending for the most part on exactly what kind of shaft a nock is being attached to. Most types of wood, fiberglass, and aluminum arrow shafts have some sort of 15-degree nock taper on the back which a nock is glued onto. The do-it-yourselfer will have to put this taper on wooden shafts with a simple tapering tool that resembles a pencil sharpener, but fiberglass and aluminum shafts usually come with commercial nock tapers. Most fiberglass shafts are designed to accept tapered aluminum nock inserts, which slip inside the back ends of these shafts. These nock inserts should be glued into fiberglass shafts with epoxy for a permanent bond, a process anyone can handle with ease. Some brands of fiberglass shafts accept special nocks with male inserts which are actually glued inside the ends of these shafts, also with epoxy. Nock tapers are swaged right into aluminum shafts by the factory, making aluminum shafts the easiest of all to work with. The bowhunter who uses aluminum shafts doesn't have to bother with tapering the ends with a tool or gluing in nock inserts. He simply glues on his nocks and goes on to the next step in assembling his arrows.

A nock should be glued to an arrow's nock taper with one of the commercial fletching glues available at archery stores. These glues usually set up within fifteen minutes, allowing a bowhunter to replace bent or broken nocks in the field or on the target range and then shoot these nocks almost immediately (see Chapter 15 for details on replacing broken nocks).

Nocks are simple to install. First, scrub the nock taper on a fiberglass or aluminum shaft with Ajax cleanser, rubbing alcohol, or another mild cleaner to remove grease and dirt. Ajax cuts grease and oil the best, and also slightly abrades an aluminum nock taper for a better bond with the nock. After the nock taper is scrubbed, wash it off in warm water and dry it with a clean cloth or paper towel. The nock tapers on wooden shafts do not have to be cleaned before nock installation—the glue soaks into the wood enough to form a very good bond. Next, *lightly* coat the nock taper with glue and press the nock over the taper, rotating it around the taper a few times to ensure good alignment with the shaft. A poorly aligned nock is the

Arrow nocks should be glued to aluminum shafts with good-quality fletching cement. Once the 15-degree nock taper is coated with cement, the nock is rotated firmly into place.

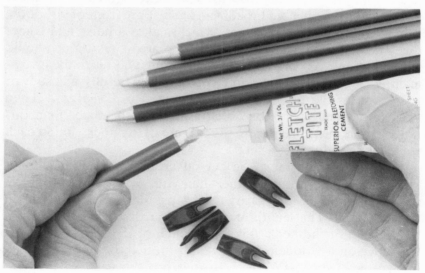

single worst cause of erratic arrow flight, so be sure the nock hugs the nock taper and isn't floating cockeyed on a heavy cushion of glue.

A shooting buddy of mine once sneaked within 30 yards of a dandy muley buck, accurately estimated the range, and let fly with cool confidence. The arrow corkscrewed out of the bow with a loud clank and sailed 2 feet to the left of the startled animal. This fellow is usually a dead-eye with his bow, so the whole affair shook him up. He examined his arrow carefully and discovered that the nock was tipped badly to one side. As a matter of fact, the nock had almost but not quite fallen off the nock taper while the glue was wet. My pal learned a costly lesson, and learned it well. To my knowledge, he's never carried another arrow with a cockeyed nock.

CUTTING THE SHAFT TO LENGTH

After you install nocks on your arrow shafts, the next step is cutting these shafts to the proper length. As mentioned in Chapter 2, proper arrow length is ¾ inch longer than your draw length (your draw length is the distance from the bottom of the nock slot on your arrow to the front of your bow's handle riser when your arrow is fully drawn). This extra ¾ inch will prevent you from bumping a big broadhead against the front of your bow when you draw back to shoot, which makes a noise and sometimes actually knocks the arrow off the arrow rest. You should already know your draw length by the time you reach the arrow-making stage, but if you don't you should carefully measure it, using one of the three methods described in Chapter 1. Then you should cut your arrow shafts off ¾ inch longer than this draw length, measuring from the bottom of the nock slot on each shaft straight down the shaft.

Wooden shafts must be cut off an inch longer than other kinds of shafts (1¾ inch longer than your draw length) to leave room for the inch-long arrowhead taper that is usually cut on the front end. The length of a finished arrow is measured from the bottom of the nock slot to the back of the arrowhead, and the taper on a wooden shaft extends an inch or so *into* a glue-on-type arrowhead. Wooden arrows are the easiest to cut to length—they can be sawed off with a carpenter's saw, hacksaw, or any other saw designed for wood. The cut on the end must be as square as you can possibly make it; use a miter box if you can to ensure a square cut.

Fiberglass shafts must be cut off with a fine-toothed hacksaw. The cut should be perfectly square to facilitate the installation of point inserts, so a miter box of some sort must be used. Rotate the shaft and score the outside all the way around before it is cut completely off; otherwise the fiberglass may fray or split away from the shaft on the bottom side as the saw blade rips through the last little bit of shaft wall.

Aluminum shafts are best cut off with a high-speed cutoff tool available through your local archery store. Some bowhunters cut aluminum shafts to length with tubing cutters, but this constricts the ends of shafts and makes point inserts very difficult to install. A point insert that is jammed forcibly into the end of a tubular aluminum shaft may work all right for a while, but places considerable outward pressure against the wall of the shaft, pressure that can eventually cause stress corrosion cracking in the wall. Stress corrosion cracking is especially likely to happen in the more expensive, tougher aluminum shafts with especially high tensile strengths—shafts made of XX75 and X7 alloys. If a bowhunter cannot obtain or afford a high-speed cutoff tool, he should carefully saw off each aluminum shaft with a miter box and a fine-toothed hacksaw, and then lightly chamfer the inside of the wall with a chamfering tool or the tip of a large high-speed drill bit. This will remove burrs from the inside of the cut and allow easy, unpressured installation of a point insert.

FLETCHING

Once your shafts are cut to length, they are ready to be fletched. Some preparation is necessary; an arrow shaft must be absolutely clean and dry when fletching is glued in place, or the fletching bond will be poor and the feathers or plastic vanes will eventually fall off the arrow.

After wooden shafts are cut to length, they should be carefully dipped in shaft lacquer to seal the wood and create a smooth, clean surface to fletch to. Shafts are usually dipped in a long, slender tube partially filled with lacquer. After being immersed in this dipping tube, they are carefully set on their front ends and leaned against their nocks to try. Once the lacquer is dry, they are ready to fletch.

Fiberglass and aluminum shafts are easy to clean prior to fletching. The best way to clean both kinds of shafts is scrubbing the back half (the half at the nock end) with a mixture of warm water and Ajax cleanser or a similar nonchlorinated abrasive cleanser. This warm-water Ajax scrub was developed by the aerospace industry to bond bare aluminum to nonmetal objects, and it works like a charm on fiberglass, bare-aluminum, and anodized-aluminum shafts. Some bowhunters use fine sandpaper to roughen and clean the fletching areas on aluminum shafts, but this process is inferior to the Ajax scrub because it puts ugly scrapes on a bare-aluminum shaft, removes the dull protective anodizing on top-quality aluminum shafts, and cleans no better than a thorough Ajax scrub. Some bowhunters also clean their fiberglass and aluminum shafts with cleaning solvent or acetone before fletching, but these powerful cleaners will literally melt a plastic nock if they touch it. The warm-water Ajax scrub is the best all-around shaft-cleaning technique.

Cleaned fiberglass and aluminum shafts should be carefully dried with a clean, lint-free cloth or left to dry in the open air. The fletching area on the shafts should not be touched again with anything prior to fletching. Even "clean" hands are covered with a film of slippery body oil which can spoil a good bond between a shaft and a feather or plastic vane. Cleaned shafts should be handled by the front half (the half away from the fletching area) and by the nock only.

A few bowhunters mistakenly believe they get a much better bond between an aluminum arrow shaft and the fletching if they coat the entire fletching area with fletching cement and let this coat dry thoroughly before attaching the fletching. However, research conducted by Easton Aluminum, Inc., by far the oldest and biggest arrow-shaft manufacturing firm in the world, indicates that feathers and plastic vanes adhere extremely well when fletched directly to clean, dry aluminum—a precoat of cement doesn't hurt anything, but doesn't help much either.

A bowhunter needs a fletching jig to fletch his arrows with. Fletching jigs are fairly simple tools which hold an arrow rigidly and allow the bowhunter to attach feathers or plastic vanes securely and uniformly. There are many fletching-jig designs available, but the best ones consist of two basic parts—a base that an arrow shaft sits in, and a clamp that holds a feather or vane in place on the shaft while the fletching glue is drying. The best fletching jigs allow a bowhunter to fletch an arrow with three feathers or vanes (the most common way), four feathers or vanes (used by some bowhunters to get better fletching clearance around some bows), and six feathers (used to make flu-flu arrows for bird hunting). A fletching jig is a handy tool to replace damaged arrow fletching, too, and every serious bowhunter should own a good one. Even the best fletching jigs are fairly inexpensive, and they don't wear out.

There are two basic kinds of clamps available for fletching jigs—straight and helical. A straight clamp holds a feather or vane between two flat plates and positions the base of the feather or vane at a slight angle to the centerline of an arrow shaft. This fletching angle is usually about 5 degrees on hunting arrows. In contrast, a helical clamp holds a feather or vane between two twisted, spiral-shaped pieces of metal, although it also positions the base of that feather or vane at a 5-degree angle to the centerline of the arrow shaft. The difference between straight and helical clamps is clear as mud to many beginners, but the two clamps result in two different kinds of fletching with slightly different flight characteristics. Straight fletching is often called straight offset fletching because it is set at an angle on the arrow shaft to turn the arrow (rifle it) as it flies through the air. However, straight fletching has no twist or spiral to it, which means it causes less air resistance when it flies through the air than helical fletching does. Helical fletching is set at an angle on an arrow shaft, too, but this fletching is also twisted or heavily spiraled. In other words, the *base* of a helical fletch lies flat on the arrow shaft along the whole length of this base, twisting this base and also twisting the rest of the feather or vane as it angles sideways along a round shaft. The base of a straight fletch is also glued to the shaft along the entire length of the feather or vane, but the base of a straight fletch does not twist to conform to the surface of the arrow shaft as it angles across it. As a result, straight fletching is not spiraled or twisted—it is merely angled on the shaft.

Helical fletching is far superior to straight offset fletching on hunting arrows because it causes more drag on the tail end of an arrow than straight offset does when fletched at the same angle. More drag means better arrow stability and better accuracy, things a bowhunter should value over slight increases in arrow speed. Arrows with straight offset fletching will fly *slightly* faster than those with helical fletching, but are not nearly as stable when used with big broadheads—they tend to wobble more when a bowhunter shoots, keep wobbling longer, and sometimes allow a large broadhead to steer the arrow way off course. When you buy a fletching jig, get one with a helical clamp—it's the only way to go.

If you decide to fletch your arrows with feathers instead of plastic vanes, the best kind to get are factory-shaped, die-cut feathers. In the olden days, a bowhunter had to buy full-sized turkey feathers, cut them to the proper length, and then glue them to an arrow shaft. After an arrow was fletched, it had to be put in a feather trimmer, which burned the feathers to the proper shape. I remember when I used to burn the feathers on my arrows, and it is not a particularly pleasant memory. Burning feathers smell exactly like burning hair. The fletching always looked good when I was done, but the house smelled terrible! Today, burning feathers is largely a thing of the past because several companies sell uniformly shaped, die-cut feathers in a variety of sizes and shapes.

Follow the instructions that came with your fletching jig when you fletch your arrows—every jig is operated differently. However, the general fletching procedure goes as follows for conventional three-fletched hunting arrows. First, place a clean arrow shaft in the jig, being careful not to touch the fletching area of the shaft with your hands. The nock usually seats firmly in a rotating cylinder in the better jigs, allowing you to turn the shaft exactly a third of a turn after the glue on each fletch is dry. Second, place a feather or plastic vane in the clamp according

The tools and materials needed for fletching arrows are simple enough—a fletching jig, fletching cement, die-cut turkey feathers, and clean, dry aluminum shafts.

to the directions that came with the jig, and run a thin bead of fletching cement down the entire base of the fletch. A little too much cement is better than not enough. Third, slip the clamp firmly in place on the base of the jig, making sure the base of the fletch is snug against the arrow shaft along the full length of the fletch. Fourth, let the fletching cement dry (drying time is usually from ten to thirty minutes, depending on the brand of glue used and the air temperature around the jig). Fifth, remove the clamp, rotate the shaft a third of a turn, and begin the process all over again. Fletching a dozen arrows with one jig takes anywhere from six to eighteen hours, depending on the drying time of the glue. After your arrows are fletched, dab a small bead of fletching cement on *each end of each fletch base* to secure the fletching to the shaft even better. Once these dabs are dry, you can attach arrowheads to your arrows.

ATTACHING THE ARROWHEAD

Arrowheads come in two basic styles—screw-in types and glue-on types. The screw-in types are much easier to install and interchange than the glue-on types, so many archers prefer them (see Chapter 2 for details). Glue-on arrowheads can also be cemented to special screw-in converters which have a glue-on taper at one end and a threaded shank at the other end. If a bowhunter prefers to use a hunting broadhead that must be glued onto a tapered point adapter, he can use these screw-in attachments to convert his broadheads into easily detachable screw-in broadheads.

If you decide to go the screw-in route, you'll need to cement screw-in point adapters to the ends of your arrow shafts. Screw-in point adapters are available for all types of arrow shafts, and are very simple to install. The kind of screw-in adapters that attach to wooden shafts slip over the ends of these shafts and are glued in place with hot-melt ferrule cement. Before you can install screw-in point adapters on your wooden shafts, you must first taper the front end of each shaft with a 5-degree tapering tool similar to the tapering tool used to form the nock taper on the other end of the shaft. Then you should heat up some hot-melt ferrule cement over a gas flame or electric stove burner until it becomes runny. Smear this warm glue on the tapered end of a wooden shaft, and then quickly slip a screw-in point adapter snugly over the end of the shaft. The whole end should then be reheated slightly over the burner to ensure a good bond. Once a screw-in point adapter is glued in place, a variety of threaded arrowheads can be screwed in and out in seconds.

Screw-in point adapters for tubular fiberglass and aluminum shafts slip *inside* these shafts, and are also glued in place with hot-melt ferrule cement. A screw-in adapter and a shaft are both warmed up, hot cement is dabbed inside the mouth of the end of the shaft, and the screw-in adapter is slipped quickly inside before the cement cools and sets up. Care should be taken not to get aluminum shafts any hotter than is necessary to keep the cement in a liquid form—too much heat can destroy special aluminum alloys, making the ends of arrows soft and weak. Some bowhunters prefer to epoxy screw-in point adapters into fiberglass shafts, because epoxy bonds well with fiberglass; however, an epoxy bond is permanent and prevents a bowhunter from switching to tapered, glue-on point adapters.

Tapered point adapters for installing glue-on-type arrow-heads are cemented into fiberglass and aluminum shafts the same way screw-in point adapters are installed. The ends of wooden shafts are already tapered to accept glue-on arrow-heads, so no adapter is necessary with these.

Glue-on arrowheads can be cemented directly to any kind of 5-degree taper with hot-melt ferrule cement. This cement is heated up, and so is the point adapter or wooden taper. The runny cement is dabbed liberally on the point taper, and the arrowhead is quickly slipped over it before the cement has a chance to cool. For the best bond, the whole end of the arrow should be warmed up again until the cement is soft, and then the end of the arrowhead should be pressed against something solid to squeeze any excess glue out from between the tapered adapter and the arrowhead. This excess glue can be scraped off warm or flaked away after the end of the arrow has cooled. Hot-melt ferrule cement bonds solidly and securely when all the parts to be glued are warmed up sufficiently.

Special care must be taken when gluing hunting broadheads to arrow shafts. A broadhead must be on a shaft *perfectly straight* or it will tend to plane off course. Big, wide-bladed

Hot-melt ferrule cement is best for installing point inserts and glue-on broadheads. All components must be warmed up to ensure a solid bond.

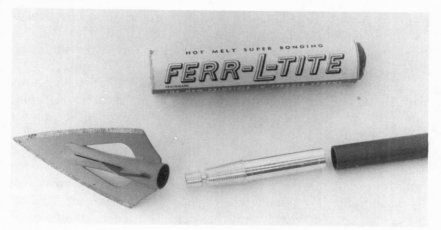

Big hunting broadheads must line up with arrow shafts to prevent erratic arrow flight. Each arrow must be spun on the tip of the broadhead to detect and eliminate any wobble where the shaft meets the back of the broadhead.

broadheads are especially bad about planing, even if the fletching on an arrow is large and heavily spiraled to help steer the arrow in the right direction. Large broadheads must be installed very, very carefully. The key is to line up the point of a broadhead *exactly* with the centerline of an arrow shaft. This will aim a big broadhead in precisely the same direction as the shaft and prevent the broadhead from steering the shaft off course.

Good screw-in broadheads automatically align with an arrow shaft, one reason many bowhunters prefer screw-in point adapters over tapered glue-on adapters. However, if you prefer to use a particular type of glue-on broadhead, you must first glue it onto the arrow shaft and then align its point with the shaft. Aligning a broadhead perfectly takes some time over a hot stove, but it's the only way to ensure that your arrow will fly accurately. I've deliberately glued big broadheads slightly off-center to see what would happen. I've seen arrows head straight for the target, then suddenly swoop to the right or left and totally miss three big bales of straw. Arrows with big, off-center broadheads will dip, dive, and perform a dozen other dipsy-doodle acts between you and the target, totally destroying your accuracy and shooting confidence.

To align a broadhead on a shaft, first install the broadhead with hot-melt ferrule cement. Second, spin the whole arrow on the point of the broadhead like a top. If the arrow shaft wobbles where it meets the back of the broadhead, the point of the broadhead is not perfectly aligned with the centerline of the shaft. The next step is reheating the end of the arrow to soften the hot-melt cement, and then moving the point of the broadhead into closer alignment with a pair of pliers. Spin the arrow on its point again, checking to see if the shaft still wobbles where the shaft and broadhead meet. Continue to reheat the end of the arrow and move the point of the broadhead around until there is *no* visible wobble where the arrow shaft and the broadhead come together when the arrow is spun on its point like a top. If there's no visible shaft wobble, the broadhead should fly well.

Arrow assembly and arrowhead installation are skills every bowhunter should know something about, even if he never builds his arrows from scratch. Then if something goes wrong with his arrows, he can at least isolate the problem, and perhaps even solve it without having to run to the nearest archery store.

Chapter 10—FINDING A PLACE TO SHOOT

Every consistently successful bowhunter shoots his bow regularly. This constant practice keeps his shooting skills from getting rusty and keeps his shooting muscles in tip-top shape. Besides, target practice can be a lot of fun. Once a beginning bowhunter buys his basic shooting equipment and gets it ready to shoot, he has to find a place where he can practice on a regular basis. Actually, he should find *several* places to shoot so he can practice by himself part of the time and with fellow bowhunters part of the time. Shooting from the same old place at the same old target butt can get boring, especially if you're by yourself.

TARGET RANGES AT HOME

The most logical place for a beginner to start shooting is at home. A backyard target range is easy to set up and provides a convenient place to shoot at lunchtime or after work. A shooting range at home lets a bowhunter tinker with his gear a little every day, perfecting his shooting skills and fine-tuning his equipment.

Any open, level stretch of ground can be used for a target range as long as it's a safe distance from areas frequented by people and pets. This stretch of ground should be at least 20 yards long, and preferably 60 to 80 yards long. A good bowhunter shoots at animals out to 40 yards, and sometimes takes shots at greater distances if the situation is right. Every bowhunter should get used to shooting at distances up to 60 yards or so—just in case.

A hunting arrow shot at a target 60 yards away rises 10 to 14 feet above the ground in midflight, so a long shooting range must have good vertical clearance to prevent arrows from hitting tree limbs, telephone wires, and other obstacles that might drape across a potential range location. Ranges that are less than 40 yards long won't present much of a clearance problem—a hunting arrow shot at 40 yards will only rise to 8 feet or so before dropping into the target. A long target range with barely enough room for an arrow to clear tree limbs and other overhead objects is a dangerous range; if a bowhunter flinches off a poor shot that flies higher than normal, the arrow can glance off overhanging junk and fly just about anywhere, including the neighbor's backyard. A 55-pound hunting bow will shoot an arrow between 250 and 300 yards when aimed at a 45-degree angle in the air, so an arrow that careens into space off an overhead tree limb can easily end up 100 yards away.

A target range should also have fairly good horizontal clearance to prevent arrows from smacking solid objects like tree trunks and buildings. The glance-off danger is not as great from objects to the sides of a range because these objects are generally close to the ground and won't deflect an arrow as high in the air. However, there is some danger involved whenever you

A backyard target range is most convenient for regular shooting practice. The conventional three-bale setup shown here is a safe distance from trees and buildings, and features a rain-proof roof to lengthen the life of the straw.

hit a solid object you didn't intend to hit and your arrow goes sailing away in a random direction. And even if you don't hurt people or property, chances are your arrow will end up bent or broken.

If you can set up a permanent target range, you won't have to worry about lugging your target butt out to the range area every time you want to shoot, and lugging the darn thing back in after your shooting session is over. However, if you live in an apartment complex or only have a yard in front of your house, you may not be able to set up a target butt and leave it up for several months at a time. As was discussed in Chapter 4, most portable commercial target butts are less than desirable for practice with a hunting bow—they don't stop fast-flying, heavy arrows very well, don't last very long, and don't allow a bowhunter to shoot broadheads. However, if you're stuck in a place where a permanent range isn't feasible, a medium-sized target matt made of Indian rope grass can be carried outdoors each day, set up on a commercial easel, and shot into repeatedly with any hunting bow under 60 pounds. Matts 30 or 36 inches in diameter are big enough for safety purposes and small enough to carry around without giving yourself a hernia.

A friend of mine who lives in the big city built a little rubber-wheeled cart just the right size to support three bales of straw. This fellow shoots just about every day, and rolls his portable butt out of the garage onto his driveway whenever the urge to fling an arrow hits him. He can shoot across his front yard into the butt at ranges up to 35 yards. He doesn't have a backyard, and feels a permanent target butt in the front yard would be an eyesore.

If you can swing it, a permanent outdoor range is the best setup. Several bales of straw or a sand-trap butt can be placed at one end of the range, providing a fairly big surface to shoot at which you don't have to drag in and out of your garage or storage shed.

A little forethought when setting up a permanent butt can prevent all kinds of problems. Once an acquaintance of mine invited me over to shoot the bull and shoot our bows, too. We talked for a while, and then stepped out back to shoot a few arrows. He had a fairly conventional three-straw-bale target butt at the other end of the range, set nicely between wooden posts. We were about 40 yards from the bales, and I watched curiously as my friend pulled back and let one go at the target. His fiberglass arrow went way low, heading for the base of the bales. Suddenly there was a loud crack like a .22 pistol going off, and I could see yellow pieces of arrow flying every which way like shrapnel from a mortar shell. My buddy cussed and we hustled down to the bales. To my amazement, they were sitting on a 3-inch-thick platform of concrete! The fiberglass arrow had hit this foundation dead-center, shattering it in a thousand pieces. My friend sheepishly explained that the concrete cost him an occasional arrow, but kept his target bales from rotting on the wet ground.

A target butt made of bales should indeed be set on some sort of platform to keep the bales high and dry. However, this platform should be made of softwood or old automobile tires to save low-flying arrows.

Most permanent target butts made of bales consist of three bales laid horizontally on top of each other with the binding wires at top and bottom. The bottom and top bales are not hit very often by arrows if a bowhunter can shoot straight—the middle bale takes the beating. When this bale wears out, it can be put on the bottom and replaced with one of the other two. By rotating bales this way, a bowhunter can make a three-bale butt last a long time.

Some bowhunters band three bales tightly together if they have access to a banding tool of some sort, and banding fairly soft, fairly lightweight bales together can help give a butt rigidity and extra tightness. However, three tight, heavy straw or hay bales will sit solidly on top of each other and really don't need to be banded together at all. It's not a bad idea to set these bales between two wooden posts to give them a little extra support, and maybe tie the tops of these posts together with rope to bend them into the bales and wedge the bales in place. Even this precaution is not really necessary if you can find big, wide, three-wire bales that stack like building blocks.

A sand-trap butt or any other kind of permanent target butt

should be set up so the target area is somewhere between 3 and 4 feet above the ground. The middle bale on a three-bale setup is automatically this high. A target 3 to 4 feet off the ground is easy to shoot at, requiring no body contortions that can ruin good shooting form. It also lets a person shoot slightly down at a target, which helps prevent an arrow from glancing up if it misses the target and hits a sidepost or nearby tree.

A permanent target butt should be protected from wet weather. Hay and straw begin to rot when they get wet, and can sometimes catch on fire because of spontaneous combustion if the weather turns warm. The sand in a sand-trap butt must also be dry so it doesn't stick to arrows. A bowhunter can simply cover his backyard target butt with a canvas or nylon tarp when he isn't shooting, or spend a little more time and build some sort of roof over the top. Any method that keeps a target butt dry is perfectly okay.

A bowhunter who uses a bowsight should carefully measure his range and mark certain distances from the target butt with wooden pegs or stakes. My own bowsights are set for 20, 30, 40, 50, and 60 yards, so my backyard range has distance markers hammered in the ground at these yardages. Distance markers help a bowhunter sight in his bow, and also give him a feel for estimating distance in the woods.

A bowhunter who has absolutely no place to set up an outdoor range can make do by setting up a range in his basement or garage. Such a range will be of limited value because of its extreme shortness, but it will at least allow a hunter to keep his shooting muscles in good shape and perfect his shooting skills out to 15 or 20 yards. A basement or garage setup must have adequate overhead lighting so a bowhunter can see both his bowsight and his target clearly. The same kinds of target butts that are used outdoors can be used indoors, too, although bales get messy unless they're wrapped in burlap or some other kind of cloth to contain the loose bits of hay or straw that come showering out when an arrow is pulled.

An indoor target range must be set up in a safe place. This seems like an unnecessary thing to say, but people do strange things sometimes, especially when they want something badly enough. A guy I know moved into a 60-foot mobile home not too long ago, and got nervous as heck when the owner of his trailer court told him he couldn't shoot his bow on the court grounds. This character dearly loves to shoot a bow, so he went to the local archery shop, bought a 24-inch Indian grass mat, and set it up on an easel *inside his new trailer*. He's a crack shot, and figured he'd never miss a 2-foot butt at 15 yards. He probably wouldn't have, either—but one day he accidentally nocked a badly bent aluminum arrow and let it fly. He told me later he didn't know what made him feel worse—the hole he put in his wife's new refrigerator, or the freeze treatment she gave him after it happened!

PUBLIC AND COMMERCIAL RANGES

Home shooting ranges are fine for regular practice, but a bowhunter should scout out other places to shoot, too. There are thousands of organized archery clubs across the country, and most own or rent target-range facilities with multiple target butts. Many maintain regulation field ranges, which consist of either fourteen to twenty-eight target butts laid out on a course similar to a golf course. A standard field range requires a bowhunter to shoot at distances varying from 20 feet to 80 yards, which gives him valuable practice at a variety of ranges he may encounter while actually bowhunting. Many field courses are in the hills, too, requiring a bowhunter to take shots across gullies, up hills, around trees, and down into canyons. This kind of practice closely simulates real hunting situations and helps a bowhunter considerably.

In a standard field round, 112 shots are taken at twenty-eight targets (four shots per target). This many shots represent a good muscle workout for a bowhunter, which will improve his accuracy if he shoots field rounds regularly. Archery clubs sponsor official shoots, but club members often shoot informally on field ranges, too, giving them valuable practice and the chance for some friendly competition at the same time.

If you don't know someone who belongs to an archery club, you can still get all the particulars about nearby clubs and range facilities from your local archery dealer. He can put you in con-

Joining a bowhunting club can give you access to indoor and outdoor shooting facilities. It can also lead to long-lasting friendships with fellow bowhunters, which leads to lots of fun on bowhunting trips.

tact with club members and direct you to various kinds of shooting ranges in your neighborhood. Most club ranges were built exclusively for club members, but a few clubs use shooting ranges open to the general public. Even if a good public range is located near you, you might want to join an archery club anyway so you can associate with fellow bowhunters and learn from the veterans in the club. Bowhunting is a loner's sport in many ways, but it can also be a pleasurable social event with members of an archery club.

Some archery clubs also shoot indoors on commercial or private shooting lanes. Commercial lanes are especially popular in areas where archery enthusiasm is high and the winters are extremely cold and long. Bowhunters and target archers in these areas shoot regularly throughout late fall, winter, and early spring, competing for prizes and keeping their shooting eyes sharp. The fanciest commercial indoor lanes have automated target butts that move up to the shooting line at the push of a button so a bowhunter can pull his arrows and mark down his target score. Good lanes also have qualified instructors on hand to help beginning bowhunters select quality shooting gear and learn to shoot properly. A bowhunter can have a lot of fun on indoor ranges, especially if the weather outside does not allow comfortable shooting.

NATURAL SHOOTING AREAS

Backyard ranges and club facilities give the bowhunter valuable shooting practice, but he should also scout around to find some *natural* places to shoot his hunting bow. One of the keys to successful bowhunting is lots of shooting practice in totally natural settings. When a bowhunter scouts for a good natural place to shoot, he should look for three basic things: an area that is legally accessible and perfectly safe to shoot in; an area

Commercial indoor lanes provide valuable off-season shooting practice as well as the chance to socialize with other enthusiastic archers.

Shooting in natural surroundings is worthwhile preseason practice. A bowhunter should dress in clothes similar to those he'll be hunting in, and take shots in heavy cover. This way, he'll know what to expect when bow seasons open.

with lots of natural targets which will not damage arrows; and an area that closely resembles the area that bowhunter intends to hunt.

My favorite natural shooting area is a typical good one. It is located along a river in fairly heavy woods that resemble good whitetail-deer habitat. It is gently rolling country full of soft sand dunes and dirt banks deposited by river overflow. This particular tract of land is private property, so there's no danger of some Sunday stroller stepping in front of me as I'm about to shoot. I've spent thousands of pleasant hours roaming this riverbank, picking out spots on sand dunes to shoot at and pretending I'm shooting live animals. The soft sand does not harm my arrows, and the natural terrain closely resembles most of the country where I bowhunt deer. I learned to estimate shooting distances accurately on this particular chunk of ground, and also learned to shoot from difficult positions.

There are undoubtedly similar natural places to shoot near you. Soft sand is the best natural target around, but soft dirt, rotten stumps, clumps of grass, and piles of soggy leaves also make good aiming points and don't damage arrows. These and other soft, natural targets are especially common along creeks and rivers.

A dedicated bowhunter shoots his bow a lot to perfect his skill and keep his muscles tuned up. He sets up a shooting range at home if he can, investigates nearby club facilities and indoor shooting lanes, and also finds a place to roam around and take potshots at sand dunes, dirt banks, and other natural targets. Once he develops these shooting places, he takes full advantage of them because he knows that each and every arrow he shoots will make him a tiny bit better at his sport.

Chapter 11—BOW-SHOOTING BASICS

To shoot a hunting bow well, you need two basic ingredients: good shooting *habits*, and lots of shooting *practice*. A bowhunter develops good shooting habits by starting out slow and easy, paying close attention to each step of his shooting style to make sure he's doing everything correctly. As time goes along, he'll have to spend less and less time actually thinking about his shooting form—every step he goes through when he shoots his bow will become programmed into his mind and body until eventually good shooting will be a subconscious habit he doesn't have to think about at all.

Most good athletes do not think about the individual movements they go through when they perform. These movements are subconscious reflexes or habits they've developed over the years through lots of practice. An athlete begins by thinking about every move he makes, but the more he practices his moves the more they become automatic reflexes and the less he has to think about them. For example, when a person first learns to drive a car, he has to think about when and how to turn corners, when and how to shift gears, and when and how to put on the brakes. However, after he drives for a few years he does these things automatically because he's done them so many times before. Driving starts out as a conscious effort and eventually becomes a physical habit.

Practice with a bow is the key to developing good shooting habits, and it is also the only way a bowhunter can keep his muscles fit enough to shoot a hunting bow well. Even if a bowhunter has good shooting habits, he cannot shoot well unless his muscles are capable of pulling back a bow and holding it back easily while he aims at the target. A bowhunter with quivering, tired muscles will never shoot accurately, even if his mind is programmed to put every arrow in the bull's-eye. A smart bowhunter realizes the importance of practice and makes a point of shooting regularly throughout the year. This way, he perfects his shooting habits so he shoots well automatically, and he also keeps his arm and shoulder muscles strong so they don't let him down when the biggest buck he's seen all year comes frisking out of the trees 30 yards away.

Learning to shoot a bow is seldom easy. It can be a slow, agonizing process at first because you have to think about every individual shooting step. You can also develop *bad* shooting habits any time during your bowhunting career. A bowhunter should strive to shoot well without thinking about it, but he must stop and analyze his shooting form every once in a while to make sure he's still doing everything correctly. Every good athlete checks his moves out occasionally to prevent problems. That's the reason most athletes have coaches, and the reason football players watch themselves on training films. They want to perform well automatically, but they must double-check to make sure their habits are still good ones.

When a bowhunter does something wrong on the target range, he instantly knows it because his arrow doesn't hit where he wanted it to. Every archer alive shoots bad shots, and every archer alive has off days when he can't seem to hit a barn door at 20 feet. All athletes have days when they're physically tired or mentally exhausted, and they should expect these periodic slumps to occur.

Archers go into slumps like other athletes, so if you have an off day, don't worry about it. Worry never got anybody anywhere. Simply quit shooting and try again later. If you have good basic shooting habits, you'll be back on target next time you go out.

However, if you shoot poorly all the time you probably have one or more bad shooting habits that are ruining your accuracy. Some bowhunters shoot well for years and then suddenly fall apart on the target range because they've somehow developed a bad shooting habit. Other bowhunters have never shot very well because they've *always* had poor shooting habits.

In either case, the way to correct the shooting problems that exist is simple enough—the bowhunter must carefully analyze his shooting form step by step to find out what's wrong, or preferably have a qualified friend watch him shoot and isolate his particular problem or problems. A few athletes are capable of discovering their bad habits on their own, but it's much, much easier if they have a coach to help them improve. If you have trouble hitting well with a bow and can't seem to figure out why, ask another bowhunter for help. Otherwise, you'll probably get frustrated and shoot worse than ever.

A beginning bowhunter should practice sensibly to prevent sore fingers and strained muscles. He should shoot only fifteen or twenty arrows per practice session to begin with, eventually building up to the point where he can shoot over a hundred arrows without stopping. He should *never* shoot after his muscles become tired and wobbly—this is a dandy way to develop bad habits. Most top bowhunters practice two or three times a week to keep their muscles in shape, spending anywhere from thirty minutes to two hours at each practice session. Too much practice can actually break muscles down instead of building them up, so every other day is about as often as anybody should shoot a heavy hunting bow.

One excitable fellow I know is a classic example of what can happen when a bowhunter shoots too much. He has fine shooting habits and practices sensibly throughout the year—until about a week before deer season opens. Then he gets fidgety and starts shooting every day, usually for hours and hours. By the time opening day rolls around, this character has sore bowstring fingers and pooped shoulder muscles. He's also a nervous wreck because his shooting has gone to hell. He calms down again after two or three days in the woods, and usually shoots a nice deer. If he gets a shot on opening day, though, he almost always blows it badly because he can't hold his bow back solidly.

Most inexperienced bowhunters practice too fast, shooting one arrow right after the other with breakneck speed. Fast shooting defeats the purpose of practicing entirely—a bowhunter who shoots arrows as fast as he can has no time to concentrate on good shooting form, and doesn't give his muscles time to recuperate between shots, either. A bowhunter should rest between shots for a minimum of forty-five seconds, letting his muscles relax and letting himself think about doing everything right on the next shot. This kind of slow practice helps a bow-hunter improve his shooting fast; fast practice usually results in slow improvement.

A beginning shooter should start practicing at 5 or 10 yards so he hits the target butt every time and builds his shooting confidence. As he gets better with his equipment, he should slowly move back until he can hit well at 20, 30, and 40 yards. He should also practice at longer ranges to see just how well he can hit at these ranges, but he should concentrate on becoming a crack shot at ranges under 40 yards. If he does this, accuracy at longer ranges will come automatically.

If a bowhunter doesn't intend to shoot the year round, he should still begin practicing at least two months before bow seasons open to strengthen his muscles and sharpen his shooting skill. The "weekend bowhunter" who grabs a bow the day before hunting season is in poor physical shape and has rusty habits, even if he's shot a bow before. He's asking for all kinds of shooting trouble in the field.

Every bowhunter develops his own unique shooting style as he goes along. However, he should carefully master the *basics* of good shooting before he experiments with different stances, anchor points, aiming techniques, and string-release methods that may or may not improve his accuracy. A bow-hunter who has never learned the following step-by-step bow-shooting basics is probably a poor to terrible shot with dozens of bad shooting habits. Breaking bad habits is ten times tougher than developing good ones, so it's vitally important that every beginner master the following steps to good shooting as soon as possible. After he does, he'll be on the road to accuracy on the range and success in the woods.

STANCE

Proper stance is the first ingredient in accurate bow-shooting. You should stand facing at 90 degrees to the target with

Holding the bow and arrow prior to drawing (Photograph courtesy of model Sherry Greiner.)   *How to stand in relation to the target (Photograph courtesy of model Sherry Greiner.)*

your feet spread comfortably from 12 to 18 inches apart. Your body weight should be evenly distributed on both feet to ensure good balance.

You should hold the handle of your bow in your left hand (if you shoot a right-hand bow) with all five fingers curled around the handle. The handle should be held firmly but not tightly—a relaxed, steady grip is best.

Place an arrow on the bowstring with your right hand, slipping the nock over the string directly under the nocking point. The arrow's cock feather should be pointing to the left (away from the bow). Put the shaft of the arrow on the bow's arrow rest, and lift the index finger of your bow hand (your left hand) to hold the arrow on the arrow rest.

Next, grip the bowstring in the first joints of your first three fingers (not your pinkie finger) with your index finger above the arrow nock and your two other fingers below the nock. This method of holding a bowstring is called the Mongolian draw, and is by far the most widely used string-holding technique.

Drawing the bow (Photograph courtesy of model Sherry Greiner.)

How to anchor properly (Photograph courtesy of model Sherry Greiner.)

When you hold the bowstring correctly, your bowstring hand will be the shape of a modified Boy Scout salute.

Swivel your head 90 degrees to face the target, leaving your feet and body where they were. Your weight should still be evenly distributed on both feet, and your bow and arrow should be resting against your left thigh with the arrow pointed toward the ground.

There are many variations to this conventional way of standing and holding the bow and bowstring. Some archers prefer an open stance, with their feet pointing slightly toward the target. Some place more weight on their front or back foot and still shoot well. Some hold a bow loosely, using a wrist strap to keep it from falling to the ground after a shot or merely touching the thumb and forefinger of their bow hand and letting the bow handle rattle loosely in their hand after they release an arrow. A few bowhunters who shoot without bowsights hold the bowstring with all three fingers below the nock (called an Apache draw), feeling they can sight down the arrow better with the arrow in this elevated position. Sighting down the arrow shaft is called "gun-barreling," and works especially well on shots under 20 yards. Although these variations work for some bowhunters, you should learn the basics of good stance before trying any variations. Most bowhunters shoot best using the standard, basic techniques.

DRAW

After you swivel your head to face the target, fully extend your bow arm and raise your bow until your bow arm is pointing directly at the target. Your bow should be held perfectly vertical if you use bowsights, but the top limb can be canted 5 or 10 degrees to the right if you shoot without sights. Canting a sightless bow lets you see the target a little better and also helps you keep your arrow on the arrow rest. Begin to pull the bowstring back toward the right side of your face (left side for left-handed shooters), keeping the bowstring firmly hooked in the groove formed by the first joints in your first three fingers. Roll the string slightly in these joints as you draw back to keep the arrow on the arrow rest, and remove the index finger of your bow hand from the arrow, wrapping it around the bow handle with the rest of your bow fingers.

Draw the bowstring all the way back to the side of your face, keeping your eyes on the target. The forearm and elbow of your bowstring arm (right arm) should be in a straight line with the arrow, not dropped low or held way up in the air. This arm position gives you maximum leverage when drawing a bow.

The main thing most beginners have trouble with when drawing a bow is keeping the arrow on the arrow rest. This problem usually corrects itself quickly as a shooter gets used to his equipment and learns to roll the bowstring in his fingers to hold the arrow against the arrow plate. Equal pressure should be put on all three bowstring fingers or the arrow may also move away from the arrow rest. Too much pressure on the top finger and too little on the bottom two fingers will make the arrow rise above the rest's arrow shelf; too much pressure on the lower fingers will pressure the arrow down on the arrow shelf, causing the arrow to fall off the shelf or bend severely in the middle and fly inaccurately.

ANCHOR

Once you draw your bow back all the way to the side of your face, you must anchor your bowstring hand solidly against your face. This makes your arms and body steadier while you aim, and also ensures that the bow and arrow are held the same way each time you shoot.

You should anchor by putting the index finger of your bowstring hand against the right corner of your mouth. This is by far the most common hunting anchor point. Your thumb should be dropped below the point of your jaw, and the point of your jaw should be nestled in the hollow between the base of your thumb and your index finger. With your bowstring hand in this position, press your whole bowstring hand firmly (but not hard) against your face, and leave it in this position while you aim at the target. Your hand should stay anchored this way until you release the arrow.

One of the most common shooting faults beginners have is failing to anchor solidly to their faces. A shooter who tries to float his bowstring hand in front or to the side of his face is bound to shake around because all the weight of the bowstring is on his arm muscles. A solid anchor transfers much of this weight to an archer's neck muscles, helping him hold a lot steadier.

A bowhunter should try to anchor exactly the same place on his face every time to ensure good accuracy. A bowhunter's anchor point is the same as the back sight on a rifle—if the anchor point or the back sight on a rifle moves around between shots, the shots will not hit the same place. A bowhunter who doesn't anchor in the same place on every shot doesn't draw all his arrows the same distance, either. Inconsistent draw lengths result in drastic changes in arrow speed, which can make arrows hit above or below the target. Practice is the key ingredient in learning to anchor the same every time you shoot. After a while one particular anchor feels good and anything else feels "funny."

The index finger in the corner of the mouth is the standard hunting anchor point, but it really doesn't matter where you anchor as long as the anchor is steady and consistent. Some

American Indians anchored on their chests, and a few modern bowhunters anchor alongside or under their chins as target archers do. However, most bowhunters find that the corner-of-the-mouth anchor is steady, consistent, and easy to use with modern bowsights. An anchor that is much higher or lower requires a hunter to attach bowsights above or below the sight window of his bow, creating all sorts of shooting and visibility problems.

No matter where you anchor your bowstring hand, your right eye (for right-handed shooters) should be in almost perfect alignment with the bowstring. In other words, you'll have to look around the inside or outside of the bowstring to aim your bow. Lining your eye up with the bowstring helps you look directly down the path of the arrow, which leads to consistent horizontal accuracy at different distances. It also helps you anchor the same place each time you shoot because you can see the fuzzy image of the string close to your eye every time you aim an arrow. If you anchor exactly the same place every time, this fuzzy string image will be in the same place every time you shoot, too—a good way to double-check the consistency of your anchor.

AIMING

You can aim in two basic ways—with bowsights, and without. A third method of aiming, called "gapping," is often mentioned in archery books, but gapping is merely a crude from of sight-shooting which requires a bowhunter to put the tip of his arrow in different places in relation to targets that are different distances away. Very few bowhunters gap-shoot these days because modern bowsights are so easy to use by comparison.

Shooting well *instinctively* calls for lots of natural talent—talent some people simply do not have. An instinctive bow shot shoots an arrow as a good quarterback throws a football—he pulls back, eyeballs the target, and lets go without consciously aiming at all. After a good instinctive shot shoots a particular bow awhile, he gets used to its trajectory and shoots it well at almost any distance within 40 or 50 yards. He merely points his bow arm in the general direction of the target, lets his mental computer move that arm to precisely the right place, and then

Aiming with a bowsight
(Photograph courtesy of model
Sherry Greiner.)

releases the arrow. He doesn't think about the distance to the target at all—the whole process is subconscious. Instinctive shooting takes lots of practice, the same as sight shooting—practice sharpens a natural instinctive shooter's talents and keeps his muscles fit. A beginning bowhunter can try shooting without a sight if he wants to see if he has natural instinctive talent. However, most bowhunters shoot much better with bowsights. There are some very good instinctive shots around, but the best sight shooters can always shoot better than the best instinctive shots, provided these sight shooters can also estimate distance correctly.

The procedure for aiming with a bowsight goes as follows. First, you must know the exact distance to your target, either by pacing it off, using a rangefinder, or estimating with your eyes. Next, you should draw and anchor as previously discussed, and then move the appropriate sight pin on your bow smoothly onto the target. It is best if you leave both eyes open while you aim—this lets you see in front of you a little better. However, if you have trouble seeing your sights with both eyes open, by all means close your left eye. As mentioned before, if you're anchoring correctly you'll be looking around the edge of the bowstring as you aim.

Once the correct sight is on target, you should hold it there a second and then release the arrow. For example, if you're standing 20 yards from a bull's-eye target, you should draw, anchor, and move your 20-yard sight pin slowly and smoothly to the center of the bull's-eye, let it rest there a second, and then let the arrow go. Most bowhunters move their sights onto target from directly above or directly below the target, but a few come in from one side or the other. How you do it makes no difference as long as you develop a consistent sight-movement pattern that gets the right sight pin on target and lets you hold it there as you release the arrow.

For yardages that are not even, a bowhunter must hold a particular sight pin a little low or a little high, or place the target directly between two pins (if he's using a sight with more than one pin). For example, if a bowhunter is using a bowsight with sight pins set for 20, 30, 40, and 50 yards, he should hold his 30-yard pin a little low if his target is 28 yards away and a little high if his target is 32 yards away. On a target exactly 25 yards away, he should set the target directly between his 20-yard and 30-yard sight pins.

The most common problem bowhunters have with using a sight is freezing, which means they develop a mental block against placing their sights directly on target. A bowhunter with a freezing problem will typically move his sight within a few inches of the bull's-eye and then "freeze up" in that position. After he freezes, he either lets go involuntarily and hits where he was aiming—off-target—or jerks his bowsights past the bull's-eye and pass-shoots it, which usually results in a bad miss. Freezing is easy enough to cure if a bowhunter has the patience and self-control to draw his bow repeatedly, aim at the target, and then undraw his bow without shooting. Freezing is strictly a psychological problem, and a freezing bowhunter who knows he isn't going to shoot can usually aim directly at the target without any trouble at all. A little aiming practice without actually letting go of the arrow usually cures freezing right away.

Neither a beginner nor an expert can practice shooting unless his bowsight is sighted in. This is extremely easy to do. Simply stand 10 or 15 yards away from a big target butt and put

Hand position after the bowstring release (Photograph courtesy of model Sherry Greiner.)

Proper follow-through stance (Photograph courtesy of model Sherry Greiner.)

your top sight pin (if your sight has several pins) on the bull's-eye. Release an arrow (proper release techniques are discussed below) and then *move your sight pin to where the arrow hits the butt*. For example, if you put the sight pin on the bull's-eye and the arrow hits a foot high and a foot to the left, move your sight pin up a little ways and to the left a little ways. Shoot several arrows, readjusting the sight until the arrows hit where you're aiming. The other sight pins below the top pin on your bowsight can be sighted in for longer ranges as you become a better shot. The lower a sight pin is in relation to the sight window on your bow, the greater the distance that particular pin will be sighted in for.

RELEASE

When you think you are perfectly on target, you should release the arrow. Releasing a bowstring is easy. Simply open your hand quickly so your bowstring fingers slip off the bow-string smoothly. Your bowstring hand will jump back along your face a few inches when you release the bowstring because your arm and shoulder muscles are pulling in that direction. The keys to a good, accurate string release are opening your hand fast and keeping your hand against your face after you release. If you open your hand sluggishly or let it fly away from your face when you release, chances are your bow arm will jump off target, causing a miss. With a good clean bowstring release, the only parts of your body that move voluntarily are your bowstring hand and bowstring arm.

FOLLOW-THROUGH

After you release the arrow, *try to keep your sight pin on target until the arrow hits the target.* This bow-shooting step is often ignored by bowhunters, but it is one of the most important ingredients in good shooting. After you release the arrow, your bow will naturally recoil to the side, but if you hold your bow up and follow through the shot, the arrow will be past the bow and on its way before the bow jumps off target. You should try to continue aiming till the arrow hits, and you should also keep your bowstring hand against your face till the arrow hits. A good follow-through usually means a good shot.

The reason for following through is easy to explain. After a bowhunter releases his arrow, that arrow is in the bow for a split-second before it flies past the front end. A bowhunter who does not consciously follow through will usually begin to drop his bow before the arrow clears the bow, deflecting the arrow slightly and sending it off the target. A shooter who does follow through will remain on target until after the arrow clears the bow, resulting in an accurate shot.

Every bowhunter should carefully practice the basics of good shooting until he has them down pat. Stance, draw, anchor, aiming technique, string release, and follow-through are like individual links in a chain—the chain is only as strong as its weakest link. If you learn all these steps correctly, you'll shoot well. If you don't, you'll be darn lucky if your freezer isn't empty at the end of bowhunting season.

Chapter 12—FINE-TUNING YOUR BOW/ARROW COMBO

After a bowhunter shoots his bow awhile and begins to perfect good shooting habits, he should start making refinements in his shooting gear to achieve the maximum in quiet, accurate performance. Fine-tuning a bow and arrow takes some time and energy, but this extra effort pays off big when you begin hunting. A superbly accurate, superbly quiet bow/arrow combination gives you an edge on game, an edge that can sometimes mean the difference between straining your body to drag out your buck and straining your brain to come up with a good alibi to explain why you *aren't* dragging out your buck. The best bowhunters are nitpicking perfectionists who tinker constantly with their shooting gear until they find that "perfect" combination that puts arrows on target with a quiet little swish.

Every bowhunter should adjust his bow on the range until his arrows fly perfectly—in other words, until they fly without wobbling. An arrow that fishtails (wobbles from side to side) and/or porpoises (wobbles up and down) is not as accurate as one that doesn't wobble at all. It doesn't fly as fast or penetrate as well. An arrow that flies straight instead of wobbling has all its energy aimed in one direction, which prevents it from shedding energy sideways as it flies. An arrow that wobbles and sheds energy sideways slows down faster than one that points all its energy at the target, making it strike lower and penetrate a shorter distance than a good-flying arrow. A wobbly arrow with a big broadhead attached also tends to plane (fly erratically) because of uneven air pressure on the sides of the broadhead's blades. A bowhunter who shoots a wobbly arrow at an animal is likely to miss his shot, and even if he scores a hit the arrow won't penetrate very deeply.

It's often tough to group wobbly, broadhead-tipped hunting arrows within a two-foot circle, let alone a nine-inch pie plate. Fine-tuning your bow and arrow leads to pie-plate accuracy at 40 yards or more—the ticket to hitting game.

If a bowhunter is shooting arrows with large, heavily spiraled fletching and the proper shaft spine (stiffness) to match his hunting bow, he's well on his way to achieving good arrow flight already (see Chapter 2 for details). If he has installed a nocking point on his bowstring in the conventional location and has adjusted his arrow rest to centershot, chances are good that his arrows will fly reasonably well (see Chapter 8 for details). And if he's developed a smooth bowstring release, his chances of getting acceptable arrow flight are even better. However, many bowhunters with the right arrows, centershot bows, and good shooting form still have to make some minor adjustments in their gear to get top-notch arrow flight.

HOW TO CHECK YOUR ARROW FLIGHT
There are three basic ways to determine how well your arrows are flying. It's difficult or impossible to detect a slight wobble in your arrows as you shoot by yourself on the range—

a hunting arrow flies too fast to be observed at close range against a medium to dark target butt. Sometimes a bowhunter can see his arrows wobble if the light is just right and they wobble badly enough, but trying to spot arrow wobble as you shoot your bow at a target is generally a poor idea. Even if you do get the right light conditions and see the back end of your arrow wobbling around, you probably won't be able to tell whether it's fishtailing, porpoising, or doing both and wobbling in a circular pattern—things you *must* know to correct an arrow-flight problem.

One fairly good way to check your arrow flight is having a friend stand behind you as you shoot at a fairly long distance— say 40 yards. He can concentrate on watching your arrows fly while you concentrate on aiming and getting a good bowstring release. In decent lighting, a person who looks over a right-handed shooter's *right* shoulder (past the right side of his bow) can usually tell whether or not an arrow is wobbling, and can often tell whether the back end is wobbling sideways, up and

Wild boars like this 216-pounder have nylon-like callous-shields across their ribs. These shields are up to one inch thick— solid barriers which stop all but the fastest, straightest-flying arrows. The author shot this burly hog just behind the right shoulder with a 70-pound compound bow, and got barely six inches of arrow penetration—just enough to reach one lung. Without good-flying arrows he would not have seriously hurt the animal, let alone killed it.

down, or in a circle. An observer should focus his eyes 15 or 20 yards in front of the shooter so he can quickly pick up the arrow with his eyes and follow it into the target. However, unless the lighting is good and your friend has sharp eyes, this method is next to worthless.

A better way to check your arrow flight is standing at one end of a big, vacant field *at least 400 yards long* and shooting a few arrows into the air across this field. Shooting into the air can be dangerous unless you have good enough visibility to ensure that no one will come wandering into the path of the arrow. If you can find a perfectly safe place, try this method, carefully watching your arrows as they fly away against the sky. An arrow silhouetted against the sky is simple to watch, and the slightest wobble can easily be detected. Having a friend along helps because he can pick up the arrow with his eye sooner than you can and detect wobbles close to the front of your bow that may straighten out by the time you see the arrow.

An arrow with heavily spiraled fletching sometimes straightens out, even if it is wobbling badly when it first leaves the bow. A wobbly arrow that straightens out within the first 10 or 15 yards of flight will be fairly accurate, but you should eliminate *all* visible wobble if possible.

A third way to check for poor arrow flight, and possibly the best way of all when done correctly, is shooting an *unfletched* arrow shaft into a target butt at close range. This target butt must be made of a homogeneous material like sand, excelsior, or soft dirt so you can tell exactly at what angle the arrow enters. An Indian rope grass mat or a straw bale has fibers running in particular directions, and these fibers tend to steer or flip an arrow off its original line of flight after it strikes.

If you have access to a nondirectional butt of some sort, proceed as follows. First, get your hands on an unfletched arrow shaft identical in every other way to your regular hunting arrows. If you make your own arrows, you can simply assemble such a shaft without fletching it. If not, carefully strip the feathers or vanes from one of your regular arrows with a knife. Next, stand about 6 feet from the butt and shoot straight into it (level with the ground), making sure you get a smooth bowstring release. If your arrow enters the butt perfectly straight, your fletched arrows should fly well. If the nock end of the arrow is slightly higher or lower than the point of the arrow, your arrow is porpoising. If the nock end is slightly to the right or left, your arrow is fishtailing. If the nock end is to one side *and* high or low, your arrow is fishtailing *and* porpoising. An unfletched shaft accentuates what a fletched arrow does, so if your un-fletched shaft is porpoising and/or fishtailing, your fletched ar-rows are probably doing the same thing.

CORRECTING ARROW-FLIGHT PROBLEMS

Correcting any arrow-flight problems you may have should be fairly easy. If your arrows are fishtailing, simply move the plate on your arrow rest in or out until the fishtailing stops. If your arrows are porpoising, move your nocking point up or down until the porpoising stops. If you've detected your arrow-flight problem by having a friend watch you shoot, or by shoot-ing into the air across an open field, your arrow-plate and/or nocking-point adjustments must be made on a trial-and-error basis. Make a slight arrow-plate or nocking-point adjustment in one particular direction, and then check your arrow flight again to see if it's worse or better. Make more adjustments and keep checking your arrow flight until the wobbling completely stops.

If you check your arrow flight with an unfletched shaft, your tuning job will be a little easier because the way the shaft enters the target butt will tell you which way to move your arrow plate and/or your nocking point. If the nock end of the unfletched shaft is slightly high, your nocking point should be moved down. If the nock is slightly low, your nocking point should be moved up. If the nock is to the right, move your arrow plate into the bow (to the right for right-handed shooters). If the nock is to the left, move your arrow plate away from the bow. Exactly how much nocking-point and/or plate adjustment it takes to achieve good arrow flight can only be found through trial and error.

It's a good idea if a bowhunter double-checks his arrow flight by using two of the three methods described earlier. For example, if he tunes his bow and arrow by using an unfletched

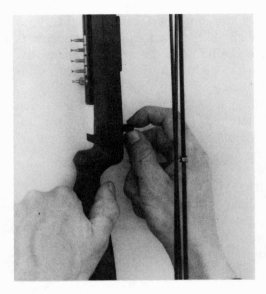

A minor adjustment of an arrow plate will normally straighten out fishtailing arrows.

shaft and a nondirectional target butt, he should also shoot his fletched arrows into the air across a field to make sure they fly right. If he notices a slight porpoise or fishtail against the sky, he can easily refine his bow tuning and turn his attention to other things.

A bowhunter should check his arrow flight every time he changes *anything* about his arrows. Arrow shafts of different materials, weights, and spines tend to have different flight characteristics, even if they are all supposed to fly well from one particular bow. If you switch from fiberglass to aluminum shafts, or switch from a lightweight aluminum shaft to a heavier aluminum shaft with a similar spine, don't take for granted that your new shafts will fly as well as the old ones did. Chances are you'll have to tune your bow all over again before the new shafts fly well. Similarly, if you change the length of your shafts or switch from one kind of arrowhead to another, the odds are good that you'll have to readjust your nocking point and/or your arrow plate to get decent arrow flight. Any changes in an arrow will affect the way that arrow bends around the arrow rest when the bowstring suddenly accelerates it out of the bow, and a bowhunter must compensate for these bend changes (sometimes called "dynamic spine" changes) by slightly readjusting his nocking point and/or his arrow plate.

Changing anything about an arrow usually makes it fly a different place, too. For this reason, some big-game bowhunters prefer to shoot one kind of broadhead the year round so they can tune and sight in their bows with this broadhead and not have to worry about tuning and sighting all over again later on. Sometimes a bowhunter lucks out and discovers that a particular kind of big-game broadhead flies the same as the field points he prefers to practice with, but a bowhunter who shoots field points in the off season usually has to retune his bow for broadheads just before big-game seasons open. For example, I prefer to bowhunt deer with four-blade broadheads that weigh 140 grains—15 grains more than the standard 125-grain field points I practice with in the off season. These broadheads are over twice as long as field points, too, which distributes their weight differently on the ends of my arrow shafts. Both my broadheads and my field points fly well with some minor arrow-plate adjustments, but the broadheads hit over a foot farther to the right than the field points do when I shoot both at 30 yards. Obviously, I have to sight my bow in all over again each time I switch from one type of arrowhead to the other.

A bowhunter who shoots on public target ranges cannot shoot broadheads the year round because broadheads are illegal on most public ranges—they are more dangerous than field points, and also tear up most kinds of target butts. And even if a bowhunter shoots at home exclusively, he may prefer field points because they don't annihilate a straw bale after a month or so of shooting. It's a minor nuisance, but a bowhunter who wants to shoot field points most of the year can easily retune and resight his bow in one afternoon just before deer season opens. The important thing is that he realize he may have to retune and resight his bow when he switches from field points to hunting broadheads.

Far too many bowhunters sashay into the woods totally unaware that their newly installed broadheads will wobble badly and hit a different place than their field points did. One of the best bowhunters I know made this mistake the first time he ever hunted deer. What happened makes an interesting story.

George practiced hard with field points for about three months before bow season, and developed into a fair to middling bow shot before opening day. He carefully scouted a likely hunting area, spotted three different whitetail bucks, and put up a roomy portable tree stand overlooking the main deer trail in that part of the woods. George also practiced a lot from a tall stepladder to get the hang of shooting down at deer. He eagerly anticipated his first crack at a buck.

At daylight on the opening day of season, George was safely strapped in his tree stand, peering this way and that with bow ready for action. He had glued new broadheads to his arrows the week before, and had spent long evenings sharpening them carefully. He nervously tested the razor edge on his arrowhead one more time, watching the late-autumn sun slowly rise above the far-off hills.

About fifteen minutes later, George caught a flicker of movement in the corner of his left eye. He slowly swiveled his head, and his heart leaped to his throat as a little forkhorn buck came prancing down the trail toward him, head down. George leaned against his safety belt, drew his 55-pound recurve bow, and aimed carefully for the buck's heart. He released smoothly, and was amazed to see his arrow sail 6 inches over the middle of the animal's back.

The deer were rutting, and the buck did a foolish thing. He turned around, sniffed the arrow curiously, and then walked nonchalantly under George's stand. George jerked another arrow from his bow quiver, snapped it on the string, and waited anxiously. A second later the buck strolled out from under the stand, walking slowly away. George aimed very carefully again, holding low on the buck's ribs where he was supposed to hold. When the sights looked right he let fly, and groaned as the arrow whizzed an inch above the buck's left ear. This time the little animal leaped in the air and galloped into the woods, flag whipping back and forth like a white handkerchief.

George sat there the rest of the day, kicking himself for his shoddy performance. No more deer showed up, and he finally climbed out of his tree and plodded to his car. He still hadn't figured things out.

He did the next day. He was on his backyard range at daylight, and proceeded to shoot a few field points into the bull's-eye at 30 yards. No problem. Then he nocked one of the arrows he'd shot at the buck, drew back, and released. The thing corkscrewed through the air and buried in the hay 18 inches high and 2 feet to the left! George's eyes got as big as saucers and he hurried into the house to call an experienced bowhunting friend for some answers.

By midafternoon George had his broadheads flying well and his bow sighted in. And eight days later he finally shot the same little buck through both lungs as it followed a doe under his tree. He's killed a deer every year since.

Ideally, a bowhunter should shoot broadheads regularly for at least two or three weeks before hunting season. This way, he can make sure his bow is sighted in well, and also make sure his broadheads group as tightly as his field points do. Sometimes all the bow tuning in the world won't make a particular broadhead shoot accurately when it's attached to a particular arrow shaft and shot from a particular bow. I once fooled around with a big four-blade broadhead for three solid weeks, moving my arrow plate and nocking point all over the place in an effort to make my arrows fly well. The darn head planed anyway—badly. The arrows weren't wobbling, either—just flitting here and there between me and the target. I could shoot 3-inch groups all day long at 20 yards with field points, but the instant I switched to that lousy broadhead my groups expanded to 8 inches. Interestingly enough, this very same broadhead flew very well from another bow I owned at the time, but not from my favorite hunting bow. I finally scrapped the head and went back to one I had confidence in.

SILENCING THE BOWSTRING

There's one other fine-tuning step a bowhunter should never overlook: silencing his bowstring. Most bows are fairly noisy to shoot unless some sort of silencing gear is attached to the string—gear designed to prevent the bowstring from twang-

Many lightweight bowstring silencers are sold at archery stores. Most are made of rubber, and most do at least a fair job of hushing a noisy string.

ing like an off-key fiddle string each time an arrow is released. A noisy bowstring can scare animals plumb out of the country, making them duck, leap over, or sidestep an arrow as they leave.

A wide variety of commercial silencers can be had at archery stores, and all work fairly well. Silencers are usually made of rubber, and come in pairs. A bowhunter should experiment with various designs and choose the *lightest* silencers that hush his bow well. Most silencers weigh very little, but all will slightly alter the way a bow shoots. Anytime you add weight to your bowstring, you slow down the string a little bit and also slow down your arrow flight. A bowhunter should make sure his bow is reasonably quiet, but he should never forget that the heavier the string silencers, the more they'll affect the performance of his bow. With extremely noisy bows, a bowhunter may have to use extra-heavy silencers, and the added weight to his bowstring in these extreme cases may actually require him to move his bowsights slightly and perhaps even move his arrow plate and/or nocking point. Bowstring silencers can definitely affect the way a bow is fine-tuned, so they must be installed on your bow long before hunting season rolls around.

Fine-tuning your bow/arrow combo takes some effort, but there's no substitute for perfect arrow flight and a quiet bow. With them you'll put game in the bag, and without them you probably won't.

Chapter 13—FINAL PREPARATION FOR A HUNT

Smoothing up your act before the big performance makes sense if you're on Broadway, and it also makes sense if you're a bowhunter. Bowhunting is a fine art, a combination of basic skill, good equipment, and painstaking preparation. A person who's a deadeye on the target range and a nitpicker about his bow and arrow is still not a bowhunter—not by any means. A bowhunter takes things one step farther and learns to use his gear in the woods as well as on the target range. By tucking in the loose ends with some final prehunt preparation, he becomes a well-equipped *bowhunter* instead of a well-equipped *shooter* with bowhunting gear.

NATURAL TARGET PRACTICE

Once a bowman develops into a fairly good shot and fine-tunes his bow/arrow combo, he should begin shooting under natural conditions that closely approximate those he expects to encounter when he actually goes bowhunting. Shooting at live game in the piny woods is an experience every beginning bowhunter should try to prepare for. Far too many bow-benders learn to shoot in the woods the hard way—they wait until hunting season opens and make their mistakes on animals they should have hung on the meat pole. Nothing can totally prepare you for the heart-pounding sensation of actually drawing on game, but some physical and mental programming can help you do the right things even when your body is trembling and your mind is numb with excitement.

The first step toward becoming a good field shot is learning to aim at animallike targets. A bowhunter can invest in several commercial animal targets, or he can make his own rough replicas out of cardboard or heavy paper. Some bowhunters feel that shooting at *any* large target area without a bull's-eye is valuable practice, and they have a valid point. The main lesson a bowhunter needs to learn is to pick out one spot on a large surface and hit it. Actually, the best thing to do is shoot at a *variety* of natural targets. A bowhunter who practices on brown paper bags exclusively might become a crack shot on paper bags and nothing else!

Whatever natural targets you decide to use, make sure you learn to shoot at one spot instead of the whole target. A beginning bowhunter's inclination is to point his bow at a *whole deer* instead of zeroing in on a spot right behind the shoulder. This "shotgun technique" is what you must learn to avoid. If you aim deliberately at a small, imaginary bull's-eye just behind a deer's shoulder, you'll probably hit that small area and kill your

Picking one particular aiming spot on a big-game animal's hide is an art within itself—an art which can be partially developed through practice on commercial animal targets.

deer. If you point your bow at the whole deer, you're likely to wound that deer or miss it completely.

A bowhunter should also learn to shoot from awkward positions. The ideal, picture-book thing to do when you see a deer is to turn your feet at 90 degrees to the animal, stand upright, and nail him with classic target-shooting form. Trouble is, this kind of shooting isn't always possible. A bowhunter might have to take a shot with his legs twisted like pretzels, or when he's kneeling, or when he's sitting on a log. A bowhunter should practice every imaginable shooting position he thinks he might have to use in the woods, and learn which ones he can actually pull off. Most of this kind of shooting can be practiced on the target range and tried again in the woods later on.

If you intend to bowhunt from a tree stand, you must figure out some way to practice at animallike targets from an elevated position. Many tree-stand hunters practice from a tall stepladder, and some actually erect tree stands in their backyards to shoot from. A few also shoot from the roofs of their houses, but this can be hazardous unless a roof is fairly flat. A guy in my bowhunting club once fell off a steep-pitched roof, broke two fingers on his bowstring hand, and had to sit out the whole deer season while everybody else was having fun. If you decide to practice from an elevated place, be sure it's a safe place.

Shooting up or down is considerably different from shooting on the flat. An arrow hits higher than normal when shot at a target below *or* above you, requiring an aiming adjustment to avoid a miss. Beginning tree-stand hunters often blow shots at close range by overshooting because they haven't practiced from high above the ground. A bowhunter who prefers to sneak along on his hind legs can also miss a shot badly if he aims dead on when an animal is sharply *above* him. Exactly where to aim on a target above or below you is tough to say—practice is the key to learning this special shooting skill. However, a good rule of thumb is this: If a target is sharply above or below you, try to figure out how far away it is *horizontally* and hold your sights accordingly. For example, if you're 30 feet above the ground in a tree stand and a buck walks under you 10 feet away from the base of your tree, aim at that buck the same as you would aim

Shooting sharply up or down makes an arrow hit higher than normal. A bowhunter must practice these kinds of shots to develop a knack for hitting objects above and below.

at a buck 10 feet away on the flat. He's 10 feet away from you horizontally, and that's the measurement that counts.

Arrows shot up or down naturally hit high, but changes in a hunter's shooting form under up/down conditions also affect point of impact. A bowhunter should always try to bend at the waist only when shooting up or down because this maintains the proper relationship between his arms, head, and bow. Bending the upper body on uphill and downhill shots can shorten or lengthen draw length, which can change arrow speed and point of impact. A bowhunter who shoots sharply down from a tree stand can easily bend at the waist by leaning into his safety belt, but a bowhunter on foot must consciously remember to do this.

A bowhunter should learn exactly where his arrows fly at extremely close ranges, too. The first year I bowhunted I didn't think of this precaution, and I blew the setup shot of a lifetime. I watched a little blacktail buck feed casually into a clump of manzanita bushes the very first morning of the season, and did have the sense to leave him alone. That evening I was huddled beside the mouth of the trail where he'd disappeared, and about seven-thirty the brush started crackling like tinfoil 30 feet in front of me. A second later the little three-point poked his nose around a bend in the trail 15 feet away and looked me right in the eye. I was decked out in new camo gear, complete with headnet, and the wind was fanning my face. Perfect. The little stinker stood there a second, squatted to relieve himself, stood up, stretched, and then turned broadside. He poked his head deep in the bushes to chomp something good, and that's when I moved.

The bow came back smoothly, and my 20-yard sight pin settled solidly behind the buck's shoulder, halfway down from the top. I let go, expecting to see the arrow disappear in his ribs. To my amazement and horror, it sailed an inch over his back and clattered through the brush behind him. I think he uprooted half the bushes in the county trying to get away! Later, I discovered that my arrow hit 8 inches high at 15 feet when I

The ultimate in shooting practice is wandering through the woods in full bowhunting attire, taking potshots at dirt banks and similar natural targets. In-the-field practice sharpens a bowhunter's shooting eye and helps him get the bugs out of his gear prior to hunting season.

used my 20-yard sight pin—more than enough to miss a little blacktail buck that probably measured 12 or 13 inches from backbone to brisket.

A bowhunter can practice many of the shooting skills he needs to learn on a backyard target range, but there's really no substitute for practicing in the woods (see Chapter 10 for details on where and how to shoot in the woods). Roving and stump-shooting allow you to take hundreds of shots at natural targets like rotten stumps, sandbanks, grass clumps, and similar soft objects. These objects will be at unknown distances, requiring you to estimate the range correctly before you can score a hit. They will also be above and below you, testing your ability to compensate and still be on target. Roving and stump-shooting cannot be considered a chore, either—slowly wandering through the woods and plinking at natural targets is loads of fun, especially if you have a fellow bowhunter to compete against. Getting good at something is usually hard work, but getting good with your bow and arrow in natural surroundings can be pure pleasure.

A bowhunter should wear his whole bowhunting getup and carry all his hunting gear when he practices in the field. This way, he learns to move and shoot well under the exact conditions he'll face when actually hunting. There are certain little habits a bowhunter develops as he sneaks along—certain ways he learns to carry his bow, nock his arrows, turn his body, and do other things when he's in particular circumstances. Most of these little techniques can turn out to be not so little when you're eyeball to eyeball with a deer, bear, elk, or some other alert animal. For example, a bowhunter who practices a lot in the woods learns to slip through thick brush and trees with his upper bow-limb tip pointed directly forward. This bow position creates a lot less noise and movement than a bow that's held crossways to the body. The way you hold your bow in heavy cover may seem like a little thing, but it only takes one slip and the jig is up on spooky animals.

Here's another example. When I first started bowhunting, I carried my bow along my left side with the broadhead very close to my pant leg. I discovered—three pairs of pants and one cut leg later—that this carrying position let my broadhead touch my pants and slice holes in them. A little preseason field practice would have let me figure out the same thing with dull practice broadheads, perhaps saving a pant leg or two and certainly saving a painful trip back to camp for bandages.

Preseason field shooting helps a bowhunter refine his moves, but it also helps him refine his equipment. As he roves and stump-shoots, he'll discover all sorts of little bugs in his gear—bugs that must be smoothed out for best results on game. There's a myriad of small equipment problems that might ruin a careful stalk or patient wait in a tree stand. The list could go on and on. Perhaps your bow quiver rattles slightly against your bow, or the wheels on your compound bow squeak, or your arrow keeps falling off a small arrow rest and clunking the bow loudly, or your arrow screeches when it slides across a slightly dusty nylon arrow plate. Perhaps you find that your bowstring knocks your hat off when you shoot downhill, or that your baggy camouflage shirt smacks the bowstring when you shoot. Perhaps your pant legs are too baggy and scrape softly against each other each time you take a step. And perhaps your belt knife or canteen clanks against your bow every time you scrunch up to slip through a small opening in the brush or trees.

These and other little bugs can be easily corrected once you discover them. A rattling bow quiver can be taped solidly to a bow to hush it up. The squeaky wheels on your compound bow can be lubricated with a good penetrating oil. A small arrow shelf can be replaced with a bigger one, or a piece of soft leather can be cemented to the bow handle in the area where the arrow strikes when it falls off the rest. A screechy nylon arrow plate can be lubricated with powdered graphite or a similar dry lubricant. You can replace your wide-brimmed hat with a smaller one or cut a chunk out of the brim. You can have somebody tailor your bowhunting shirts and pants to remove unnecessary bagginess, or simply buy tighter-fitting duds. And you can reposition your knife and canteen on your belt so they don't hammer your bow when you sneak through thick cover. An ingenious bowhunter can always correct minor equipment problems once he shoots awhile in the woods to discover these problems in the first place. And after he does correct these problems, he and his equipment will become one smoothly functioning unit, a unit ready to go bowhunting.

CAMOUFLAGING YOUR SHOOTING EQUIPMENT

I should say *almost* ready. There's one other thing you must do to your bow, bow quiver, and any other shiny and/or light-colored parts of your shooting equipment—you must carefully camouflage them. This step is best saved until after you've shot awhile in the woods and have all the little bugs out of your gear. Otherwise, some of the additions you've made to your bow and other equipment may stand out like sore thumbs against otherwise perfectly camouflaged gear. A good example is a shiny metal hunting-bow stabilizer. If you decide to install one late in the game to help your shooting, it's a lot easier to camouflage it with the rest of your gear instead of taking special pains to go back and dull it down separately.

Most bows and bow accessories are designed to appeal to a customer's eye across a store counter, not to fade into the woodwork as they ought to. Hunting bows, arrow quivers, and other bow accessories usually have shiny, light-colored surfaces that literally flash warning signals to game. Especially bad are the highly polished limbs on hunting bows. A few archery companies offer dull-finished hunting bows and bow quivers on a special-order basis, but most bows and bow accessories must be camouflaged after you buy them. The only major exceptions to this are modern aluminum hunting arrows, which are dull-anodized in woodsy colors to prevent game from seeing them.

The simplest, quickest, and *least* effective way to camouflage a hunting bow is slipping a camouflaged bow sock over each shiny bow limb. Cloth bow socks cover the worst of the shine on a bow, and work fairly well if a bowhunter plans to sit in a tree stand above an animal's direct line of sight. However, they do nothing to cover up smaller shiny or light-colored parts of your hunting gear.

Several kinds of dull-finished camouflage tape are available at archery stores, and this stuff can be plastered over most eye-catching parts of your gear. Camouflage bow tape will not damage the finish on a good-quality hunting bow, regardless of what old wives' tales say. Tape is a bit messy coming off sometimes, leaving sticky adhesive all over your bow that must be removed with a mild solvent and elbow grease. The main objection to camouflage tape is that it takes so long to install and cannot be installed on some parts of a bow. For example, cutting bits and pieces of tape to neatly cover a compound bow can take hours and hours, and things like the wheels and cables cannot be covered with tape at all. Using camo tape is an okay way to conceal your bow, bow quiver, and other eye-catching gear, but it is not the best way, all things considered.

Camouflaging your nice, new, shiny hunting bow the *best* way takes courage. You might have to grit your teeth, wring your hands, and maybe even cry a little, but if you want the ultimate in bow camouflage you'll spray-paint your bow. Very few beginners like the idea of attacking a fine-looking, glossy recurve or compound bow with a spray can of dull paint, but this is the only way to completely cut the shine and the light colorations on every part of your bow, bow quiver, and other shooting aids. Most veteran bowhunters don't even think about spray painting their bows any more—they just do it and know it's better than using bow socks or camo tape.

Several companies sell regular bow-camouflaging paints, and some of these can actually be scrubbed off with special paint removers supplied by these companies. The idea that you can safely remove the paint from your shiny new hunting bow may be comforting, but nobody I know of has ever actually stripped the paint from his hunting bow. There's simply no reason to do such a thing.

One friend of mine was frightened to death of spray-painting his hunting bow. The bow was attractive, all right, with a fancy rosewood handle riser and smooth, epoxy-finished limbs. However, you could have shaved in the reflection of those limbs, and my pal realized he had to do something. He shopped around and found some dull water-base paints that were supposed to be easily removable with soap and lukewarm water. He dabbed this stuff all over his bow with a brush and then went hunting. Only trouble was, he picked a rainy day. By noon his clothes, arrows, and half the bushes in the country were covered with paint. The only thing that wasn't covered was his bow!

A variety of paints work well on bows and other shooting gear, both special bow paints and most other nonglare primer paints and lacquers sold for use on auto bodies and other metal objects. Spray paints are easier to apply than paints that come in cans, and also apply more evenly. A bowhunter needs two basic shades of paint for the best camo paint job—a medium color like light brown or green, and a very dark color like deep brown or black.

First, he should carefully clean up his bow, quiver, and any other objects to be sprayed to ensure that the paint adheres well. Dust and other loose crud should be blown or wiped off the bow and accessories, and then all surfaces to be painted should be carefully wiped clean with an unsoiled cloth soaked in rubbing alcohol. After these surfaces are cleaned and allowed to dry, they should not be touched again. Even "clean" hands can deposit body oil that ruins a good paint job. If you must handle equipment ready to spray-paint, do so with a clean cloth or paper towel between your hand and that equipment. Equipment to be sprayed should be suspended from a clothesline or hung by ropes or wires from some overhead object to let you paint from all angles without touching the equipment.

There's an awful lot of baloney in print about how a bow should be painted. Elaborate instructions are laid out on page after page, instructions to ensure that you do everything *just right* and don't make little mistakes that will ruin your hunting season. Most of these careful instructions are so much bunk, the ramblings of someone who loves painting bows more than hunting with them. Typical tricky bow-camouflage techniques include carefully spraying a small part of your bow with one color, then climbing a nearby tree to find a certain-sized leaf, climbing back down, holding that leaf over the already-painted section of your bow, and carefully (don't move the leaf!) spraying a darker color around it. This 20-minute process only camouflages 1/16 of your bow—the rest comes later—but you do have a perfect green leaf on your bow, surrounded by a pretty black background. You also have spray paint all over your fingernails and twenty minutes less to paint the other 15/16 of your hunting bow.

Spray-painting your hunting bow and other gear in a *practical* camouflage pattern should take you a total of twenty minutes. Simply cover the gear with a thin coat of your lighter spray paint (following the spraying instructions on the can), and then paint dark spots and stripes here and there over the lighter paint. The outcome will be a nonglare paint job with about 50 percent medium color and 50 percent dark color. It will blend with almost any background and will last a long time.

You should let fresh camo paint cure for at least twenty-four hours before handling it, so it won't rub off or glaze over when you shoot your bow and fuss with your other gear. Such a paint job should be cleaned with alcohol and touched up every so often in areas where the paint has become chipped, scraped off, or shiny from lots of wear. Most paints let off faint chemical

A dull, two-tone paint job takes very little time to apply and effectively tones down the shiny, light-colored surfaces on a brand-new hunting bow. The camo colors used here are light brown and black, a good combination for average hunting situations.

odors for a week or two after they're applied, so you should make an effort to camouflage your bow at least two weeks ahead of bow season to prevent animals from smelling the paint.

The only other part of your bow that may need to be camouflaged is the bowstring. Most commercial hunting bowstrings are made of black, green, or brown materials these days so they blend with the woods. However, some are still manufactured with traditional white Dacron strands, and these bowstrings must be carefully rubbed with a dark wax crayon to tone them down. A white bowstring stands out starkly against a medium-to-dark background, seriously jeopardizing a bowhunter's chances of success.

After you learn to shoot and move in the woods, get the little bugs out of your bowhunting gear, and camouflage your equipment, the next thing to do is start assembling all the gear you need to take on your bowhunt. Deciding what you really need and what is excess baggage will take a little time. The key is carrying as little as possible with you to avoid bulging pockets and noisy contraptions dangling all over your body. Many bow-hunters make up permanent in-the-field equipment checklists so they can go on hunt after hunt without having to refigure what they need to carry.

The only other thing you must do before a big-game bow-hunt is make sure your broadheads are shaving-sharp. Broadhead preparation is one of the very most important parts of successful bowhunting, and will be discussed completely in Chapter 14.

Chapter 14—SHARP BROADHEADS— The Key to Big-Game Success

This is probably the single most important chapter in this book. The vast majority of bowhunters are big-game bowhunters— deer hunters in particular—and as a result, the vast majority of bowhunters hunt with broadheads attached to the ends of their arrows. There are dozens of broadhead designs available at archery stores, and many of them are big, streamlined arrowheads made of adequate steel to do an efficient, humane job of stopping animals. However, *no* broadhead is worth a plugged nickel on animals unless it is shaving-sharp—so sharp it's almost scary to handle.

If the perfect hunting broadhead did exist, it would do the following things. First, it would penetrate very deeply into flesh. Second, it would cut off everything it touched cleanly without shoving tissue aside or ripping and tearing. Third, it would cause massive hemorrhaging (bleeding) in an animal with little or no clotting to slow down rapid blood flow. Fourth, it would inflict no pain at all. And fifth, it would create a wound that would heal quickly and cleanly if an animal did not die immediately after being hit.

Unfortunately, the perfect hunting broadhead does not exist, but a truly sharp one comes very close. Broadhead design does have a certain influence on the five things a broadhead should do well. However, whether or not a broadhead comes close to fulfilling these duties depends overwhelmingly on one thing—how sharp its edges are. The keenness and type of edge on a broadhead both determine whether it's a dependable game-getter or a miserable flop. Broadhead design enters in significantly only if a particular model has steel too soft to be sharpened properly, has a bizarre shape that makes sharpening impossible, has excessively small blades that cut an excessively small hole, or has less than three cutting edges to open a reasonably big wound channel. The edge is the most important thing on a broadhead because the edge is what kills animals.

CHARACTERISTICS OF VARIOUS BROADHEAD EDGES

There are only three basic kinds of edges a broadhead can have—a dull edge, a coarse, ragged edge, or a smooth, honed edge. All three edges are formed when two flat or semi-flat edge tapers come together at a particular angle, creating a ridge of steel. The angle at which these edge tapers meet partially determines how well an edge cuts and how long it stays sharp. However, almost all broadhead edges are formed at an angle somewhere between 18 and 22 degrees, so we won't discuss edge angle here. The only broadheads with poor edge angles are those that use real shaving-type razor blades in their construction. Such blades have edges ground at too slim an angle to hold their sharpness well. A razor blade's edge shaves hair well enough, but rolls over and dulls instantly when it hits ribs or anything else that's solid in an animal. The edge is the important thing on a broadhead, and each kind of edge has certain unique characteristics a bowhunter should be aware of.

A dull edge pretty well speaks for itself. It cuts hot butter reasonably well, and that's about all. A dull edge is really not an edge at all, technically speaking, because it is not really a ridge between two edge tapers. A dull edge has flats and valleys all over it which can readily be seen when this edge is held under a strong light. A true edge reflects little or no light, but a dull one is covered with little nicks and smooth spots that do reflect light. All commercial broadheads that are not specially presharpened in machines have dull edges when they come from the factory, and should be carefully sharpened before a hunt. Some cheap broadheads are made of steel so soft that they can never be brought to an easy-cutting, keen edge. These have fairly dull edges even when carefully worked with a file, whetstone, and fine sharpening steel. And broadhead edges *always* become dull whenever they collide with anything solid after a missed shot, even when the steel is good. As will be shown a little later in this chapter, a dull edge is totally worthless in bowhunting—in fact, it's worse than worthless.

A coarse, ragged edge is the sort of edge produced by careful sharpening with a fine-toothed file, a coarse butcher's steel, or a disk-type knife sharpener. This edge reflects very little light when properly sharpened, but has hundreds of tiny, ragged steel burrs along its length which can be detected through a powerful magnifying glass. A coarse, ragged edge is perhaps the very best edge for cutting meat because it has serrations similar to those on a steak-knife blade. In fact, a coarse, ragged edge is preferred by almost all commercial butchers because it neatly saws through meat and is easy to touch up with a coarse butcher's steel. Some bowhunters still mistakenly believe a ragged edge is the best kind of edge to put on a hunting broadhead, and in the past the ragged-edge/smooth-edge debate was a common one around archery shops and hunting camps. However, *a ragged broadhead edge is an inferior edge to a smooth broadhead edge in every way*. This is not supposition; it is hard fact which will be proved a little later in this chapter.

A smooth, honed edge is the kind of edge produced by a medium-to-fine whetstone used in conjunction with either a fine sharpening steel or some sort of knife strop or razor strop. When correctly sharpened it reflects no light, even when viewed under a magnifying glass. This is the sort of edge found on razor blades, old-fashioned straight razors, surgical scalpels, and other tools designed to slice instead of saw through semi-soft materials. A smooth, honed edge is found on most commercial presharpened broadheads, and can be put on any good unsharpened broadhead with some skill and the proper tools. A smooth, honed edge is by far the best edge a broadhead can have—and again, this is a statement of fact, not opinion.

In order to understand how important the edge on a broadhead really is, a person must first understand something about how an arrow kills big game. A living animal is an incredibly complex organism, but it is composed of two basic things—living body cells which survive on oxygen, and a complicated circulation system which carries oxygen-rich blood from the lungs to these body cells in arteries. Once this blood is drained of oxygen by the body cells, it is pumped back to the lungs in blood veins, and the lungs supply this blood with another load of oxygen. An animal's heart keeps this blood circulation system going constantly to keep giving the body cells the oxygen they need to survive.

When a broadhead penetrates an animal's heart, it stops this blood pump instantly, which in turn stops the blood from flowing through the lungs, which in turn cuts off the oxygen supply to an animal's body tissues. This results in extremely quick death. An arrow that penetrates one or both lungs collapses these balloon-like vital organs, and again stops the flow of oxygen-rich blood to an animal's body cells. And again, that animal dies within seconds.

Even if a sharp broadhead misses the heart and lungs, it can still cause a quick, humane kill if it cuts lots of arteries and veins or cuts an organ that lots of blood flows through—an organ like the liver. Cutting these blood centers drains an animal of its life blood—which again robs the animal's body of oxygen and again kills it fast. Unless a broadhead hits an animal's brain or spine, it *always* kills by disrupting the blood-circulation system. Brain and spine shots disrupt an animal's central nervous system, killing quickly by shock instead of blood loss. However, the key terms when you discuss how a broadhead kills are blood circulation and blood loss. If an arrow stops blood circulation by damaging the lungs or heart, an animal will die fast. If an arrow causes excessive blood loss, an animal will also die fast. This explanation is somewhat oversimplified, but basically explains how a broadhead kills game.

Let's compare the three basic kinds of broadhead edges (dull, ragged, and smooth) in each of the five categories a broadhead should perform well in (penetrating deeply, cutting cleanly, causing rapid blood loss, inflicting little or no pain, and promoting rapid healing with nonfatal hits). This comparison can be a real eye-opener, and destroys all sorts of myths about the kind of edge a broadhead should have.

A broadhead must penetrate deeply so it can reach one or more vital organs in an animal's body and cut off a maximum number of blood vessels (veins and arteries) on the way. Penetration increases blood loss, and also increases the odds that an arrow shot into an animal's rear end will reach the vital organs at the front end (heart, lungs, and liver). A dull-edged broadhead penetrates the least in flesh because its flattened edges create friction against flesh, slowing an arrow down fast. A ragged-edged broadhead penetrates much better than a dull broadhead, but the microscopic steel burrs on a ragged edge still cause friction as they grab and tear flesh, again slowing an arrow down. A well-sharpened smooth edge penetrates the best, creating very little friction as it slices through flesh. There's simply nothing on a smooth edge to hang up on as it slides through body tissue.

Cutting ability is also a very important broadhead trait. This is the ability of a broadhead to slice off everything it touches as it penetrates an animal's body. A dull broadhead tends to push flesh out of the way as it plows through an animal, especially the tough, flexible walls of arteries and blood veins. A dull broadhead can hit these blood vessels without actually cutting them—and without cut blood vessels, an animal will not bleed. A ragged edge does cut everything it touches, or put more correctly, it saws through everything it touches. This is the main reason some bowhunters still cling to the notion that a ragged edge is best for bowhunting—it snags and rips blood vessels instead of sliding over them as a dull edge will. A properly sharpened ragged edge actually reaches out and tears flesh, so it makes an even bigger wound channel than a smooth, sharp edge. However, a smooth, sharp edge cuts everything it touches—even flexible blood vessels—and probably penetrates more than enough extra distance to top the cutting performance of a ragged edge. And even if a ragged edge does destroy more tissue than a smooth edge in some situations, it still comes up short in the next, and most important, requirement of a good broadhead edge.

The most important thing a broadhead must do to kill quickly and humanely is cause rapid and continuous blood loss in an animal. The main thing that stops or slows bleeding in a wound is the coagulation (clotting) of the blood, which blocks the ends of cut blood vessels and prevents blood from flowing freely out of that wound. The chemical reactions that trigger blood clotting in a wound are very complex, but every bow-hunter should understand the basic causes of blood clotting so he can use a broadhead edge that causes the least amount of clotting and the greatest amount of blood loss.

Blood is composed of four basic substances—red blood cells, white blood cells, platelets, and plasma. The rest of the tissue in an animal's body is composed of body cells, which survive on oxygen and nutrients supplied by the blood. All body cells and the platelet cells in the blood contain a chemical called thromboplastin, which is released when these cells are broken or damaged by a cut, bruise, or some other kind of wound. For example, when a broadhead penetrates an animal's body, it rips, tears, or cuts (depending on the type of edge) billions of body cells and blood platelets, which in turn release thromboplastin. This thromboplastin mixes with certain substances in the blood's plasma, triggering an instantaneous chemical chain re-action which forms a threadlike substance called fibrin. This fibrin bunches up near the ends of severed blood vessels like lumps of twine in clogged drainpipes, blocking blood flow out of these vessels. It also "ties up" other blood cells and makes blood turn to a jellylike substance. The chemical reaction that occurs between thromboplastin and substances in blood plasma is coagulation, and can be compared to the chemical process that causes epoxy glue to set up.

Now comes the important part. The more body cells and platelet cells that are damaged in a wound, the more clotting occurs. This is fairly obvious, because the more of these cells that are damaged, the more thromboplastin is released into the blood and the more fibrin is formed. Remember, fibrin is the twinelike stuff that plugs up the ends of blood vessels and makes blood get jellylike. In other words, *the more tissue damaged in a wound, the greater the clotting that occurs*. So a broadhead that cuts a hole of a particular size and length and damages 10 billion body cells in the process causes considerably less clotting and considerably more bleeding than a broadhead that cuts the same-size hole, penetrates the same distance, and damages 50 billion cells. This is solid fact.

A "messy" wound that damages a lot of body cells also causes more pronounced vascular spasms than a "clean" wound, which in turn also causes more extensive clotting. A blood vessel which is ripped in two expands and contracts violently for several inches away from the rip, and may continue these vascular spasms for as long as twenty minutes after a wound is made. In contrast, a blood vessel that is sliced off cleanly experiences no vascular spasms or very minor ones of very short duration. In other words, the more cells that are damaged in a cut blood vessel, the more that vessel "quivers" or has spasms after it is cut. Vascular spasms are triggered by the nervous system, and they break millions of platelet cells in a blood vessel. Remember, platelet cells contain thromboplastin. So when vascular spasms occur in a blood vessel, blood clotting occurs *inside* that vessel for several inches away from the actual wound. This clotting inside the vessel is a fairly violent reaction in itself, which causes still other platelets to break open, releasing even more thromboplastin and causing more clotting. This chain reaction of clotting around a wound is what causes the discolored, blood-shot meat every hunter is familiar with. The discoloration in the meat around a wound is simply clotted blood inside blood vessels.

Because of the great amount of blood clotting in a ragged wound and the clotting caused by vascular spasms for several inches around that wound, a wound made with a dull or ragged instrument plugs up incredibly fast compared to a wound caused by a smooth, sharp edge. In a nutshell, a smooth, sharp broadhead edge damages a minimum of body cells in an animal, causing a minimum of blood clotting and a tremendous volume of blood loss. A dull broadhead hacks its way through the flesh and causes maximum cell damage and minimum bleeding. A coarse, ragged broadhead edge also causes a lot of cell damage as it rips and saws through an animal, which produces quick blood clotting and a plugged-up wound. It is debatable whether a dull broadhead edge or a ragged broadhead edge causes more cell damage, because they both cause a lot; however, a smooth, sharp edge is far superior to the other two when it comes to cutting well without destroying cells. This means it is also far superior when it comes to causing rapid and continuous blood loss—the thing that kills animals.

Anyone who has cut himself on various kinds of edges already knows that a smooth, sharp edge causes a cut that bleeds and bleeds and bleeds. The best example of this is cutting yourself when you shave. It seems as though a nick with a razor blade will *never* stop bleeding—this is because that nick has damaged very few body cells and doesn't release much thromboplastin to cause blood clotting. On the other hand, a cut with a dull pocket knife stops bleeding very fast because it damages lots of body cells, which in turn causes very fast blood clotting.

I have to kill one more old myth before moving on, a myth I used to believe myself. It has often been written that a cleanly cut blood vessel bleeds more freely than a raggedly cut blood vessel because the end of the cleanly cut vessel is more open than the end of the raggedly cut vessel. People who voice this theory usually liken a blood vessel to a water pipe, saying that a water pipe with a cleanly sawed end lets water flow out quicker and smoother than a water pipe with a mashed-down, ragged end. This argument would make sense if a blood vessel were like a water pipe, but it is not. Doctors and veterinarians I've talked to all discount this old theory. Fact is, a blood vessel is a very elastic, flexible tube, so tattered ends simply move out of the way when blood flows out—they don't get in the way and slow or block blood flow at all. What blocks blood flow is the massive clotting going on around this tattered end.

The fourth thing a broadhead should do is cause little or no pain. Pain is a difficult thing to discuss because it is strictly a state of mind. The nerves around a damaged part of the body send electrical impulses to the brain, and the brain interprets these impulses into the unpleasant feeling we call pain. Nobody is really sure if an animal feels pain as we know it, or really experiences anything unpleasant at all when a part of its body is injured. You'd have to get inside an animal's head to find that out. However, if animals *are* capable of experiencing pain as we know it, a broadhead should be designed to cause as little as possible.

According to the medical authorities I've talked to, a

smooth, sharp edge *doesn't* cause much pain, if any at all, when an animal is hit fatally and dies reasonably fast. The reason is similar to the reason a smooth, sharp edge causes rapid blood loss. A smooth edge cuts through nerves cleanly, damaging very few nerve cells. The more nerve cells that are damaged in a wound, the stronger the impulses that shoot to the brain, and the more pain that is felt. A razor blade doesn't hurt to speak of when it nicks a man's face because it cuts nerves cleanly. In contrast, a dull or ragged edge tears and rips nerves as it penetrates, which causes considerable pain. A cut with a ragged edge may very well be the most painful of all because it tears nerves instead of plowing around them as a dull edge does. As mentioned before, most professional butchers prefer the ragged, serrated edge put on a knife by a coarse knife-sharpening steel because it cuts meat well—and these men readily admit that when they cut their fingers with such an edge, it hurts like hell. The butchers I've talked to also say that a similar cut with a sharp, smooth edge produces little or no pain. Again, the smooth, sharp edge comes out on top.

The fifth and final thing a broadhead should do is produce a wound that heals cleanly and rapidly if the broadhead does not kill with reasonable speed. One of the biggest misconceptions non-bowhunters have about this sport is that it cripples a lot of animals that eventually die a slow, agonizing death. Not true! The survival rate for arrow-hit animals that get away is exceedingly high—much higher than the survival rate for animals hit in poor places with rifles. An arrowhead doesn't pulverize body tissue as a bullet does, so the wound has a much better chance of healing up. And again, it's the smooth, sharp broadhead edge that yields the best recovery rate and the quickest healing. There are three reasons for this. First, a smooth, sharp edge cuts a minimum of cells, which means there is less tissue that has to heal up than in a cut made with a dull or ragged edge. Second, a cut made with a smooth edge bleeds more freely before the blood coagulates and closes the wound. This extra bleeding helps cleanse the wound of bacteria, which are the main cause of infection in a cut. And third, a smooth, sharp edge drags a minimum of bacteria into a wound as it penetrates.

Bacteria are all over the place, and literally cover an animal's hide and hair. A dull or ragged edge drags some of this hide and hair into a wound, introducing a lot of infection-causing bacteria to that wound. A smooth edge has no uneven surfaces or steel burrs for bacteria-laden gunk to cling to, so it creates a wound which is less likely to become infected.

HOW TO SHARPEN A BROADHEAD

It's obvious that a smooth, sharp edge is the *only* kind of edge a bowhunter should consider having on his broadheads. He can attain such an edge in one of two ways—either by carefully sharpening his broadheads, or by buying sturdy factory-sharpened broadheads. A hundred years ago, sharpening knives, scythes, and other steel cutting tools was part of most men's daily chores, so most men were very proficient at this art. However, the majority of people today do not even carry pocket knives because they live in urban centers where knives and other edged tools are not often used. As a result, the majority of modern men *are not* proficient knife sharpeners. Sharpening steel edges takes a certain amount of talent and lots of skill—skill acquired through practice. If you are not a practiced sharpener, you must spend lots of time learning this art before you can put a shaving-sharp edge on an unsharpened factory broadhead.

Once mastered, broadhead sharpening is fairly easy and fairly fast. The standard way to sharpen a broadhead goes as follows. First, use the arrow shaft as a handle and file the edge tapers of a broadhead to an 18-to-22-degree angle with a mill file, using the ferrule (center section) of the broadhead as a file guide. Most broadhead ferrules are just the right diameter to give you the proper edge angle if you lightly rest your file against them as you work. Bring each blade to a reasonably sharp edge with the file, then stroke the file backward along each edge taper to remove any large steel burrs on the edge. Next, carefully hone both sides of each edge with a medium-to-fine whetstone like a soft Arkansas stone. This honing process can be done totally by hand or with the help of a sharpening guide available at sporting-goods stores. The whetstone should be placed on a

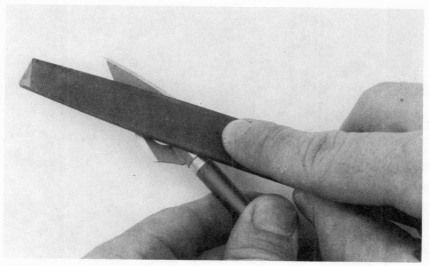

Filing broadhead edge tapers

solid surface like a tabletop, and the broadhead edges should be stroked repeatedly into the stone with firm, even pressure. A whetstone slowly removes steel from edge tapers, smoothing them and making the resulting edge very sharp. Once the edges of a broadhead seem to be sharp, each edge taper should be stropped on a fine knife-sharpening steel, razor strop, or piece of leather to "iron" or gloss over each taper (remove any small steel burrs that are still clinging to the edge). A fine knife-sharpening steel is used the same way as a whetstone—each edge taper is stroked repeatedly into the steel with a smooth, slicing action. To strop an edge on a razor strop or piece of leather, briskly stroke each edge taper backward (away from the edge) across the stropping surface several times. When properly done, the filing, honing, and stropping processes result in a very, very sharp broadhead with smooth edges.

The sharpness (keenness) of a smooth broadhead edge can be checked in a number of ways. The most common is attempting to shave hair from your arm or leg. If a broadhead's edges shave hair easily, it is sharp enough to hunt with. Another widely used method of checking sharpness is lightly dragging a

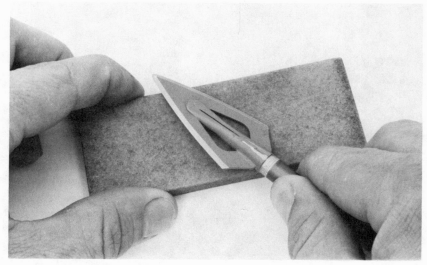

Honing edge tapers on a whetstone

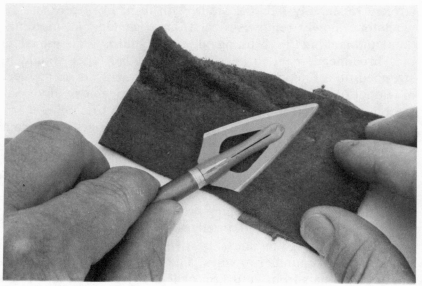

Stropping edge tapers on a piece of leather

broadhead's edges across your thumbnail. If each edge "grabs" or digs into your nail instead of sliding smoothly over it, it is sharp enough to take game. A third way of testing a broadhead is holding a rectangular piece of medium-weight typing paper by an upper corner and trying to slice the paper in two from top to bottom. If a broadhead's edges all cut paper easily, it is also ready to take afield. If one of these sharpness tests fails on an edge, you must rework this dull edge on a whetstone, restrop it, and retest it until it does pass the sharpness test. *Every edge* on every one of your hunting broadheads must be shaving-sharp *along its entire length*—otherwise, you're greatly increasing the odds of hitting and losing animals.

Sharpening broadheads correctly takes talent and skill, and it also takes time. Even the best broadhead sharpeners spend at least fifteen minutes on a medium-sized four-blade broadhead before they're satisfied with all the edges. Because of the skill and time required to properly sharpen broadheads, more and

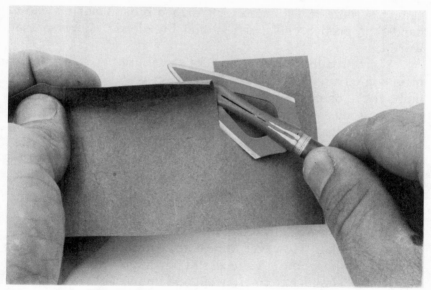

Testing broadhead sharpness on medium-weight paper

The best factory-sharpened broadheads feature replaceable, shaving-sharp blades.

more bowhunters are using sturdy, factory-sharpened broadheads with smooth, shaving-sharp edges. The best factory-sharpened broadheads have three or four replaceable blades which are honed to shaving-sharp edges by special machines. Unless you are *positive* you can put a smooth, razor-sharp edge on an unsharpened broadhead, you owe it to yourself and the game you hunt to use factory-sharpened broadheads instead of hand-sharpened broadheads. A dull broadhead is worse than worthless.

Your broadheads must be kept sharp, too. A sharp broadhead edge that is accidentally dragged across a bow quiver, tree limb, rock, or any other solid object instantly becomes a dull edge, and must either be replaced (in the case of factory-sharpened broadheads) or carefully resharpened. Broadhead edges can also become dull *in minutes* if they get wet and begin to rust. A bowhunter should carefully oil his broadheads to prevent edge-destroying rust, and he should frequently check these edges, using one of the sharpness tests mentioned above.

Making sure your broadheads are sharp takes time, patience, and skill. However, unless they are sharp you have no business in the woods. A successful bowhunter uses top-quality equipment, shoots extremely well, and knows how to hunt. But he has another edge, too—the shaving-sharp edge on the business end of his arrow.

Chapter 15—EQUIPMENT CARE, REPAIR, AND STORAGE

Bowhunting equipment is a snap to care for. The trick to keeping your bow, arrows, and shooting accessories in tip-top shape is learning a few basic facts about how and how not to maintain, repair, and store this gear. After that, the upkeep will be as easy as rolling off a log.

BOW CARE

A bow is the most complex piece of equipment any bow-hunter owns, but it is still a fairly simple, reliable tool. The only things that can easily be abused on a recurve bow are the limbs and the bowstring, and on a compound bow you can only add the moving parts and cables to this list. *Major* malfunctions like cracked, bent, and broken handle risers do occur occasionally, but these are usually caused by poor factory design or assembly—not by owner abuse.

Bowstrings wear out eventually, requiring a bowhunter to install a new one immediately. Shooting a worn-out bowstring is a little like sitting on a powder keg—you never know when things might blow up. If a bowstring breaks while you're shooting, you'll remember the experience, that's for sure. There'll be an explosion of noise in your face, the bow will kick like a mule, and you'll be vaguely aware of things whipping around your noggin—things like bits of string and steel cables (if you're shooting a compound bow). Bowstring failure probably won't damage your bow, but it might damage your nerves and the nerves of anybody else in the immediate vicinity. It will also frighten an animal if you happen to be shooting at one.

Any bowstring with frayed or broken strands is a definite hazard and should be replaced immediately. Strings with worn spots in the serving (the wrapping around the strands at both ends and in the middle) should also be replaced. A recurve bow is much tougher on a bowstring than most compound bows— I've broken dozens of strings in recurves, but have yet to break one in a compound bow. The most common wear points on a recurve string are where the string meets each bow limb, where the arrow is nocked, and where the string slaps a bowhunter's armguard. These friction points get considerable pounding and should be checked periodically for wear. A bowstring in a compound bow doesn't slap the limbs on either end, so these places are not likely to wear through. The nocking area on a compound bowstring does not get as much abuse, either, largely because compound bows do not kick an arrow in the rear end all at once as recurve bows do, which leads to less friction wear. Compound bowstrings do sometimes break where the string hits the armguard, however, so keep a close watch on this particular part of the string if you shoot a compound bow.

As mentioned in Chapter 8, bowstrings should be waxed about once a month with regular bowstring wax. This lubricates the individual strands and prevents them from weakening as they rub together when a bow is shot. Bowstring wax also forms a protective coating on a bowstring which prevents rough objects like tree limbs, rocks, and pickup doors from easily fraying the outside strands.

Most hunting bowstrings are made of 16 heavy-duty Dacron strands. All strands work together to take up the shock of shooting an arrow, and one broken strand can result in complete bowstring breakage.

A bowhunter must take special pains not to cut his bowstring with a sharp broadhead. This comical, embarrassing, and sometimes maddening mistake happens hundreds of times each year across the country, usually when a bowhunter takes his arrow off the bowstring to maneuver through heavy cover or when he's trying to nock an arrow to get off a shot at an animal. A normally calm acquaintance of mine got excited a few years back and pulled this little stunt.

Jim was driving his open jeep down a steep hill when a huge muley buck suddenly leaped out of the brush directly in front of the bumper. The big animal milled around in the road, trying to decide which way to run. Jim yanked the emergency brake, setting the jeep on its nose and throwing duffel out both sides. He grabbed his recurve bow off the seat beside him and dove over the side, jerking an arrow out of the quiver as he stumbled around the front fender. The buck was still wheeling this way and that, barely 15 yards away. Jim whipped his arrow around the bowstring to nock it—and sliced the string neatly in two. The limbs snapped forward with a mighty bang, one limb tip smacking him hard in the leg and the other clanging the fender of the jeep. He stood there with his mouth open while the old buck stood broadside, looked at him for what seemed like hours, and finally ambled back into the brush the way he'd come. Jim was one sick bowhunter, and learned then and there to carefully steer broadheads clear of his bowstring.

The limbs are the most important part of a bow, and also the easiest to damage. Bow limbs can be knocked around quite a bit without suffering any, but certain things will ruin them very quickly indeed.

The glue that bonds the fiberglass and wood laminations in modern bow limbs is very sensitive to heat, so a bowhunter must be extremely careful to keep his bow reasonably cool. The limbs on both recurve and compound bows will delaminate when exposed to extremely high temperatures, totally destroying them. Ordinary hot weather won't hurt a bow at all, but leaving it in a hot car, especially under the windshield, will usually do it within minutes.

A bow left too near a campfire can also delaminate. This

particular tragedy happened to me on a wilderness bowhunt a few years back, causing considerable inconvenience. The guide was looking at my compound bow, and after he was through he innocently set it on a rock about a foot from a blazing pile of pine logs. I poked my head out of my tent about thirty minutes later and felt my heart sink as I gazed at the poor old bow. All four laminations on both limbs had popped apart, making it about as useful as a club. The next day we rode 18 miles out to retrieve my spare bow, and 18 miles back in to base camp. I was rubbing a very sore behind when I finally slipped the backup bow in my tent and headed for the cook shack.

Drawing a bow and letting go of the bowstring without an arrow on the string is also a surefire way to damage the limbs. Dry-firing a recurve or compound bow like this sends violent vibrations through the limbs, vibrations which can snap them off, crack them severely, make the laminations fly apart, and/or twist them out of shape. A bowhunter should never draw the bowstring and let go without an arrow in place. One dry-fire and his bow could very well become a worthless hunk of wood and fiberglass.

Leaving a recurve bow strung for long periods of time is not a good idea, although modern recurves are rugged bows and can be left strung for several days without hurting them at all. When a recurve bow is left strung for a long time, its limbs can develop a set and lose some of their cast, which means they lose some of their springiness and the ability to snap back to their original position as fast as they once could. A bow that loses cast can still be shot, but it won't shoot arrows as fast as it originally did. Old recurve bows and longbows made of yew, lemonwood, and other springy bow woods were especially likely to develop limb sets, so much so that bowhunters in the past often left their bows unstrung unless they knew they were close to game. The modern bowhunter has it a lot easier—as long as he strings his recurve before he begins hunting and unstrings it after the day is done, his bow should never lose cast.

Some bow manufacturers suggest that the limbs on their compound bows be "relaxed" before these bows are stored for extended periods of time. This also prevents limb sets, reduced cast, and slower arrow speeds.

Some kinds of compound bows cannot be overdrawn without damaging the limbs, either. These particular designs are set for certain draw lengths, and when they are drawn beyond these recommended lengths their cable-and-wheel assemblies exert terrific force on the limbs—force which can snap the limbs in two or crack them severely. If you decide to use a compound bow, be sure to read the manufacturer's literature to learn about any special limb care you should give it.

Stringing a recurve bow improperly can also ruin its limbs. The correct way to string a recurve is using some sort of bow-stringer—not stringing by hand. The old step-through and push-pull bow-stringing methods illustrated in some archery books are surefire ways to permanently twist one or both limbs on a recurve bow unless a bowhunter is an expert at these techniques. A twisted recurve limb sometimes causes the bowstring to jump off the bow—an interesting experience to say the least—and can sometimes develop into a cracked or broken limb as a bow is shot over and over.

The steel cables on compound bows occasionally break, although this happens less and less frequently as bow companies perfect their bows and the way cables are attached to wheels and bowstrings. A bowhunter should not concern himself particularly with cable breakage, but he *should* keep an eye on the cables in his compound bow to make certain they don't become badly frayed. Breakage usually occurs near the union point of a cable and the bowstring or a cable and the bow.

The moving parts of compound bows also require occasional lubrication to prevent rust, wear, and unnecessary noise. Penetrating oil is best to use where metal meets metal, and a dry lubricant like graphite or baby powder works best where plastic meets plastic or plastic meets metal. Plastic sometimes gets squeaky when lubricated with oil, but it is completely quiet when lubricated with graphite or baby powder.

Both recurve bows and compound bows should be stored in cool, dry places by hanging them vertically from the bow-

Metal-to-metal friction points like the weight adjustment bolts on a compound bow should be lubricated regularly with penetrating oil.

string or a cable, by resting them horizontally on both limbs across two pegs, or by laying them on their sides on a flat surface or in a commercial bow case. Bows should never be stored by setting them vertically on a limb tip or a compound wheel—this storage position can eventually warp the lower limb on a recurve bow and possibly damage the lower wheel and/or limb of a compound bow. Takedown bows of various sorts are the simplest to store safely because they can be dismantled and packed neatly in a small case.

ARROW CARE

Arrows are quite easy to care for, especially arrows with fiberglass or aluminum shafts. Arrows with wooden shafts are more prone to warp and break, which means they must be handled with kid gloves.

A little common sense is the key when using your arrows. Obviously, any arrow shot into a solid object like a large rock will probably shatter like glass or bend like a pup's hind leg. An arrow that is stepped on or sat on will generally give up the ghost, too. Arrows should be handled carefully and shot wisely at all times to prevent breakage or bending.

Nocks are made of fairly soft plastic, so they can become cut, bent, or broken when they collide with anything sharp or solid. A bowhunter should check his nocks frequently to make sure they are in good condition, and replace any that are not. Replacing nocks is easy enough—simply cut them off the nock taper on the back of a shaft with a sharp knife, reclean the nock taper with Ajax cleanser (if the taper is made of aluminum), and install another nock with nock cement. The whole process takes a minute or two, and the cement should be dry within fifteen minutes.

Good fletching is a must for good arrow flight, so a bow-hunter should make sure his fletching retains its original shape and size. Plastic vanes are incredibly durable and wear like iron, but they can become torn or cut during target sessions when other arrows hit them directly. A bowhunter must remove dam-

Damaged nocks should be removed with a pocket knife and replaced using good-quality fletching cement.

aged vanes with a sharp knife, clean the fletching area with Ajax (in the case of fiberglass and aluminum arrows), and glue on another vane in a fletching jig (see Chapter 9 for details).

Feather fletching is more durable than plastic when smacked by another arrow, but feathers tend to mat down and lose their shape when they're squashed against something solid for a while or when they get wet. A bowhunter should always transport arrows with feather fletching in commercial arrow boxes so the feathers do not touch anything solid and mash down. Arrows fletched with feathers must also be loaded in a bow quiver with particular care so these feathers don't rest against other feathers or the bow quiver and become misshapen. Feathers can be partially waterproofed with a coat of hair spray or commercial fletching waterproofer, but a lot of rain can make them wilt like old lettuce anyway. Bowhunters who prefer to hunt with feathers usually cover them with a plastic sandwich bag or something similar when it rains; otherwise, they're risking poor arrow flight and missed animals. Feathers also begin to wear out after lots of target shooting. A worn feather fletch

The steam from a teapot quickly returns matted feather fletching to its original shape. Simply hold misshapen feathers a couple of inches from the spout and slowly rotate the arrow shaft until the feathers bounce back.

will not stabilize an arrow well, and should be removed as soon as its outer edge becomes tattered.

Both plastic vanes and feathers should be thoroughly washed in warm water after they penetrate an animal and become covered with blood, or whenever they get excessively dirty. Plastic can be dried in seconds with a clean cloth, but feathers must be dried slowly in the open air and then steamed back to their original shape over a teapot spout. Any matted or misshapen feather fletch will pop back to its original shape when carefully steamed, too, and will retain that shape when dried in the open air.

Arrow shafts must be inspected regularly to make sure they are straight. To test the straightness of an arrow shaft, either roll it across a flat surface like a tabletop, or lightly touch your index finger to your thumb and spin the shaft across the V formed by your fingernail and thumbnail. If a shaft visibly wobbles as it rolls across the table, or if you can feel it wobble as it spins across your fingernails, it is too crooked for good accuracy. Incidentally, learning to spin an arrow across your nails takes practice, but is by far the best way to check the straightness of an arrow because the slightest wobbles telegraph through your nails. If you can't get the hang of testing arrows this way, have your local archery dealer show you how.

Wooden shafts are notorious for warping in wet weather, and must be checked for straightness regularly. Badly warped shafts should be discarded, but a shaft with a slight warp can sometimes be salvaged. You should heat it up first over a stove burner, being careful not to singe the wood. Then carefully bend it back to shape over the palm of your hand or your knee, first sighting down the shaft in good light to detect the direction of the bend, and then bending the shaft in the opposite direction. Repeat this process, spinning the shaft across your thumbnail and fingernail until it seems to be straight. This technique is far from surefire because wood tends to creep back to its original warped condition—which is one reason most bowhunters prefer aluminum or fiberglass shafts.

Fiberglass shafts do not warp appreciably—they are either straight or broken. However, a fiberglass shaft that hits something solid will occasionally crack badly without actually break-ing in two. A cracked fiberglass shaft is not always accurate and is extremely dangerous to shoot. A fellow I met at an archery shop had a big bandage around his left forearm, and I asked why. He said he drew a fiberglass arrow in his bow, let it fly, and had the arrow disintegrate while still in his bow. His arm ended up full of fiberglass splinters—splinters that would take months to fester and pop out. This kind of experience is fairly common. A cracked fiberglass shaft will often fly apart when the bowstring raps it in the rear end, startling and often injuring a bowhunter in the process. Fiberglass shafts that smack solid objects should be carefully inspected immediately along their entire length, and should be thrown away if they are cracked or splintered.

Aluminum shafts are very durable, especially those made of XX75 alloy, but they occasionally become bent when they strike solid objects. In a pinch, a bowhunter can straighten an aluminum shaft reasonably well by sighting down the shaft in good light to see which way it's bent, bending it in the opposite direction over his knee or the palm of his hand, spinning it across his fingernails, and repeating this process until the shaft spins reasonably well. However, bent aluminum shafts are best straightened on a commercial arrow-straightening device sold at archery stores. Most archery shops also straighten aluminum shafts for a small fee as a service to their regular customers, and a practiced professional can straighten an aluminum arrow as good as new. It's a good idea to practice straightening aluminum shafts by hand just in case you get caught in the woods with nothing but bent arrows; however, the best procedure is to pack your bent shafts back to civilization and let a pro work them over carefully.

Fiberglass and aluminum shafts which become dirty or cov-ered with blood can be washed with soap and warm water, then dried with a clean cloth or paper towel. Wooden shafts can also be washed, but they must be dried very quickly to prevent water from soaking in and causing a warp.

As mentioned in the previous chapter, hunting broadheads should be carefully oiled to keep them shaving-sharp and ready to shoot at game. Some bowhunters sharpen a lot of broadheads prior to bow season, oil them carefully, and then wrap them in toilet paper or cover the edges with masking tape to protect these edges from dulling clanks and scrapes. Sharp broadheads should always be protected with toilet-paper wrapping, commercial broadhead covers, or masking tape whenever they are stored or transported. Other types of arrowheads are simple steel, rubber, or plastic affairs which need no special care.

Broadheads, field points, and other wedge-shaped arrowheads sometimes become tightly imbedded in trees, logs, hard stumps, wooden fence posts, and similar objects when bowhunters miss shots. If a bowhunter is carrying a commercial arrowhead puller, he can usually salvage a stuck broadhead or field point by using this handy tool. If he doesn't own an arrowhead puller, he can still salvage all but the arrowhead by either heating it off with matches or a cigarette lighter, or simply unscrewing it from the shaft. Screw-in point adapter systems are especially handy when you bury a broadhead in a tree because you can unscrew the shaft in the twinkle of an eye and install another sharp broadhead in about the same length of time.

A broadhead that's deeply buried in a tree or stump is darn near impossible to pull free—even with pliers. Screw-in broadheads solve this problem, letting a bowhunter quickly unscrew his shaft and go about his business.

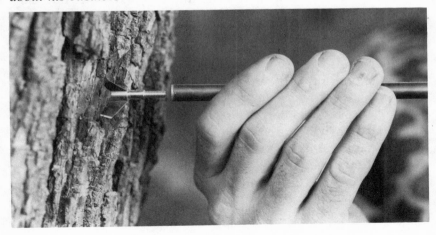

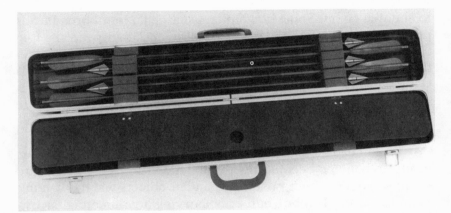

Broadhead-tipped hunting arrows should be stored and transported in sturdy boxes with individual arrow clips. This particular arrow box is a heavy-duty plastic job with foam-rubber arrow keepers— ideal protection for shafts, fletching, and sharp broadhead blades.

A bowhunter should inspect a broadhead after he shoots it into something solid to make sure it isn't bent. Bent broadheads can sometimes be straightened with pliers by a patient bowhunter, but any that cannot be straightened should be thrown away. A slightly bent broadhead will usually fly erratically, and more than one bowhunter has mistakenly resharpened one and shot it at game—much to his regret. Broadheads that become dirty or bloody should be washed off with soap and water and carefully dried. Blood is especially corrosive and must be removed before it severely rusts an otherwise good broadhead.

Hunting arrows should be stored and transported in one of two ways—either in sturdy arrow boxes which hold each arrow individually in rubber, cardboard, or metal clips, or in an arrow quiver that also holds arrows snugly and securely. A wide variety of arrow containers are sold at archery stores, all the way from inexpensive cardboard boxes to very expensive metal or plastic cases. As long as an arrow container protects arrows from rattling together, getting damp, and becoming damaged by careless handling, that container is a good one. Most bow quivers are designed to detach quickly from a bow so they can be used as storage units, and a good bow quiver with a protective broadhead cap and dependable arrow clamps is just the ticket for transporting and storing a few sharp broadhead-tipped hunting arrows. So are good hip and back quivers.

ACCESSORY CARE

Bow-shooting accessories like shooting gloves and tabs, armguards, powder pouches, and target quivers require little or no maintenance. As long as such items are stored in a dry place, they last a long, long time, and when they do wear out they are simply discarded and replaced. For example, the armguard I'm using now is over five years old, has been stepped on by horses, mules, and me, has been drenched in rainstorms, has fallen in at least one campfire—but still serves me well. My shooting tab is fairly new, but only because the old one got carted off one night by an adventurous packrat in central Montana. Quality shooting accessories last and last and last.

If you follow a few basic rules when handling bows, arrows, and shooting accessories, these simple tools will serve you well for years and years.

Part III—BOWHUNTING KNOW-HOW

Chapter 16—THE GAME

Just about any kind of animal or bird can be hunted successfully with a modern bow and arrow. Most dyed-in-the-wool bowhunters try to sample as many kinds of bowhunting as they possibly can to add spice to their sport and give them a maximum number of hours in the field. The majority of bowhunters concentrate on deer and other big-game animals, but many also bowhunt fish, birds, small game, and varmints. All these species are fun to hunt, and most require considerable shooting and hunting ability to score.

Bowfishing is popular offbeat entertainment among bowhunters because it provides exciting springtime sport. Fish like carp, gar, eels, sharks, and suckers can be hunted the year round in many areas, allowing a dedicated bowhunter to practice his skills when normal bowhunting seasons are closed. These or similar "rough fish" can be found almost anywhere there's water, and make tough targets when shot at from dry land or boats. Fish like gar and carp can be downright difficult to approach and hit, but are usually easy enough to find at certain times of the year. Bowfishing can be a fish-in-a-barrel operation when fish like carp spawn in shallow water, but it usually takes special hunting and shooting talents. Approaching fish requires a bowhunter to dress in camouflage gear, move slowly, and take care not to make too much noise by splashing up the water or clumping his feet on the bottom of a boat. Balancing precariously on a slippery mudbank or the bow of a boat while you aim a heavy fiberglass or steel fish arrow complete with fishing line and a heavy barbed point can be quite an experience, and so can fighting a fish when you score a hit. A 40-pound carp, 80-pound gar, or 100-pound shark puts up quite a tussle, often scooting a small boat around like a rubber duck in a bathtub.

    Game birds are shot regularly by a few bowmen who have developed a knack for picking moving targets out of the air. Pheasants, quail, grouse, wild turkeys, ducks, and geese are some of the more commonly bowhunted birds. Almost any bow-hunter can find at least a couple of these game birds in his neck of the woods, and he owes it to himself to give them a try. Even if he shoots deliberately with a bowsight, chances are he'll get a few shots at some of these birds as they sit on the ground. Turkeys and grouse are almost always shot on the ground, and pheasants, quail, ducks, and geese sometimes sit in the open, too. Most game birds have excellent eyesight and good ears, making a hunter work hard for shots. And hitting any game bird in the air or on the ground is a supreme shooting challenge, even if a bowhunter is skillful enough to get within range. Sneaking close to a small, alert bird like a quail and scoring a solid hit is extremely satisfying, and also puts tasty meat on the table. Even a fairly dumb game bird like a blue grouse is worthwhile to

Shooting at fish from the bobbing bow of a small boat is a difficult, interesting sport. (Photograph courtesy of Bear Archery Co.)

Ground-dwelling birds like blue grouse make difficult targets as they strut around in heavy cover. However, a back-country bowman can often take enough of these for regular meals.

bowhunt. I've lived off arrow-shot grouse in the backwoods of Montana and Colorado for several weeks at a time. Bowhunting birds can be gratifying in a number of ways.

Small game hunting is one of the best ways to practice for big-game seasons. Rabbits, squirrels, groundhogs, prairie dogs, and similar animals under 10 pounds have many things in common with deer and other big-game animals—they use their eyes, ears, and/or noses to detect danger, and disappear quickly when a bowman makes a hunting or shooting mistake. Small game is extremely abundant all over North America, giving bowhunters everywhere the chance to sharpen up their hunting and shooting skills and have fun doing it. My favorite pastime before deer season is stalking ground squirrels, little 2-pound critters that scamper to and fro in late spring. It takes considerable stealth to catfoot within 30 yards of these wily little buggers, and pinpoint accuracy to nail 'em with a field point or blunt-tipped

Ground squirrels are abundant in many parts of North America, providing top shooting practice for a serious bowhunter. It is not unusual to take 100 shots or more in one pleasant afternoon in a heavily populated ground-squirrel area.

arrow. After a few weeks of practice on ground squirrels, deer actually seem easy to hit.

Varmints like gray foxes, red foxes, coyotes, bobcats, and raccoons are also favorite targets of bowhunters. These alert predators live all over this continent, making them easy to locate with a little scouting. They are generally lured into bow range with a varmint call, and usually approach with all their senses perked up to see, hear, and smell what's going on. Varmints make tough targets to draw on and hit because they normally see a bowhunter move and streak for safety like greased thunderbolts. Varmints can be bowhunted throughout late fall, winter, and early spring in most areas, letting a bowhunter fill these "dead" months with lively entertainment.

Big-game hunting is the main event, though fish, birds, small game, and varmints are worthwhile sideshow attractions. Large animals are glamorous and make attractive trophies, and most are also at least fairly challenging to hunt with a bow. A big animal helps fill the freezer and cut down food bills, too—a worthwhile bonus if a bowhunter does his stuff and scores a kill.

Besides, there's a special kind of thrill in big-game bowhunting, an indescribable inner tingle that mushrooms into temple-pounding excitement when a large animal steps into view at close range. At that moment, all those agonizing months of shooting practice and equipment preparation suddenly become well worthwhile.

All big-game animals have something to offer a bowhunter, but they are not created equal—not by a long shot! For example, a cagey whitetail buck will make a bull moose look like a spastic numbskull every time. A whitetail has extremely sharp eyes, fine-tuned ears, and a wonderfully sensitive nose. He also has an agile brain to interpret these senses and a nimble body to disappear in the twinkle of an eye when danger approaches. On the other hand, a bull moose has terrible eyesight, only fair ears,

The author shot this well-furred red fox at 25 yards with a flat-flying aluminum arrow from a 70-pound compound bow. Foxes and similar predators come readily to a carefully blown varmint call, but represent fairly small targets to aim at and have the perplexing habit of dodging a slow-moving arrow.

and a fairly sensitive nose. His huge noggin houses a pea-sized brain which is slow to interpret data from his mediocre senses and tell his sluggish body to lumber away to safety. A moose is likely to get shot even by an uncoordinated bowhunter in size 16 brogans; a whitetail deer can sneak out from under an experienced bowhunter's nose without being seen or heard. A bowhunter should try as many kinds of big-game bowhunting as possible, but he should know something about the animals he's after so he isn't disappointed in the outcome.

Bison and musk-oxen have to qualify as the bumbling idiots of the North American big-game world. These stupid beasts are virtually no challenge to shoot with a bow once a bowhunter finds them to shoot. It was no accident that bison were nearly annihilated in the 1800s by market gunners—these big cattle are dunderheaded fools. The sole reason they are still shot on game ranches dotted across this continent is a sentimental one—the Indians and our forefathers shot buffalo, so some bowhunters like to bump one off for tradition's sake, plus all the good meat a buffalo provides. Musk-oxen are sometimes tough to locate in their northern haunts, but once found they generally mill around and allow a bowhunter to take his time and pick the animal he wants to shoot. A north-country musk-oxen hunt can be a memorable experience, but the actual hunting and shooting leave a lot to be desired.

Exotic animals are raised on game farms in Texas, California, and other fairly warm states. Bowhunting is a difficult game, so many bowhunters concentrate on fairly easy animals like Spanish goats, mouflon sheep, Corsican sheep, and other so-called exotics. These and similar animals can be a fair test of skill for beginning bowhunters, and occasionally give experienced bowhunters fits, too. However, most exotics have mediocre senses and medium-poor intelligence, making them something less than the cream of the big-game animals. I enjoy bowhunting Spanish goats as much as the next man, but these and similar animals have received far too much praise in sporting magazines and books. They are convenient to hunt and give a bowhunter reasonable shooting practice, and some of them taste pretty good when turned over to an expert cook. However, it

Exotic animals like these Spanish goats are extremely abundant on some game farms and private ranches, providing hunters with plenty of action and attractive trophy heads.

is not accurate to put them in the same class with whitetail deer, elk, black bear, and other slippery creatures that have a knack for making good bowhunters look like ding-a-lings.

Wild pigs of various types are extremely intelligent animals, but they are severely handicapped by their terrible eyesight and poor ears. Feral hogs (domestic hogs gone wild), European wild boars, and javelinas all have exceptional noses, but a bowhunter who spots these pigs and moves in from the downwind side can generally get a good close shot. Bowhunters enjoy hunting these animals because they are often difficult to find, and even when they're found, getting within range without letting the wind mess up the works can be tough. Besides, a young wild pig makes some of the best eating you ever had, and old boar makes an impressive, ferocious-looking trophy on the wall. Wild pigs don't rank with the most difficult animals, but they are interesting to hunt with a bow.

Moose derive their glamour from the magnificent north-country where they live, the gorgeous racks of horns on their heads, and the half-ton of tasty meat lumbering along underneath. A moose is fairly easy to hunt, requiring a bowhunter to keep the wind right, and not much else. One thing that does make moose hunting a challenge is trophy hunting—searching diligently for one oversized bull that makes all the others look like youngsters. The selective bowhunter can enjoy days and days in moose country, look at dozens of bulls, and finally take one that meets his specifications. The moose is not tough to sneak up on and shoot, but he can be very interesting to bowhunt if a hunter gets persnickety about the size of the horns.

Caribou are very similar to moose—big, beautiful, and dumb. They have decent eyes, decent noses, and very poor ears. However, most of these picture-book nincompoops inhabit the open plains of Canada and Alaska, which makes approaching them an interesting chore to say the least. They also have the disconcerting habit of moving great distances without warning, walking at a ground-gobbling pace that no man can match. It isn't unusual for a bowhunter to stalk a herd of caribou for hours, almost get within bow range, then suddenly feel his heart sink as the animals take a notion to move miles away and bed up again. You can't ever figure caribou, which makes them less than surefire to bowhunt. They are also among the most beautiful trophies in North America.

Brown bear and grizzly bear are sometimes very difficult to locate, especially in areas not too far from civilization. However, these big northern bruins are not too difficult to bowhunt once they are found. They have a lot in common with wild pigs—their eyes are terrible, their ears poor, and their noses extremely good. They make exceptionally fine trophies and are very exciting to bowhunt. Part of this excitement comes from the fact that they're big, beautiful animals, and part from the fact that they can chew your leg off if you miss or make a poor shot. A lot of animals are more difficult to bowhunt than these big bears, but none is more exciting.

Rocky Mountain goats are interesting animals. They inhabit some of the steepest, most inaccessible terrain in North America, but are really quite easy to bowhunt if a hunter is in excellent physical condition and has the ability to shoot sharply up and down hills. A mountain goat has good eyes, a fair nose, and poor ears. He is not an intelligent animal—in fact, he's fairly dull-witted. A goat doesn't make a spectacular trophy, but he's a favorite of bowhunters because he's easy to find in Canada and southern Alaska and represents a reasonable bowhunting challenge with a reasonably good chance of scoring.

Wild mountain sheep have been grossly overrated for years by outdoor writers and guides. Dall, Stone, and bighorn sheep are beautiful animals, inhabit some of the most magnificent country in North America, and taste incredibly good. However, they are not very bright when compared to deer and some other creatures, and don't have very good senses, either. A sheep's main line of defense is his eyes, which are excellent. His nose and ears are fairly good.

Even before I hunted wild sheep I suspected they might not be the super-smart, super-slippery animals they are usually cracked up to be. At the turn of the century these animals were almost wiped out by market gunners on some parts of our continent—bighorns in particular—and you just don't wipe out smart, elusive animals like elk, blacktail deer, and whitetail deer. You wipe out easier animals, like sheep. North-country guides have naturally perpetuated the sheep-are-tough myth to serve their own purposes; some hunters will not pay vast sums of money to go after easy animals. However, the fact is that a very, very high percentage of nonresident hunters—both riflemen and bowhunters—score on sheep. Last time I checked, over 80 percent of the nonresident sheep hunters in Alaska were successful, and parts of Canada produced almost as well. These success figures are bound to slide as more and more sheep are taken from the north country, but the fact remains that 80 percent success on any kind of animal is phenomenally high.

A bowhunting buddy of mine moved from Montana to Alaska several years ago, thrilled at the chance to try for the glamour animals in this far-off land. Since then he has shot seven Dall sheep with his bow and arrow, plus most of the other north-country animals. I talked to him not long ago and he admitted that the elk, whitetail deer, and mule deer in his native Montana beat anything in Alaska hands down. When I quizzed him about sheep, he shook his head. "There's no comparison with an elk or a whitetail," he stated flatly. "Sheep are pretty animals, but they're a lot easier than most of the game I hunted back home."

Bowhunting sheep is largely a matter of being in the right area and having lots of stamina. These animals do have good eyes, and a bowhunter sometimes has to watch them for several days before they move into an area that allows a stalk. However, Dall, Stone, and bighorn sheep are fairly easy to approach in rough, broken terrain.

Black bear have poor eyes, but their ears are quite good and their noses are excellent. The black bear is also intelligent and wastes no time in getting away when he knows danger is nearby. A well-furred black bear also makes a nice trophy rug, and tastes good too unless he's an ol' grandpappy. Another good thing about the black bear is his incredibly large range—he inhabits almost all of the upper half of North America, as well as the Pacific Coast Mountains, the Rocky Mountains, and parts of the East. Almost any bowhunter who wants to take a crack at a black bear can, and at a reasonably low cost, too.

Black bear are bowhunted in three basic ways—on foot, over bait, and with hounds. Still-hunting (hunting on foot) and baiting bear can be a real challenge, especially with hunter-wise bear. Baiting a bear to a smelly pile of meat is not a particularly glamorous technique, but it is not always an easy one. Bear tend to be nocturnal in all but the most remote areas, which means they are not at all dependable about coming to bait during daylight hours. Finding one to stalk on foot is also very challenging.

Chasing, treeing, and then shooting any animal with the help of hound dogs cannot be considered bowhunting—not at all. This kind of sport is enjoyable and very effective, but the bowman who shoots a bear out of a tree after dogs put it there is merely shooting a bear with a bow and arrow—not bowhunting that bear. I've personally shot half a dozen black bear from trees with a bow, partly because I love to listen to good hound dogs run, and partly because I love to eat bear meat. However, I would never pretend I bowhunted those bear—I merely shot them with a bow as they sat 30 feet or so above my head. The dogs did the hunting and I did the shooting.

Mountain lions (cougars) are almost always hunted with the help of hounds. As a result, I cannot consider the cougar a bowhuntable animal at all—he's much too elusive and thinly populated to be taken on purpose with a bow.

Mule deer are sometimes sneered at by Eastern bowhunters because they are not as nervous and high-strung as the Eastern whitetail deer. However, the Western mule deer prefers high, open country with a view, making it difficult to get a close shot at a mature buck with two or three hunting seasons under his hide. A mule deer has very good eyes, excellent ears, and a superb nose. He is not nearly as predictable as a whitetail deer, either, making him difficult or impossible to bowhunt from tree stands and ground blinds. A mature muley *isn't* as edgy as a mature whitetail, so he doesn't present quite the bowhunting challenge that a whitetail does when both are hunted on foot. Muley hunting often requires shooting over 40 yards, though, so the bowhunter who heads West after this big deer should practice his long-range shooting skills.

Pronghorn antelope require the longest shooting. This fleet-footed animal inhabits open plains country, and can be exceedingly tough to get close to. A pronghorn has phenomenal eyesight, fair ears, and a fair nose. He is not a very intelligent animal, but his eyesight and incredible ground speed make him a toughie to bowhunt. The best way to take a pronghorn is by sitting near a watering hole, although these animals can sometimes be approached on foot in broken country. They are also extremely curious, and can often be "flagged" into range by a bowhunter who stays out of sight and waves a hat or white handkerchief in the air. I once flagged a nice buck pronghorn within 30 yards simply by holding a white handkerchief in my teeth and letting the wind blow it around. I was standing upright on flat, bare ground, but the curious animal made the mistake of walking right to me anyway. I'd like to report that this was his *last* mistake, but the quick little devil dodged my arrow and took off like a raped ape. The pronghorn is a beautiful creature, good to eat, and one of the most difficult game animals a bowhunter can pit his skills against.

Elk have good eyes, good ears, and fine noses, plus quick

*The pronghorn antelope is difficult to bowhunt because of his love
for open ground and his incredibly fast feet. The author stalked this
14-inch, record-book buck for over six hours before getting a decent
shot and nailing him high through the spine at 60 yards.*

brains to interpret these senses and give hunters the slip. A big
bull elk before or after the rut is tough to bag. An elk is also a
herd animal, meaning a bowhunter after elk usually contends
with a dozen or more sets of eyes, ears, and nostrils instead of
just one. Elk are spectacularly beautiful, especially the biggest
bulls, and also provide meat on a par with the best beefsteak.

Like all lovesick males, a bull elk in the rut gets downright
daffy, making him a lot easier to hunt than normal. Bugling in
or sneaking up on a squealing, sex-crazed bull elk borders on
dirty pool because the animal is totally preoccupied with hot
little cow elk. Bowhunting bull elk in the rut is exciting business,
but nowhere near the challenge of taking these animals when
they are sane and sober.

Blacktail deer are the most underrated big-game animals on
this continent, mainly because they inhabit a narrow band of
Pacific Coast Mountains far from where most bowhunters live.
These dinky deer are nearly as spooky as whitetail deer and

don't have the whitetail's predictable habits. Their senses are all extremely sharp, and they have quick brains and quick bodies to save them from the sneakiest bowhunters. On top of all this, blacktails prefer to live in dense forests and heavy brush, making them tough to see and even tougher to sneak close to. The blacktail deer is one of the most difficult animals to bowhunt.

Whitetail deer have been touted for years as the most elusive game in North America, and I agree wholeheartedly. The nifty part is, this beautiful, cagey animal is also the most widespread big-game animal on our continent, letting every bowhunter take a crack at him. The whitetail has superb eyesight, superb ears, and a superb sense of smell. He is also high-strung, intelligent, and fast on his feet. A bowhunter who shoots a whitetail deer can congratulate himself, especially if he sneaks up on the animal.

Whitetails are generally bowhunted from tree stands because they are extremely predictable. Tree-stand hunting for whitetails is not nearly as challenging as hunting them on your two hind legs because an elevated stand puts a bowhunter above a deer's line of sight and usually prevents a deer from catching a telltale whiff of human odor. However, watching whitetail deer before season so you can dope out their habits and select a suitable tree-stand location *is* enjoyable and challenging, and herein lies much of the pleasure bowhunters get from hunting whitetails out of stands.

A bowhunter should be aware of the extensive hunting possibilities provided by the fish, birds, small game, varmints, and big game on this continent. By doing so, he can hunt the year round, perfect his bowhunting skills, and have a barrel of fun doing it!

Chapter 17—BOWHUNTING BASICS

A good bowhunter has three basic things working for him—an intimate knowledge of the game he hunts, the skills necessary to find and get close to that game, and the patience and sheer determination to keep on trying until he gets the shot he wants. Successful bowhunting is largely a matter of common sense and practical experience in the field, but a beginning bowhunter has to understand a few basics before he can head for the woods and begin perfecting his hunting technique.

ALL ABOUT AN ANIMAL'S DEFENSE SYSTEM

All animals have three main lines of defense—eyes, ears, and nose. Some creatures are extremely alert in all categories, and some have one or two senses that dominate (see Chapter 16 for details). A bowhunter must learn all he can about an animal's three-point defense system so he can successfully penetrate it and take home the bacon.

Virtually all game animals and most birds are color-blind, but most have at least fairly good black-and-white vision. White-tail deer, wild sheep, and pronghorn antelope are among the animals with superb eyesight, and the various bears, wild pigs, and moose are some of the animals with medium-to-poor eyesight. However, any animal can zero in on a badly concealed bowhunter, especially if that hunter is moving quickly. Animals with poorer eyesight sometimes fail to see slow movement, but even the nearsighted pig can pick up movements at fairly close range. As discussed in Chapter 5, a bowhunter must take pains to wear the proper clothes so he blends into the shrubbery and avoids detection.

Proper clothing is a must, but a bowhunter should also develop the knack of staying out of an animal's sight completely. The best-dressed bowhunter in the world will startle the wits out of any animal if he silhouettes himself against the sky, and if he plans to sneak along through the underbrush, he should pick a route that at least partially obscures his body from the eyes of game. A bowhunter who walks along in the sunlight when he could be in the shadows is making a big mistake because he's contrasting his well-lighted body against a very dark background. A bowhunter who trudges down the top of a ridge when he could be lurking along the back side of that ridge with just his eyes and ears poked above the skyline is also jeopardizing his chances of success. Proper clothing is necessary to avoid being seen by animals, but silhouetting yourself or moving through the open unless it's absolutely necessary is a definite blunder. The best situation of all is staying totally out of sight of an animal until just before you take a shot, either by catching

A bowhunter silhouetted against the sky makes a pretty picture, but scares the living daylights out of game. He's much better off lurking in the shadows below the skyline.

the animal with its head behind a solid obstruction like a tree, log, or bush, or by moving in on the back side of a ridge or from behind a big rock or brushpile.

A bowhunter should always move with the speed of a snail, even if he's well dressed and either concealed behind something or deep in the shadows. Sharp-eyed animals like deer can pick up a bowhunter hotfooting it through the underbrush, even if that bowhunter is camo-clad from head to toe and makes no noise. Quick movement is the worst when a bowhunter doesn't blend in with his background, but it never does a bowhunter any good to move fast unless he has to run a footrace to intercept a fast-moving creature like a caribou. If a bowhunter does have to move fast to get in good shooting position, he should try to do his moving when an animal cannot see him at all.

Different animals have different degrees of peripheral vision (the ability to see to the sides). Prey animals like deer, elk, and antelope have their eyes set on the sides of their heads so they can see to the sides and slightly behind them. This extra-big arc of vision allows a prey animal to see predators before they strike. In contrast, a predator like a black bear, coyote, fox, wolf, or man has eyes set in the front of the head to give superior depth perception and the ability to spring at an animal and score a kill. The bowhunter who goes after deer and other prey animals should remember that these animals can pick up side movement extremely well. For example, if a hunter is trying to sneak within range of a mule deer in fairly open terrain, he should *never* move unless the deer has its head behind a log or bush, or is facing directly away. A relaxed, broadside deer will spot the slightest movement to the side or slightly behind him, even if his head is down in a feeding position. The bowhunter who's stalking bear or calling coyotes should also be careful not to move at the wrong time, but should realize that these predators cannot pick up side movements nearly as well as deer can.

Very few animals look up, so a bowhunter who somehow gets above game has a definite edge. The fact that animals do not expect danger from above makes tree-stand hunting a deadly technique, and also makes hunting high ridges very effective. In heavily timbered, hard-hunted Eastern states, whitetail deer

A bowhunter should carefully watch a deer's ears. This blacktail's ears are intensely cupped forward . . . which means he's alert and coiled like a bedspring. A relaxed deer holds its ears back and flops them around, letting a bowhunter know he hasn't been detected.

have become somewhat wary of overhead danger, but a tree-stander still has a real advantage over a man on the ground.

Some animals have extremely sensitive ears, ears capable of picking up sounds a bowhunter may not even know he's making. Generally speaking, the larger an animal's ears are in proportion to its body, the better it hears. Deer of all kinds have big, cupped ears that detect tiny sounds with ease. In contrast, grizzly bear and caribou have small ears and do not hear especially well. A bowhunter should pay close attention to how well the animals he hunts can hear, and take pains to be quieter than he has to be to avoid detection.

Some kinds of noises scare the dickens out of animals, others are ignored by animals, and still others actually attract animals. Hunter-wise creatures like whitetail deer have learned to run from metallic clinks, the sound of rough fabric scraping against bushes, and other obviously human-made noises. However, the woods are full of natural sounds which do not disturb animals at all. For example, a bowhunter who trudges along steadily through a carpet of dry autumn leaves sounds like what he is, but if he moves with the speed of a turtle and rustles a leaf once in a while, he might get away with it even if a deer hears the sound. Wild sheep are used to the sound of falling rock, and I've created minor rockslides within 100 yards of Dall rams on several occasions without disturbing them in the least. However, the clank of a compound bow's metal eccentric wheel against a rock can send a sheep packing. The *type* of sound is the key.

Some kinds of game, especially those in the rut, are drawn irresistibly to certain sounds. Rutting whitetail bucks sometimes come running when a bowhunter rattles two antlers together. Lovesick bull elk come charging to a skillfully blown bugle, and blacktail deer often respond to the imitation of a fawn squealing in pain. A bull moose in the rut suckers readily to the artificial

A feeding animal makes a lot of racket—racket that partially covers up the noise a bowhunter makes. The author sneaked within 50 yards of this huge record-book mule deer and shot it through both lungs as it fed noisily on a bush. He has also shot bucks after they bedded down, but this is a far more ticklish task.

moan of a cow in heat, and wild turkey gobblers can be lured within range with seductive hen clucks during their spring mating season. A bowhunter who thoroughly knows his game can use sounds to his advantage as well as trying to keep quiet.

Unless a bowhunter wants to lure game within range, he should take pains to be completely silent. If he's in a tree stand, he should keep movement to a minimum and avoid scuffing his feet across his platform. Many bowhunters carpet their stands to hush their movements, or wear soft-soled shoes when standing on wood or metal. A stalking bowhunter is best off keeping a solid barrier like a ridge between him and game. Such a barrier blocks off sound and lets him move into position without being heard, even when the footing is noisy. The best time to get the drop on animals without being heard is when these animals are up and feeding. For instance, a feeding deer makes a world of noise and blots out much of a bowhunter's noise with his own. On the reverse side of the coin, an animal that is bedded down may be almost impossible to approach on foot because the critter can hear the slightest sound a hunter makes. Sneaking up on bedded animals is possible, however, provided a bowhunter has the patience to go slow and watch his Ps and Qs.

One of the most exciting stalks I've ever made proves my point. I spotted three dandy muley bucks high above me one frosty morning in central Montana. The animals milled around and finally bedded under a small ledge at the base of a naked dome of noisy rockslides. I hustled up a deep ravine that ran past them, keeping out of sight and hearing. I eventually topped out on the dome of shale, moving in behind and above the bucks. The last 100 yards of the sneak was sharply downhill across loose shale. As Western hunters already know, this damnable stuff clinks maliciously when you breathe on it, let alone step on it, and the only way I could move was stooping over carefully before each step, hollowing out a new foothold one rock at a time with my fingers, and then gingerly planting one foot in the fresh little stair-step. A full forty-five minutes later I finally stepped out on the ledge above the bucks, hovering above them like a red-tailed hawk after a meadow mouse. A second later I shot a very good four-pointer as he snoozed in his bed only 7

BOWHUNTING

feet below me. One careless mistake on that sneak and the outcome would have been entirely different.

As a bowhunter gains experience, he automatically learns how to walk without making noise. The proper footgear helps an awful lot, but walking technique is important, too. A bowhunter should move slowly, picking his feet up high to avoid scraping them against dead branches and other junk on the forest floor. He should always put his feet down gingerly, feeling his way along. A skillful bowhunter can move silently without watching his feet, which lets him keep his eyes peeled for game.

An animal's sense of smell is usually its foremost defense mechanism. This is especially true of whitetails and other kinds of deer. A deer will sometimes linger around and actually relax again after seeing or hearing something that alarms him, but give him a snootful of human odor and you can kiss him good-bye. An animal with a good nose may doubt what he sees and what he hears on occasion, but a hunter's body odor is unmistakable.

An experienced bowhunter keeps track of wind direction at all times and either hunts directly into the wind or sideways to it. In both cases, the animals in front of the hunter cannot possibly smell him unless the breezes radically shift direction. Using odor-masking scents (see Chapter 7) can help a bowhunter if the wind does shift suddenly, but he should never travel with the wind on purpose. If he does, he'll see fleeing animals or none at all. Some bowhunters claim they can actually lure animals within range by using the right artificial scents, especially during the mating season. I know for a fact that rut-goofy whitetail bucks can be attracted to doe-in-heat scent, especially if a bowhunter is high above the ground where this scent has been squirted. Similarly, a black bear is attracted to a smelly pile of meat or fruit like a hunk of steel to a magnet, making this a very effective hunting technique wherever it is legal.

A tree stand helps keep a bowhunter's scent in air currents above an animal's nose, which is another reason tree-stand hunting is so effective. A bowhunter on foot has a tougher row to hoe because he's moving in the same air belt with his prey. In very slight breezes, a hunter must continually check wind direction by tapping his powder pouch, tossing dust, leaves, or

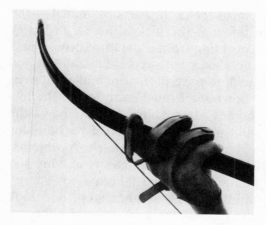

A thread tied to the upper limb-tip of a bow acts as a simple wind sock, keeping a bowhunter constantly informed about the direction of prevailing breezes.

grass in the air, or watching a little thread he has tied to the upper limb tip of his bow. A lightweight thread acts like a wind sock and eliminates the hassle and movement involved in tossing debris in the air.

LEARNING TO USE YOUR OWN SENSES

Once a bowhunter knows about an animal's three-pronged defense system, he can concentrate on penetrating that defense system and getting a good shot. Moving within 30 or 40 yards of an alert game animal seldom happens by accident. Approaching this close requires a bowhunter to use his own senses and intelligence to close the gap. As a bowhunter perfects his art, he develops a knack for seeing animals before they see him, hearing them and pinpointing their location, and actually smelling them on occasion when they happen to be nearby. He also learns to see and understand various kinds of sign like tracks, droppings, fresh animal beds, and less obvious clues to an animal's whereabouts. As these skills become more finely tuned, a bowhunter gets better and better at his sport—and enjoys it more and more.

Learning to see game takes practice. How perfect a bowhunter's eyes are is far less important than his ability to recognize what he sees. I know several fine bowhunters with severe eyesight problems, and these nimrods can instantly spot animals that an unskilled man with perfect vision would never see. An experienced woodsman looks for parts of animals—the tip of an antler flashing in the sun, the flick of an ear in heavy trees, a wet, shiny nose protruding from a patch of brush, or a set of legs planted like grape stakes between a deadfall log and the ground. Live animals seldom pose in the open like the ones on picture postcards, so a bowhunter must learn to see the bits and pieces. This ability comes after hours and hours in the woods, so a beginner should not get frustrated if he bumbles repeatedly at first. Time will solve his game-spotting problems.

One of the main difficulties a beginner has is moving too fast when he's sneaking along. He should take a step, survey the terrain around him carefully, take another step, and look carefully again. All too often beginners and experts alike get excited when they're close to game and move too quickly, re-

Wild hogs and most other animals make telltale noises as they feed, fight, and relax. Jim Easton, well-known president of Easton Aluminum arrow-shaft company, took this trophy boar after hearing another boar squealing and thus locating a concentration of pigs.

vealing themselves to animals before they see those animals. This problem is compounded when a bowhunter is stalking one particular animal and bumps unexpectedly into another. One of the first stalks I ever attempted taught me this lesson with a vengeance.

I spotted the big forkhorn at the head of a huge boulderfield. The fat, velvet-horned buck was feeding on oak brush, the morning sun frosting his heavy, even rack like sugar on a doughnut. The wind was blowing from him to me, and the walking was completely quiet across big, smooth rocks. The buck was in a slight hollow, too—a setup! I trotted up the rock face noiselessly, eyes riveted on the thick horn tips that bobbed up and down above the brush. I almost made it, too. The buck was less than 30 yards away when a violent snort to my right scared me half out of my socks. A fat little doe was standing 20 yards to the side, eyeballing me with total contempt. Does are illegal game in my native California, so all I could do was stand there with my teeth in my mouth while the belligerent pipsqueak blew again and again, stamping her front foot occasionally for emphasis. The horn tips ahead swiveled my way, and I could see the buck's ear tips quiver as he listened intently. Then his gorgeous horns slowly turned and melted into the brush like a puff of cigar smoke on an evening breeze. I cussed my luck, and vowed to go slower next time so I could keep an eye out for other deer.

A bowman should use his ears to good advantage as he sits in a tree or moves slowly across the ground. Relaxed animals can be very noisy, crunching their feet, rustling brush with their bodies, and wheezing, coughing, and uttering other audible sounds. Alert bowhunters very often hear animals long before they see them, giving them time to get ready for a shot. Bugling bull elk are especially noisy creatures, but almost all animals make sounds that give them away. I remember one time when I went hog hunting with my good friend Jim Easton, president of the world-famous Easton Aluminum arrow-shaft company. We were sitting on a rimrock high above a brush-choked ravine one evening, glassing for pigs. Suddenly a shrill squeal echoed across the canyon, followed by a series of grunts. We zeroed in

Elk and many other animals enjoy loafing in and around waterholes (above). Such water-loving creatures leave hundreds of tracks in the mud to let a bowhunter know they aren't far away (below). (Above photograph courtesy of Phlor-Phauna Photos.)

on the spot with our binoculars, and a few minutes later a nice boar waddled into sight about 500 yards away. We didn't get that particular hog, but Jim shot a good tusker in the same general area the next day.

Another time I was sitting on a ridge, carefully watching six blacktail bucks feed 200 yards away. All at once I heard the sound of heavy breathing directly behind me, and felt the hackles on my neck rise up like porcupine quills. I slowly swiveled my head, and was startled to see a medium-sized black bear shuffling across the ridge directly behind me, barely 15 yards away. The shaggy animal never saw me, and when he turned straight away I put an orange-anodized aluminum arrow through him lengthwise at 25 yards. His jet-black hide is hanging on the wall beside me as I write this book.

Humans have poor to mediocre noses, but some animals let off enough odor to be detected by a bowman with a sharp sniffer. Two notable examples are elk and wild hogs, which leave behind a barnyard smell that lingers for several minutes. A hunter who knows this can slow up when he smells these animals, confident that they're somewhere nearby.

Animals of all kinds make sign—sign that proves they're in an area, and sign that sometimes lets a bowhunter follow them and score. All animals leave tracks and droppings, and most also leave beds where they lie up in midday. They also scrape off hair on tree trunks, barbed-wire fences, and other snaggy objects. Whitetail bucks and other antlered animals leave rubs when they strip the bark from trees with their antlers during the rut, and some species also urinate in scrapes during the rut to attract members of the opposite sex. Black bear tear stumps apart to find beetles and other tasty morsels, wild pigs root up the ground in search of subterranean tidbits, and migratory animals like caribou beat deep trails in the ground with their feet. These and other telltale signs help a sharp-eyed bowhunter, letting him actually follow fresh sign or lie in wait till an animal returns. An intimate knowledge of animal sign is one of the most valuable tools a bowhunter can possess, and must be acquired through months and months of hunting practice coupled with careful, intelligent observation.

A bowhunter learns many valuable hunting lessons as time goes along. He learns most of these by blundering repeatedly and benefiting from his mistakes. The most important thing a bowhunter can do is *not give up*. This sport is very demanding, but sheer determination and a "try, try again" attitude will always beat the odds. And once a bowhunter *does* beat the odds, he gains self-confidence and performs a little better next time around. Eventually he becomes a really good bowhunter, a skillful predator with an intimate knowledge of wild animals and a keen awareness of his own capabilities.

Chapter 18—SPECIFIC BOWHUNTING METHODS

Once a bowhunter learns a few basics about the animals he's after and the skills he needs to score, he's ready to zero in on game with one or more specific bowhunting methods. Which methods work best for a bowhunter depends on many things, including the game to be hunted, the terrain, the time of year, how skillful and patient that bowhunter is, and local bowhunting laws. As a bowhunter becomes more and more familiar with particular kinds of game in particular hunting areas, he learns which hunting methods flop and which ones work like a charm. Here are a few basic guidelines to follow when deciding which hunting methods will do you the most good.

STAND HUNTING

Stand hunting is one of the easiest bowhunting techniques, especially when a stand is elevated above an animal's line of sight and smell. This bowhunting method also happens to be one of the most surefire ways to bag game, provided a bowhunter knows when and where to take a stand.

A stand hunter simply locates himself in a promising game area and sits patiently until game arrives. He doesn't have to be a quiet walker, and doesn't have to be quite as alert with his eyes and ears as a bowhunter who sneaks along through the woods. A stand hunter lets game come to him, uncomplicating the bowhunting process considerably and putting most of the burden on the animal. For instance, a whitetail buck in the dry autumn woods has to be mighty sharp to locate a well-concealed, motionless bowhunter nestled in front of a bush by a game trail. The same buck would be difficult or impossible to approach on foot across the noisy forest floor. Ambushing game

*A bowhunter who takes a
stand in a tree instead of
on the ground is much
less likely to be spotted by
sharp-eyed animals like
whitetail deer.*

by remaining motionless in a tree stand or on the ground can be
a very effective way to hunt.

Stand hunting is most effective on creatures of habit like
whitetail deer, pronghorn antelope, and nonrutting elk. These
and other animals tend to feed, water, and bed in the same
places day after day, letting a smart bowhunter observe their
movement patterns and lay a careful ambush. Much of the challenge of stand hunting is mapping out the strategy to waylay a
particular animal—after the plan is carried out, the shooting is
often easy. Top places to wait for whitetail deer and other predictable animals are waterholes, saddles in ridges, field edges,
and ravines with well-used game trails. A bowhunter can locate
such hotspots by observing animals from a distance before hunting season and/or carefully checking animal sign in likely areas
to see if these areas are being used. A heavily used trail, wa-
terhole, or feeding area is always littered with tracks, droppings,
and other signs of use.

If there's an unusually high density of animals in a particular area, taking a stand almost anywhere can be productive. Blacktail deer are not very predictable creatures, but one of the best blacktail bucks I ever shot came strolling by as I sat beside a bush, eating my lunch. I somehow got rid of my baloney sandwich, gathered up my bow, nocked an arrow, and got off a shot before the fat four-point walked out of range. I wasn't purposefully stand hunting, but I saw over a hundred deer that day and know I could have had several other shots if I had planted myself in almost any spot and waited patiently. However, the woods were damp, which made sneaking easy, and shooting my buck from a stand was purely accident.

When a bowhunter decides to put up a temporary or permanent tree stand, he should make sure his stand is well above the area where game is likely to pass by. Most bowhunters prefer stands at least 15 feet high, and a safer bet is 20 or 30 feet.

The author shot this fat trophy whitetail from a stand at the edge of an alfalfa field. He watched the buck for a solid week before ambushing the animal in its favorite feeding area.

An elevated stand of any sort should be located where animals cannot see it without looking up. A poorly placed tree stand in a ravine might well be *below* the ridges on either side, defeating the purpose of the stand by letting ridge-running animals see a bowhunter and possibly smell him too. Similarly, a bowhunter who decides to take a stand on the ground should pay strict attention to the wind direction and plant himself where animals are not likely to smell him. For more information on how to set up a tree stand and take a stand on the ground, see Chapter 6.

As a rule, the best times to sit on stand are morning and evening. This is when most animals move around the most, going from a feeding area to a watering area, a feeding area to a bedding area, a bedding area to a watering area, and so on. However, there are notable exceptions to the morning/evening rule. For example, when creatures like deer, elk, and moose are in the rut, they sometimes move around all day long, giving a stand hunter hours and hours of fruitful hunting time. When lots of bowhunters are milling around the woods, animals also tend to keep moving, doubling or tripling a stand hunter's odds of cashing in. One time I accidentally took a stand in hunter-crowded woods and accidentally got close to a buck. The incident was a bit embarrassing at the time, but the story is a classic.

It was after one o'clock on opening afternoon of California's August mule-deer season. I was moseying along below a high ribbon of rimrock, eyes peeled for the flicker of an ear or the flash of a tail swatting pesky summer flies. The plateau above was crawling with eager bowhunters, but I had the steep lower country to myself.

All at once, I felt nature's call. I ducked under a stunted pine tree, dropping my drawers after carefully laying my old recurve bow on a convenient bush to one side. I was just fumbling in my pocket for toilet paper when I suddenly heard rocks clatter directly above. I rolled my eyeballs and was amazed and shocked to see a deer's legs moving along under the trees, 15 feet above me. I slowly stretched to grab my bow—and felt my heart sink as I realized it was just out of reach. I was mentally kicking myself when the animal stepped into view, and I froze helplessly in a twisted, uncomfortable crouch.

The sunlight danced on the big three-point's even rack as he looked my way with a blank expression on his grizzled face. Then he looked over his shoulder. I was huddled under the tree, and was pretty well camouflaged except for my white BVDs. The wind was also perfect, blowing directly from the buck to me. The animal stood still a second, then walked down the hill toward me, passing barely 5 feet away. As he gingerly stepped over the tip of my bow (no kidding) and slipped on past, I made a frantic dive for the old recurve—and landed flat on my face. I'm sure that poor buck came close to coronary arrest!

HUNTING OVER BAIT

Baiting is a variation of stand hunting. Baiting laws vary considerably from one area to another, but the legal baiting of black bear, deer, wild pigs, and other creatures can be very rewarding. In some densely wooded areas it's the only way a bowhunter can score consistently. The trick is putting out bait in a convenient location and then sitting in a tree stand or ground blind near this bait. Black bear are the most commonly baited animals because they come readily to smelly meat, rotten fruit, and other "tasty" stuff deposited in a place sheltered by trees and brush. Black bear in hard-hunted areas are next to impossible to see unless they're baited because they generally move at night. Bear baiting in a lightly hunted area like northern Canada can be exceedingly easy, but a hunter-shy black usually comes slipping to a bait just at dark with the caution of a cat burglar. A bowhunter must be well concealed, stay totally quiet, and have the wind in his favor before he has a prayer of scoring on such wary game.

Wild hogs can be lured to corn, fruit, meat, and similar baits, and deer sometimes come to alfalfa hay, apples, and other nutritious foods. These animals have very keen noses and home in on baits quickly. Before baiting any kind of animal, be sure this hunting practice is legal in your area.

CALLING

Another brand of stand hunting is calling game. This is a unique sport because the game is actually hunting the hunter.

A calling bowhunter must be extremely well concealed because the creatures he calls are doing their level best to see him.

A fair percentage of animals and birds can be called within bow range if a bowhunter knows his stuff. Wild creatures respond to various calls for various reasons. A coyote, fox, or similar predator will come running to the sound of a dying rabbit because he figures he'll get a free meal. A bull elk will sometimes actually charge a bowhunter who imitates the bugle of another lovesick bull, mainly because the bull is out of his head with the urge to fight any and all comers that might try to steal his cows. A rutting whitetail buck might respond to the sounds of antlers banging together because he thinks there are two bucks fighting over a doe and figures he might get a piece of the action. A bull moose will come galloping to the moan of a cow in heat, for obvious reasons. He'll also run to the sound of water poured quickly from a pan or a little catch basin fashioned from a piece of birch bark because this sounds like a receptive cow urinating on the ground. Blacktail deer can often be attracted to the mournful bleats of a fawn in pain, especially if they are called in very heavy brush or trees. Ducks and geese can be

A bowhunter can coax most predators to the artificial squeals of a dying rabbit (left). When coyotes and other long-toothed meat-eaters hear a varmint call, they immediately think there's a free meal not far away (right).

lured to a skillfully laid decoy set with the calls of feeding waterfowl, and wild tom turkeys are real suckers for the lovelorn cluck of a seductive hen.

These and other calls can be imitated by a bowhunter, giving him the unique thrill of seeing animals and birds come looking for him. A few talented bowmen I know can utter animal calls with nothing more than their mouths; however, most of us do not have plastic vocal cords and must buy our calls.

Game calling is a fine art, an art every bowhunter should try. A game caller can have a lot of fun, learn a lot about animals in the process, and put more game in the bag at the same time.

STILL-HUNTING

Still-hunting is more challenging than stand hunting because a still-hunter is an active predator moving along through the woods in search of game. A still-hunter must pussyfoot into the wind, making no noise and watching carefully for animals ahead and to the sides. An animal has the advantage in this kind of situation because a bowhunter is moving instead of staying still. If he makes one little error in the way he walks or fails to care-

fully watch surrounding terrain, he'll tip off animals and come
up empty-handed.

Still-hunting works best on unpredictable animals that prefer fairly dense cover. This method is effective on blacktail deer,
for example, because these animals do not have regular movement patterns and usually live in heavy brush or trees. A successful blacktail hunter goes after these deer on foot, covering
lots of ground, eventually slipping within range of a deer, and
then shooting it before it spots him. Still-hunting is also a dandy
way to try for wild pigs, moose, and other unpredictable critters
that love heavy cover. This technique works on predictable animals like whitetail deer, too, provided a bowhunter has the
sneaking talent to make it pay.

The bowhunter who prefers a challenge will enjoy still-hunting. This method requires both sneaking skill and the ability to
see game before game sees you. It also requires intense concentration at all times. A tree-stand hunter can relax while he
waits for game, but a still-hunter can never relax. He's an active
hunter practicing an intricate art where one little mistake can
ruin the whole show.

Still-hunting works best when animals are up and moving
in early morning and late evening. A moving, feeding deer is
much easier to sneak up to than a bedded animal, and often
gives a still-hunter an easy shot. In contrast, a bedded animal
is darn tough to slip up on, and darn tough to see even when a
bowhunter moves within spitting distance. Bedded animals like
deer, elk, pigs, and other forest dwellers often "stick tight" as
a bowhunter moseys past, freezing until the hunter is gone and
then either slipping away quietly or staying put till the evening
feeding hours. One morning a few years ago I watched nine wild
hogs disappear in a living-room-sized blackberry thicket. I
walked around the patch a couple of times, peering into the
dense mess carefully. Nothing happened. I picked up a fist-sized
rock and heaved it in the berries. Still nothing. A dozen rocks
later the hogs were still nowhere to be seen. I stayed near the
thicket all day, and just before sundown those hogs came tiptoeing out of that berry patch like puffs of fog. Thirty minutes
later I shot the biggest one as I still-hunted through the woods

A still-hunter must proceed slowly with eyes peeled for nearby game (above left), spotting animals through nooks and crannies in the heavy woods before they spot him (above right).

in the direction they had gone. The long-tusked boar weighed 194 pounds field-dressed, a good pig for that particular area.

One interesting and effective variation of still-hunting is quietly floating along a stream or lakeshore in a boat. Bowhunting from a boat is silent and deadly on deer, moose, and other animals that frequent shorelines. It is also the only way to bowhunt some kinds of fish. For example, a gar in the 100-pound class is every bit as elusive as a trophy whitetail deer, and usually requires a noiseless approach far from shoreline in a small canoe or flat-bottomed fishing boat.

JUMPSHOOTING

Jumpshooting is a popular sport with a few good bowhunters who shoot instinctively and hunt extra-spooky animals in heavy cover. An average bowhunter who uses a bowsight should *never* shoot at running animals, but a few instinctive bow shots are good enough to consistently hit small moving targets at close range. Using a bowsight is a deliberate technique that requires a hunter to draw, anchor, aim carefully, and then release. However, the best instinctive shots can draw, anchor, and release in one fluid motion, a lightning-fast technique that's tailor-made for flying birds and running animals. My friend Duke Savora, designer of the famous presharpened Savora Swept-Wing broadhead, has this uncanny knack for hitting small moving targets. He's a busy man, and tells me he prefers to bowhunt near his Washington-based archery company to save time. The deer in this metropolitan area are spooky as all get-out, but that doesn't bother Duke. He eases along through the heavy brush and trees like slow molasses, which often rattles the nerves of deer bedded nearby. Some of these animals get nervous enough to leap up and race away through the trees, giving Duke plenty of time to strike like a rattlesnake after a

Stalking works best in fairly open, mountainous country. A bowhunter should climb to a high point in such terrain, look for game, and then plan a stalk once an animal is located.

rabbit. Shooting at running game results in misses and poor hits unless you shoot as well as my buddy Duke, but if you're *consistently* deadly on moving targets and hunt nervous animals in heavy brush, jumpshooting may be perfect for you.

STALKING

Stalking is perhaps the single most exciting way to bowhunt. This method is similar to still-hunting, except that animals are spotted at a distance in fairly open country and then carefully approached. A still-hunter suddenly finds himself within good bow range of an animal in heavy cover—a stalker uses his eyes and good binoculars to find an animal at long range, and then purposefully sneaks within bow range of that animal. Many trophy bowhunters prefer to stalk because they can size up animals ahead of time and decide whether or not a sneak is worthwhile.

Stalking works best in fairly open mountain country where a bowhunter can get up high and look over lots of ground. Most Western animals are taken by stalking because most live in fairly open country. Western whitetail deer, mule deer, high-country elk, Western black bear, pronghorn antelope, wild sheep, mountain goats, and similar animals can all be bagged by a sharp-eyed bowhunter with good stalking skills.

Once an animal is found, a stalking bowhunter must carefully plot an approach route that keeps the animal from seeing, hearing, or smelling him. Planning such a stalk can be complicated, exciting business, and the actual approach is even more exciting. Your heart beats faster and faster as you get closer and closer, and you often see an animal off and on for several hours as you pick your way into range. This technique tests a bowhunter's nerves and every ounce of his sneaking skill. He must watch his target animal carefully and also keep an eye out for other animals along the way. He must move slowly, walk noiselessly, pay close attention to wind direction, and hug natural cover to avoid being seen.

Like still-hunting, stalking is often most productive in morning and evening, provided an animal decides to stay put in one small area. Many stalks are foiled when game takes a notion to move a long distance at a fast pace. This usually happens in late

Trophy hunters prefer stalking because they can size up racks before planning an approach. Author Adams spotted this dandy blacktail buck as it fed in a small opening between heavy patches of brush. He used this natural cover to sneak within 25 yards of the animal, and then shot it behind the right shoulder as it angled away. It scored near the top of the bowhunter's record list.

morning when animals have eaten their fill and suddenly decide to go get a drink or bed down for the day. Bedded animals can be successfully stalked, but the stalker must be very lucky. All too often a bowhunter bumps into other bedded animals between him and his target animal, blocking him off from the animal he wants or scaring his target animal out of the country. Successful stalking is extremely satisfying, takes a world of patience and talent, and happens to be my favorite method of bowhunting.

DRIVING

A group of bowhunters can sometimes drive whitetail deer, black bear, wild pigs, and other shy animals in extra-heavy cover where other bowhunting methods are not too productive.

For example, dense jungles typical of the Deep South are much too thick for stand hunting or still-hunting, but a few men moving noisily through this heavy cover can sometimes push game past bowhunters located along key escape routes. Successful game drives require bowhunters to know exactly how animals move in a particular patch of woods when pressured from a particular direction. The bowhunters on stand must also have the wind in their favor or they'll seldom see anything at all.

Driving deer and other animals has advantages and disadvantages. This technique lets an organized group of bowhunters hunt from dawn till dark, an advantage for gung-ho bowmen who prefer to hunt all day long. Driving often gives bowhunters point-blank shots at animals, too. However, driven animals are always tense and often run past a stander, making aiming and releasing an arrow difficult at best. Driving is productive in cover too heavy for other bowhunting techniques, but rarely works the best in more open terrain.

BOWHUNTING WITH HOUNDS

Quite a few bowhunters shoot black bear, cougars, and other treeing game with the use of hound dogs. However, as I mentioned in Chapter 16, this hunting technique cannot be considered bowhunting—it is *dog hunting* and *bow-shooting*. Following good hounds is an exciting and worthwhile sport. However, shooting an animal that is treed or bayed by hounds is usually easy, even with a bow. I've shot black bear out of trees on several occasions, and I have no regrets. But the excitement of the chase and the tasty bear meat were what made the experience worthwhile, not the point-blank bow-shooting.

A careful bowhunter makes a point of being good at several basic hunting methods. This gives him the flexibility to match a particular method to a particular kind of game in a particular kind of terrain—which usually leads to success.

Chapter 19—THE ART OF SHOOTING AT GAME

Shooting at game is an art within itself, a complicated and demanding move that takes just a split-second to accomplish and often decides the outcome of months of careful planning. Every bowhunter should know how far he should shoot, where to aim on animals, when to let an arrow go, and how to cope with special shooting problems he may encounter. Add a little luck to these requirements and he just might score a good hit!

Practical shooting ranges are tough to discuss because different bowhunters have different limitations. One man might be the kiss of death out to 70 yards, and another might not be accurate past 30. A man might be a crack shot out to 50 yards when he's in a tree stand and knows exactly how far it is to various landmarks around his stand, but this same man on unfamiliar ground might have trouble estimating yardage and making shots past 25 yards. Every bowhunter should learn his own capabilities on the range and in the field prior to actually hunting, so he can be confident in the shots he decides to take and be able to pass up longer shots with equal confidence.

The average deer shot in the East is less than 30 yards away from a bowhunter, but Western averages tend to be longer because of more open terrain and the fact that Western bowhunters must stalk their game instead of ambushing it from tree stands. An average-to-good bowhunter can usually hit game out to 40 yards with fair regularity, but shots longer than this are usually iffy propositions at best. And no matter how good a shot you are, an alerted animal is very likely to move before your arrow arrives if the distance is over 40 yards. A fast-shooting compound bow cuts the odds of missing or poorly hitting a moving animal, but isn't a cure-all by any means.

A good rule of thumb when shooting at game is this: If you can hit a standard-sized, 9-inch paper plate almost every time at a particular distance, you are capable of vitally hitting a deer-sized animal at this same distance. If you miss a 9-inch plate very often at 40 yards (for example), then you're running a big risk of missing or crippling a deer at this same range. One of the best ways to determine your shooting limitations is bowhunting little varmints like woodchucks and ground squirrels in the off season. This kind of practice is an even more realistic gauge of your shooting ability than "punching paper" because it introduces the element of excitement a bowhunter feels when he draws on a living target.

No matter how good a shot you are, you're best off to pass up a shot if you think you can get a better one by waiting awhile or sneaking closer. A closer animal is always easier to hit than one that's farther away, giving a bowhunter a greater margin of

Taking a bead on game is the high point of any bowhunt. What happens next will depend on how well you've prepared and how well the animal cooperates.

shooting error. It's very possible for a superb bowshot to nail a broadside buck at 70 or 80 yards, but the slightest shooting error at these ranges will cause a miss or poor hit. A 20-yard shot at the same animal would let a bowhunter make a slight aiming or shooting error and still score a vital hit.

WHERE TO AIM ON AN ANIMAL

A bowhunter should always try to put his arrow in an animal's chest cavity. This portion of the body houses the lungs and heart, which instantly cease to function when skewered with a sharp broadhead. The chest cavity is also the single largest vital area on any animal, giving a bowhunter a fairly big target to aim at. The chest cavity can always be reached with a well-directed arrow unless an animal is facing directly away (see diagrams).

A solid hit in an animal's ham also produces a quick death, provided a broadhead has a sharp, smooth edge (see Chapter 14 for details on various kinds of broadhead edges). The big femoral arteries run down the insides of an animal's hind legs, and lots of other blood vessels branch off from these arteries to supply the ham tissue with oxygen. An animal hit directly in the ham generally drops within seconds from massive hemorrhaging.

Hits in spine or brain literally knock an animal off its feet, paralyzing the creature or killing it instantly because of severe shock to its central nervous system. The spine and brain are small targets and should never be aimed at unless a bowhunter has no other kind of shot. One of the first bucks I ever killed with a bow presented this shooting problem. The little deer fed out of a thicket 25 yards away, directly behind a doe. Then he rose on his hind legs to nip an overhead leaf. His chest cavity was shielded by branches and his hams were behind the doe. I pulled back, aimed quickly at his spine, and let fly. The arrow hit with a crack and literally lifted the animal off his feet. He landed upside down with all four hooves aimed at the sky, very dead indeed.

The neck is a poor place to aim on any animal because it's a small target and consists largely of nonvital tissue. An arrow

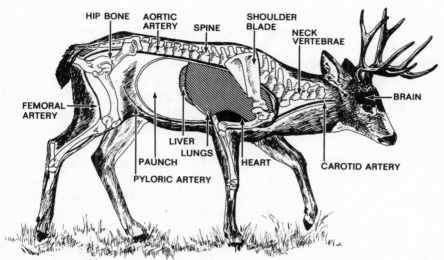

HIP BONE AORTIC ARTERY SPINE SHOULDER BLADE NECK VERTEBRAE

FEMORAL ARTERY

BRAIN

LIVER LUNGS

PAUNCH HEART

PYLORIC ARTERY CAROTID ARTERY

The anatomy of a broadside deer

that hits the spine in the neck area kills well, and so does an arrow that cuts the carotid artery. However, a deer with a cut windpipe or flesh wound in the lower neck region can go for miles before dropping—if it drops at all. Stay away from shots in the neck area.

The shoulder blade on big-game animals is thick enough to stop arrows cold from all but the heaviest bows. An animal hit in the shoulder blade will usually survive nicely, even if the broadhead imbeds permanently in the bone. A creature hit in the shoulder never drops unless the arrow penetrates all the way through to the lungs. An arrow will occasionally penetrate the edge of an animal's shoulder bone and reach vital flesh, but a bowhunter is best off aiming a couple of inches away from the shoulder blade to make sure his arrow slips around it. A solid shoulder hit is bad news.

The worst news of all is a paunch (gut) hit. Only one major artery runs through the paunch (the pyloric artery), and if a broadhead misses this an animal can go for miles before it dies. A paunch hit almost always kills an animal, but seldom right away. Beginning bowhunters sometimes get excited and aim for

the middle of a deer, and the middle of a deer is unfortunately
where the paunch happens to be. A bowman who takes a shot
at a running animal is risking a paunch hit unless he shoots extremely well on moving targets. An animal shot at long range
will sometimes take one step forward before the arrow smacks
home, which also results in a gut hit. A superb tracker can
sometimes walk down a gut-shot animal, but such an animal
leaves almost no blood and usually loses all but the most skillful
bowhunters.

The liver sits just in front of the paunch and immediately
behind the chest cavity. This vital organ filters all the blood in
an animal's body, so a hit here causes extremely fast blood loss
and very quick death. However, nobody should aim for the liver
on purpose because this organ is fairly small and sits right
against the paunch. Bowhunters sometimes hit the liver by mistake when an arrow narrowly misses the lungs, and when this
happens they get their animal.

One nifty thing about the lungs is that they're bordered on
three sides by other vital organs—the heart below, the spine and
aortic artery above, and the liver behind. The lungs are the best
to aim at because they're the biggest vital area, and let a bowhunter score even if he misses them high, low, or slightly behind.

Superficial hits in the lower legs and around the edges of
an animal's body generally cause minor muscle damage and heal
up quickly. A bowhunter should always aim at solid blocks of
flesh—there are simply not enough big blood vessels in surface
muscle to cause the massive bleeding necessary to drop game.

A bowhunter should carefully study the illustrations in this
chapter so he knows how to aim on animals standing in different
positions. Deer and other creatures are often shot broadside,
but just as often present other body angles to a bowhunter.

The place to aim on a broadside animal is 2 or 3 inches
behind the shoulder and exactly halfway between the backline
and chestline. A hit here will catch both lungs, and a near miss
will also catch both lungs. Aiming too close to the shoulder can
result in a shoulder-blade hit if the arrow goes slightly astray,
which can mean a lost animal.

The best shot of all is the quartering-away shot. An animal

The broadside shot

The angling-away shot

The angling-toward-you shot   *The chest-on, head-up shot*

that's angling away cannot see a bowhunter draw his bow under most circumstances, and also presents a bowhunter with the biggest vital area because the shoulder blade is completely out of the way. The place to aim on an animal that's quartering away is halfway between the backline and chestline in a direct line with the far shoulder. This shot will hit the back of one lung and the front of the other, and possibly nick the liver too.

An animal angling toward you presents a ticklish problem. The shoulder blade covers up most of the lungs in this situation, which means you must slip your arrow directly in front of the shoulder to hit the lungs. A perfectly placed shot along the back edge of the shoulder will also catch one lung and the edge of the liver, but risks a gut shot and inevitably plugs the exit hole with nonbleeding paunch material. A plugged exit hole often means a skimpy blood trail, doubling the trouble it takes to find a dead animal.

A chest-on animal with its head up presents a fairly large vital target, but can easily see a bowhunter move as he draws

The chest-on, head-down shot   *The rear-end shot*

his bow. If an animal stands around and lets a bowhunter aim at its chest, he should hold dead center where the neck joins the body. A hit here will catch one or both lungs, and also the liver if the arrow penetrates well. A chest-on animal with its head down is easier to draw on without being seen, but covers most or all of the chest cavity with its neck. A bowhunter can sometimes slip an arrow between the shoulder blade and neck if the animal has its head turned slightly to one side. The best shot on a deer with its head down and directly toward you is right between its ear tips—an arrow placed here should sever the spine.

Many bowhunters worry about a rear-end shot, but a deer or another big-game animal with its butt toward you should be in one heap of trouble. A deer facing directly away cannot easily see a bowhunter move, and presents both vital hams for a man to shoot at. A bowhunter should aim for the middle of the ham area presented on a horizontal line even with the middle of the animal's tail. A critter angling slightly to one side should be smacked in the center of the inside ham (see diagram). A critter

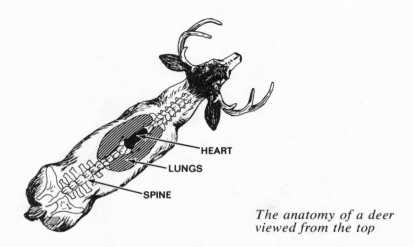

*The anatomy of a deer
viewed from the top*

facing directly away should be hit just below the anus where the two hams join.

Those skeptical of the rear-end shot should talk to my hunting pal Rod Skelton. Rod's an extremely talented hunter and a superb shot with a bow. A few years ago he told me about a buck he shot during the last hour of the last day of season. The deer was facing directly away at 55 yards, chewing on some low oak bushes. Rod realized the buck might not get any closer to his tree stand, so he pulled back, aimed carefully at the middle of the buck's tail, and let his arrow go. It sailed through the air and hit the deer exactly where Rod had aimed. The buck raced straight away, and the arrow fell out immediately. Rod said he was starting to worry when the deer suddenly folded like a dove centered with a tight pattern of No. 8 shot. The deer ran less than 50 yards before dying, and a careful autopsy showed that the arrow had penetrated less than 5 inches. However, Rod's razor-sharp broadhead had cut both femoral arteries where they joined under the tail, draining the buck of blood in less than five seconds. I've personally shot over a dozen deer in the rear end, and none went over 100 yards before keeling over.

A bowhunter in a tree stand occasionally has to shoot straight down at a deer as the animal strolls underneath him. By using a safety belt, a bowhunter can bend at the waist and make such a shot count, provided he knows where to aim. A deer's vitals sit farther back than one might think when viewing that animal from directly above. The correct place to hit such an animal is in the spine just behind both shoulders. This hit will paralyze a deer, and a near miss to either side will still hit one lung and possibly the heart, too.

WHEN TO TAKE A SHOT

A bowhunter should know exactly where to aim on an animal, and he should also know exactly when to take his shot. Attempting a shot at the wrong time can have disastrous consequences, even when an animal is standing still within point-blank range.

The act of drawing and aiming creates a lot of game-spooking movement, so a bowhunter should time this movement carefully to avoid being seen. Animals facing directly away or quartering sharply away cannot see a hunter move, but broadside and head-on animals definitely can. A bowhunter should bide his time and wait for an animal to put its head behind a stump, log, bush, or another solid object. If this isn't possible, he should wait until the animal looks directly away or at least turns its head partially away before he draws to shoot. A deer that spots a bowhunter draw won't always run away, but its muscles will tighten up like a bowstring, giving it a chance to dodge the arrow when the hunter releases his shot.

Occasionally an animal leaves no choice but to draw and hope for the best. I once shot a big eight-point whitetail buck that walked within 35 yards of my stand and then started feeding. The animal was head-on to me in a wide-open alfalfa field, and it was almost dark. I took a chance and drew my bow. The big brute threw up his head instantly, his muscles bunched to run. I aimed hastily at his chest and let go. The buck completely swapped ends like a frightened coyote before the arrow arrived, but I lucked out and hit him in the biggest part of the right ham. He ran about 90 yards and piled up.

A bowman who isn't confident in a particular shot should always wait until an animal turns and presents a better body angle. For example, if a deer is angling toward you at fairly long

Author Adams followed this big bull elk for almost two hours before taking a shot. He was within long bow range most of the time, but waited for a broadside shot over open ground. The result was a perfect hit through both lungs at 60 yards. The animal ran 120 yards and piled up like a sack of potatoes.

range, the best bet is waiting until the deer turns broadside or begins to angle away. As already mentioned, the angling-to-you shot requires pinpoint accuracy, accuracy that isn't always possible.

SPECIAL SHOOTING PROBLEMS

A bowhunter will encounter some special shooting problems as time goes by, problems he should anticipate and be ready for. It's nice to shoot from an upright, classic stance, but overhead obstacles like tree limbs sometimes force a bowhunter to crouch or kneel and/or drastically cant his bow. As discussed in Chapter 13, a bowhunter should practice a variety of awkward shooting positions to increase his versatility.

Bowhunters sometimes get close to game in heavy brush. It is darn near impossible to punch an arrow through brush and kill an animal. Even if an arrow penetrates brush without deflecting badly, the broadhead will be dull and penetration into the animal will be shallow. A bowhunter in heavy cover should always wait for a clear shot.

In some instances a hunter who knows the exact trajectory of his arrows can lob an arrow over an obstacle and score a hit. For instance, I once killed a pronghorn antelope that was standing beyond a low hill. The animal was 60 yards away, and all I could see were its horns and ear tips. I held my 60-yard sight pin where I knew the animal's chest cavity was and scored a solid hit through both lungs after the arrow arched over the hill and dropped out of sight. A bowhunter can sometimes do the same thing when animals stand beyond bushes, logs, and other solid objects. The key is knowing exactly where your arrow will be at different yardages and figuring out whether or not it will clear all obstacles between you and your target.

A bowfisherman has a special aiming problem to contend with—the image refraction caused by water. Fish which are more than 6 or 8 inches below the surface are actually lower than they appear to be, requiring a bowman to aim slightly below the image he sees to score a hit. How much lower he should aim depends on the angle of the shot and how deep a fish is submerged. Lots of practice on deep-water fish is the only way to get good at this type of shooting. Fortunately, fish like carp, gar, and sharks are usually shot as they spawn in very shallow water or roll near the surface.

Shooting at game is a delicate art, an art that often determines the outcome of a bowhunt. A bowhunter should be prepared for a variety of shooting situations to prevent major mishaps in the field.

Chapter 20—AFTER THE SHOT

Knowing when and where to shoot at game is important, and so is knowing what to do after a shot is taken. Good bowhunters seldom if ever lose hard-hit animals because they know how to proceed after they score a hit.

HOW TO TELL WHERE YOUR ARROW HITS

One key to getting game is knowing exactly where your arrow goes after you release it. Many bowhunters prefer arrows with bright, easily seen fletching so they can track these arrows as they fly and see where they hit. Some hunters like white fletching, but a better choice for most situations is a bright, medium-hued fletching like fluorescent orange. Such a fletching is extremely easy to see as it flies through the air, yet doesn't catch an animal's eye when it's carried in a quiver with other arrows. White fletching is the easiest to see just after dawn and just before dark, but can flash a warning to close-range animals. A tree-stand hunter can get away with using white feathers or plastic vanes, but a bowhunter on the ground should use other colors, especially when hunting alert animals like whitetail deer.

If an arrow hits an animal, it is often possible to see that arrow protruding from the animal as it turns and runs away. A bowhunter should try to spot his arrow in an animal whenever he doesn't actually see it hit, so that he'll know exactly what kind of hit he got and be better able to follow up his shot correctly.

If a bowhunter misses his shot, the jig may be up—but not necessarily. Sometimes animals mill around for several seconds after an arrow clatters nearby, confused about what made the noise and where the noise came from. And occasionally an animal will act especially unsophisticated. An excitable acquaintance of mine once missed a young muley buck *twelve times* before the little stinker decided to trot away. I've never been lucky enough to find a deer that dumb, but other hunters assure me they do exist. In any case, a bowhunter who sees his arrow miss the mark should quickly nock another and get ready to shoot a second time. An animal is especially likely to stand around if an arrow sails over its back and hits beyond. An arrow that kicks up gravel or dirt at an animal's feet is more likely to startle the critter and send it packing.

If a bowhunter loses sight of his arrow because of the terrain, the vegetation, or the time of day, he can still tell a lot about where it hit by listening carefully. Arrows that clatter shale or rattle through the bushes make distinctive sounds a bowhunter learns to recognize. Arrows also make different sounds when they smack different parts of an animal's body. An arrow that slices through an animal's ribcage makes a noise like that made when you plunk your fingers against a ripe watermelon. A hit in the ham makes a similar but slightly more solid sound. A hit in a bony area like the head, spine, or shoulder often cracks sharply like a hardball thrown against a cement wall. An arrow that hits the point of the chest also cracks solidly, but with a slightly lower pitch. A hit in the gut area usually makes a sickening liquid splat like a water balloon exploding on the side of a house. When an arrow barely creases an animal, it seldom makes an audible sound at all unless it nicks a bone near the surface.

Another telltale clue to where you hit is how an animal reacts after a shot. An animal that is missed completely either stands stock still to try to locate the source of the disturbance, mills around in confusion, or runs away with an even, medium-to-quick pace. A hit in the lungs, heart, or liver usually produces a frantic death run of 50 to 200 yards with the animal holding its body lower to the ground than normal and really pouring on the coal. An animal hit in lungs, heart, or liver often runs blindly, too, plowing into bushes, trees, and other obstacles a scared, healthy creature skirts around. A ham-shot animal often drops its hindquarters slightly and also drops its head, either running

An animal that races off after you shoot may be dead on its feet.
For example, a deer hit through heart or lungs almost always covers
50 yards or more before keeling over.

or walking off in this unnatural body position. A ham-shot creature seldom runs away full-tilt like a chest-shot animal. An animal shot in the shoulder blade usually flinches violently and
takes off like a scalded cat, but holds its body higher and bends
its knees less than a chest-shot animal. A hit in the paunch
almost always causes an animal to hump up in the middle and
either run off at an uneven pace or walk away with a lowered
head. Solid spine and brain shots will flatten any animal instantly
if the hunting bow used is heavy enough to penetrate bone.
Minor flesh wounds in the edges of the neck, back, brisket, and
hams usually put an animal in high gear, but the reaction to
these hits varies considerably from situation to situation.

    These are the most typical reactions to various kinds of

hits, but cannot be regarded as gospel. For example, I once shot a deer through both lungs at 35 yards, and it went on feeding as if nothing at all had happened! I quickly nocked another arrow and was aiming a second time when the animal suddenly collapsed as if beaned with a 12-pound sledge. Animal reactions are reliable most of the time, but not always.

If a bowhunter can take a second shot within good range, he should do it, even if he thinks his animal is dead on its feet. A few years ago I sneaked up on a wild pig in a knee-deep barley field and shot the critter at less than 10 yards. The shot felt good and I was totally convinced the arrow had hit him in the lungs. However, I shot again when the animal paused 40 yards away. My second arrow smacked the hog in the left ham, and he dropped after running another 30 yards. When I got to the 175-pound porker, I was amazed to discover that my first arrow had barely nicked the top of his back. I had simply held too high the first time. I thanked my lucky stars I'd followed up with another try.

After you do your shooting, stay exactly where you shot from and watch the animal move off, noting the exact escape route it takes. Listen carefully to track it even farther by sound. The more exactly you can trace an animal's movements, the easier it will be to find if it is mortally hit and leaves little or no sign to follow.

TRACKING A HIT ANIMAL

There's been a lot of mumbo-jumbo written about how long to wait before following up a hard-hit animal. As explained in Chapter 14, a really sharp arrowhead does its work extremely fast, generally dropping a chest-shot animal in ten seconds or less. A hit in the ham also kills fast, often within a minute or two. The key to quick, humane kills is a sharp, well-honed broadhead that cuts a fairly large hole—such a broadhead opens a wound that keeps on bleeding till an animal drops.

No matter what kind of hit a bowhunter makes, he should wait a minimum of thirty minutes before following up a shot. If he's reasonably sure his animal is hit through the lungs or heart, the last 29½ minutes of this wait will simply be insurance in case his arrow narrowly missed these vital organs and passed through a less vital zone like the band of muscle between the lungs and spine. Such a hit will also kill, but not as quickly as a direct hit in organs like lungs, heart, and liver. A bowhunter who races after an animal hit in a "slow-kill" zone like the edge of the chest cavity will only succeed in pushing that animal a long ways before it drops, which means the blood trail will be skimpy and hard to follow. Not long after I first started bow-hunting I made a dandy sneak on a little muley buck, took a 30-yard broadside shot, and saw the arrow pass clear through the buck's chest, very low and half a foot behind the heart. The buck ran off, and I mistakenly went after him immediately, following his tracks in the soft dirt on the mountainside. There was

A sharp broadhead through the chest cavity kills the biggest animals with lightning-fast efficiency. The author hit this record-sized Canada moose squarely through the heart as it angled away at 50 yards. The 1,200-pound beast took four steps and collapsed.

very little blood. About 100 yards farther on, I finally spotted
the animal. He was lying down with his nose in the dirt, apparently dying. I decided to walk up and finish him off—which was
my second mistake. I was still 40 yards away when the deer
suddenly leaped up and charged down the hill at full tilt, disappearing in a sea of brush thick enough to choke a chipmunk.
I spent the rest of the morning searching for that little deer, and
finally found him dead, 50 yards inside the thicket. The arrow
had hit the edge of the chest cavity about 5 inches behind the
heart and had just missed the pyloric artery. The buck had died
of suffocation within five minutes, and if I'd been smart enough
to wait 30 minutes before following, he would have expired in
the open and less than 200 yards from where he was hit.

Some bowhunters pound their fists and strongly argue that
a deer hit in the rear end must be followed at once to keep the
wound open and increase bleeding. All my experience says no
to this particular theory, for a couple of reasons. First, a really
sharp broadhead with a smooth edge cuts a wound that doesn't
stop bleeding just because an animal stops moving. A deer shot
in the ham with a sharp broadhead usually lies down and dies
within minutes after it's hit unless it is dogged by a persistent
bowhunter. True, a running deer whips an arrow around in its
ham, keeping the wound open and making that deer's heart
pump blood a little faster. However, an animal that is pushed
by a bowhunter covers at least five to ten times as much ground
as an animal that is left alone, which means it must bleed five
to ten times as much to leave a blood trail that's comparable to
the trail left by a deer that is not pushed. And no matter how
hot the pursuit, a deer won't bleed five to ten times more than
it will when left alone.

Furthermore, the more an arrow flops around in a wound
as an animal runs through the woods, the more tissue damage
is caused in that wound and the quicker blood clotting occurs
(see Chapter 14 for details on why blood clots). If a bowhunter
hits a deer in the ham with a *dull* broadhead, he might be best
off following that animal at once—a dull broadhead won't produce a constant blood flow, and following immediately might
keep the wound open and help a hunter out. However, a bow-

hunter should *never* hunt with dull arrows, so he should never follow animals at once.

I normally leave a chest-shot animal 30 minutes, a ham-shot animal an hour, and a gut-shot animal three hours. An animal hit in the paunch will either die very quickly from a cut pyloric artery, or will eventually lie down and stiffen up. A three-hour wait lets a gut-shot animal lie down, calm down, and stiffen enough to give a bowman a decent chance of trailing it down and sneaking within range for a finishing shot.

When a bowhunter hits an animal through the chest, he normally sits down in the spot he shot from and waits anxiously for 30 minutes or so. If evidence indicates that his wait should be longer, he often heads back to camp for lunch or goes to find his hunting buddies. If you take a shot from the ground and decide to leave the scene for a while, be sure to carefully mark the spot you shot from with toilet paper, fluorescent tape, or something else that's simple to find. It is sometimes very easy to lose the spot you shot from, especially in heavy woods. And if you lose that spot, you have absolutely no idea where to start looking for your animal. It's also a good idea to mark the place you shot from even if you *don't* go anywhere. This lets you easily retrace your steps to where you made the shot if trailing becomes difficult and you decide to start over again.

A tree-stand hunter has no trouble relocating the place he shot from, but he sometimes loses track of where his animal was after he climbs down to follow that animal. Terrain looks entirely different when viewed from the air, and a bowhunter who climbs out of his tree may become confused about where his animal was when he took his shot. Many tree-standers carry a special bright-colored arrow with them at all times to shoot into the ground where an animal was last seen. When they climb out of their tree, finding this bright arrow is generally easy even if the countryside looks different than it did before.

Once a bowhunter waits the appropriate length of time after he thinks he has scored a hit, he should go directly to the place where his animal was when he shot and mark that spot clearly with a shred of toilet paper, a white handkerchief, or another noticeable object. Then he should slowly cast about for signs of a hit. Occasionally he'll find his unbloodied arrow sticking in the ground, a tree, or a stump, indicating that he actually missed his shot. An arrow that passes all the way through an animal is usually bloody or at least sticky from other body fluids.

With luck, a hit animal will leave a good blood trail away from the hit site, a trail that is easy to follow all the way to the downed animal. However, fatally hit animals sometimes leave *no blood at all,* and often leave fairly skimpy blood trails. This is especially true if they are hit high through the chest—in such a case they often bleed internally and leave little or no blood on the ground. The old bowhunting myth that hard-hit deer always leave buckets of blood is just that—a myth.

Blood from a wound often drips to the ground, but just as often it ends up on objects above the ground. A bowhunter should carefully examine the ground for blood, but he should also pay close attention to bushes, high grass, logs, stumps, and tree trunks along an animal's escape route. Blood squirting from a severed artery or oozing from a vein is sometimes sprayed or smeared on objects several feet above the ground, and this possibility should not be overlooked when a blood trail is hard to follow.

If a bowhunter finds no blood in the area where he hit his animal, he should look for other clues to help him follow the trail and indicate exactly where he hit. A sharp broadhead always cuts a little hair as it enters and exits an animal's body, and this hair falls to the ground and/or ends up on tree trunks and bushes as an animal races away. A bowhunter can often establish the fact that he did hit an animal by finding a little hair near the hit site, and can sometimes actually follow an animal a little distance by finding additional bits of hair. He may also be able to tell where he hit an animal by the hair he finds, provided he's thoroughly familiar with the hair distribution on that animal. For example, the belly hair on a deer is long and white, and the hair on a deer's sides is short and gray. Long white hair on the ground can mean a low gut hit, and short gray hair can mean a solid hit in the ham or chest. Likewise, hair sticking to a bloody arrow found near the hit site can be convincing evidence of where an animal is hit, especially if a bowhunter has other evidence to go on—like the sound of the arrow striking and the way the animal ran off.

If blood and hair cannot be found, a bowhunter must try to follow his animal's tracks to the end of the trail. This is usually possible in soft soil or snow if a hunter has sharp eyes and a little tracking know-how. In snow, tracks show up extremely well and a bowhunter is often able to see every individual track an animal makes as it runs away. In dirt, an occasional scuff mark or splayed, wide-toed track may be all a bowhunter has to follow. Deer and other split-hoofed animals leave wide tracks whenever they run because their toes spread as they hit with their feet. Such tracks are easy to differentiate from other tracks in an area, helping a bowhunter do his job.

In an area literally covered with the tracks of deer or other kinds of game, a bowhunter may have some difficulty following one particular set of tracks even if his animal is running. If so, he'll have to pay close attention to other little tracking signs. For example, the fresh tracks of a running deer will be farther apart than "normal" tracks because the animal is taking longer strides, and the scuffed-up dirt in these tracks will be a slightly darker color than the surrounding soil and the soil in older tracks. Fresh tracks are darker because surface soil is drier than kicked-up soil, and therefore a little lighter in coloration. Even a fresh running track made in hot dust will be a little darker than the rest of the dust because dust holds a little moisture below the surface. I once shot a nine-point whitetail buck high through both lungs as he lay in his bed, watched him leap up and run off, and saw him drop almost 200 yards away. I was curious to see what kind of trail he had left, so I inspected his escape route carefully. I could not find one drop of blood between me and that deer, but there were enough fresh, dark running tracks to lead me to him.

This incident was fairly unusual. A bowhunter sometimes finds no blood at first as he follows up a good hit, but he'll usually begin finding a little blood here and there after he's gone some distance. An animal hit through the chest can bleed internally for quite a while, but it generally starts pumping blood outside after its chest fills up partway.

A bowhunter can usually track down a fatally hit animal in soft dirt or snow, even if there's little or no blood to be found.

On the other hand, blood may be plentiful at the beginning of a trail and slowly peter out completely. A good blood trail that gets skimpier and eventually disappears is usually the sign of a superficial muscle wound, a wound that will heal up quickly. Even the best bowhunters occasionally nick animals around the edges, but these animals survive nicely when hit with a smoothly sharpened broadhead (see Chapter 14 for details).

The type and color of blood an animal leaves often indicates where it has been hit. Bubbly pink blood indicates a solid lung hit, and means your animal is somewhere nearby. Bright-red blood indicates an artery hit, and also means your animal is dead if blood is dropping in fair quantities. Arteries are under extremely high pressure, which means that artery blood is usually squirted on the ground and surrounding objects rather than dripped. In contrast, a vein hit leaves dark-red blood, the kind of blood which is found on a trail that eventually peters out. Vein blood is not under high pressure like artery blood, which means it seeps to the surface and drips to the ground rather than spurting from a wound. The veins in an animal's body are much closer to the surface than the arteries are, so a superficial edge hit cuts veins, not arteries. A solid artery hit keeps bleeding profusely till an animal drops because of blood pressure—a wound in small surface veins usually bleeds quickly for a little while and then clots up. A hit in a large vein like the jugular in the neck will kill an animal fast, dropping a steady flow of dark blood. A direct heart hit also leaves fairly dark blood, and this blood is usually dropped in tremendous quantities. A gut hit sometimes leaves a little dark vein blood, too, as well as body fluids of other colors. The one exception to this is a pyloric-artery hit, which bleeds bright-red.

No matter where a bowhunter thinks he has hit an animal, and no matter how dismal the prospect looks, he should try to follow the trail with dogged determination. If his broadheads are sharp, his odds of finding a well-hit animal are close to 100 percent if he moves along slowly, determined not to overlook one shred of sign. An animal that runs off fast can lose a lot of blood without leaving much in any one spot, and an animal that runs off fast can die within ten seconds and still cover 100 to 200 yards before keeling over. A bowhunter should not expect

Following a skimpy blood trail is made easier if you leap-frog two white handkerchiefs. This way, you can look ahead for new sign without losing the last sign you found.

a foot-wide blood trail to follow or a deep, clear set of tracks
leading all the way to his prize. He may have to analyze bits
and pieces of sign and move at a painstakingly slow pace to get
his animal, but if he's patient enough he will almost always
succeed. And if he exerts superhuman effort and still doesn't
find an animal, chances are overwhelmingly good that the creature is not seriously hurt and will survive.

When following a trail, a bowhunter should always stay to
one side of the trail to avoid stomping on and destroying sign.
He should always mark the last sign he has found on a tough-
to-follow trail with toilet paper, a handkerchief, or some other
easily seen object. In heavy woods it is incredibly easy to entirely lose track of where a trail is as you cast about for more
sign—this is the reason for carefully marking the last sign you
find. The easiest way to follow a skimpy trail is leapfrogging
two markers—leaving one beside the last blood, track, or hair
you've found, and taking another marker with you to place by
any sign you find farther ahead. By leap-frogging two handkerchiefs or similar markers, you can systematically ferret out a
trail without ever losing it.

Wounded animals often follow established game trails as
they run away, but a bowhunter should never try to second-
guess where a hurt animal will go. Mortally hit deer sometimes
run uphill until they drop, others head cross-country through
heavy cover, and others go one particular direction for a while
and then head directly back in the direction they came from. A
bowhunter who relies too heavily on where he thinks an animal
will go instead of the sign at hand will usually bollix himself up
and lose a poor trail repeatedly.

If worse comes to worst and you can't find *any* sign to help
you find your animal, you should very carefully criss-cross the
general area where you think that animal went, keeping your
eyes open for sign and the animal itself. This is where some
prior precaution can pay off. If you carefully watched your animal race away after the hit and tried to track it even farther by
sound, you can pinpoint the area where it is most likely to be.
I've found several animals stone dead within a few yards of
where I heard them moving last—animals that spilled no blood

A bowhunter with sharp broadheads can have total confidence when he scores a solid hit. If his trailing skills are up to snuff he should find his animal before very long.

and ran across hard, rocky ground without leaving any tracks. Finding such animals is seldom easy, but persistence pays off.

Special trailing problems created by weather or time of day can complicate a bowhunter's life considerably. A sudden rainstorm or snowstorm can easily wash away or cover up all sign an animal has left behind, including blood, hair, and tracks. If precipitation threatens to destroy a wounded animal's trail, you have no choice but to follow that animal *immediately* and hope it dies quickly. An animal hit just before dark is another matter, however. If you score a good hit late in the evening, you should follow the normal trailing steps outlined in this chapter, including a wait of thirty minutes or more before following. Then you can either follow your animal by lantern light, or wait for the crack of dawn.

A lantern makes trailing surprisingly easy at night—blood shows up well and so does most other sign. A flashlight doesn't work nearly as well because it has a narrow beam, but can be used in a pinch with fair results. Deer-sized animals will keep all night without spoiling in all but the warmest weather, but big, insulated animals like elk, black bear, and wild pigs can sour unless they're found and field-dressed within two or three hours after they die. I've trailed a fair number of animals with flashlights and lanterns, but prefer to wait till morning if the weather is cool and the animal is fairly small.

After a bowhunter lets an arrow go, he should watch and listen for telltale clues about where that arrow hits and where his animal goes. Unless he's absolutely certain he has missed his shot, he should sit tight for at least thirty minutes, and then go directly to the hit site after carefully marking the spot he shot from. With luck, he'll have a good blood trail to follow to his animal. If the trail is skimpy, he should patiently search for loose hair, tracks, little drops of blood, and other trailing clues, marking any new sign he finds with a handkerchief or something similar. If there's no sign at all to follow and a bowman knows he's made a good hit, he should go to the last place he saw or heard his animal and carefully criss-cross the area until he finds his prize. A bowhunter can always count on a sharp broadhead that hits a vital spot—all he has to do after such a hit is search confidently and patiently until he locates his animal.

Chapter 21—CARE OF ARROW-SHOT GAME

Proper care of arrow-shot game is an extremely important part of bowhunting, every bit as important as shooting well and knowing how to hunt. Taking care of an animal or bird immediately after the kill results in tasty, succulent meat, which adds one more pleasing dimension to the whole bowhunting experience. A man who shoots game himself and correctly handles the meat from field to freezer is practicing an ancient hunting heritage, a sacred outdoor art which is rapidly vanishing in our day and age of cellophane-wrapped beefsteak and professional butchers.

FIELD-DRESSING GAME

The tools needed to care for game between the woods and the meat locker are simple indeed. Every bowhunter should carry a small hunting knife with him at all times to make gutting, skinning, and other operations easy. A rank beginner usually makes the mistake of toting a huge toad-sticker on his belt—a long, heavy knife that slaps his hip obnoxiously and serves no practical purpose. A medium-to-small knife with a blade between 2 and 4 inches long will do everything a hunter needs to do on the biggest animals, and can be tucked away in a small belt sheath or a pants pocket. The only other tool a bowhunter really needs is a small meat saw to sever bones when quartering animals and detaching antlers and horns from an animal's head. A few hunters use a hatchet instead of a saw, but it requires considerable skill to do a safe, clean job of cutting bone with a hatchet.

Every kind of bird and animal should be field-dressed immediately after the kill. The field-dressing process removes a creature's paunch (stomach) and intestine. Field-dressing a big-game animal promptly is *especially* important because it lets the animal's body cavity cool out rapidly to prevent meat from spoiling, and also keeps the animal's innards from quickly bloating and secreting unpleasant belly juices into surrounding meat. Every type of animal and bird is shaped differently, so field-dressing procedures vary from species to species. The entire field-dressing process is difficult to adequately illustrate with photos or drawings, and a beginner will learn it best by watching an experienced hunter field-dress an animal or bird.

Although exact field-dressing moves should be learned first-hand for best results, the basic procedure for field-dressing deer and other big animals is fairly simple to explain. First, you roll an animal on its back with its belly to the sky, propping up the head and shoulders slightly on a hill, rock, or bush so the animal's innards roll away from the carcass when they're pulled out. Next, cut a straight slit down the middle of the animal's belly from the point of the brisket (back of the ribcage) all the way to the anus, *being careful to cut only the hide and not the thin layer of muscle between the hide and the paunch*. This belly slit should go alongside a male animal's genitals, and straight through a female's genitals. Once this slit is made in the hide, cut a 2-inch slit through the muscle layer between the hide and the paunch. This slit is usually made just forward of the animal's genitals. Next, slip your first two fingers between the paunch and this muscle layer, spreading these fingers like a slingshot. A couple of fingers between the belly muscle and the belly itself hold the belly away from the muscle you are cutting, keeping your knife from pricking the paunch and releasing stomach fluids onto the surrounding meat. Insert your knife tip between these two fingers and slit the belly muscle from genitals to brisket, moving your fingers along with the knife. As this muscle casing is split, the paunch will roll partway out of the animal. The next step is to reach up into the body cavity ahead of the paunch and feel around until you find the esophagus (the tube that connects the throat with the paunch). Cut this tube off, and the paunch and intestine will roll out of the animal. The end of the intestine should be cut off where it enters the inside of the anus, or the

The exact techniques for field-dressing deer vary considerably, but the basic procedure is the same. First, slit the belly hide from genitals to brisket (left). Next, carefully slice the muscle layer that encases the paunch, being extra-careful to keep your knife-tip away from the paunch with two fingers (right). After that, it's a simple matter to disengage the paunch at both ends and roll it free.

whole anus can be reamed out like the core of an apple with your knife. There are many variations to the field-dressing process, but as long as you open an animal's belly and disengage the paunch at the esophagus and anus without rupturing the paunch and flooding the body cavity with stomach acids and other fluids, you'll be okay.

You *won't* be okay if you leave your deer ungutted, though. Several seasons ago I was lounging around in the living room when a loud banging started on my door. When I opened it I was greeted with the grinning mug of my next-door neighbor, who had just returned from his first out-of-state big-game hunt.

"Come on out and see what I've got!" he urged excitedly. I trotted out the door, and a minute later I poked my head into his garage.

Holy Toledo! A nice four-point muley buck was strapped across the hood of his jeep station wagon—guts, feathers, and all! The animal was bloated up like a poisoned pup, and the faint smell of rotten gut flooded the room. My buddy was a total greenhorn at this hunting business, and I broke the news as tactfully as I could. His deer was completely spoiled, the result of a twenty-four-hour drive across three states with the ungutted critter dangled across the hot hood of his rig. All he salvaged from the mess was a nice set of antlers.

Heat is the number one enemy of wild meat, and should be avoided at all costs from the time an animal is killed to the time it is cut up and frozen. Heat quickly activates bacteria in meat, which in turn quickly breaks down the proteins in that meat and causes spoilage. My next-door neighbor committed a double blunder when he carted his deer home. First, he didn't field-dress the animal, which prevented the carcass from cooling

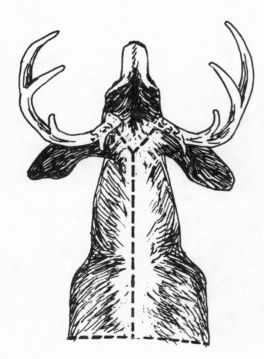

An animal with horns or antlers should be carefully caped by making an incision in the hide completely around the animal behind the shoulders and down the backs of both front legs. A second incision should then be made up the center of the spine to a point even with the backs of the ears, and two incisions should be cut from this point to each horn base in slingshot fashion. The hide should be carefully peeled from the shoulders and neck, and the head cut off where the neck joins the skull.

quickly. And second, he draped it over his car's hood, by far the hottest place on any vehicle.

Big, insulated animals like elk, moose, and bear are usually split all the way up under the chin after field dressing so they can cool out more easily. To do this, simply lengthen the belly incision to the throat by sawing through the middle of the chest. Once the chest is opened up, the lungs and heart can be removed with a knife, and the ribs can be propped apart with a short stick to accelerate cooling. The animal's windpipe should also be cut out to let the neck meat chill faster. *Warning: If you want a taxidermist to mount your animal's head, do not split the animal from brisket to throat.* This will ruin the cape completely. If the weather is warm and you're afraid your animal might spoil, first remove the animal's cape and head properly (see illustration on previous page), and then split the chest open. If you want to save the hide for a rug, go ahead and split the chest—this is one of the incisions you'll make in the hide anyway.

A big animal in steep, remote country can be dragged over cliffs and similar obstacles with a rope tied to a horse.

TRANSPORTING THE CARCASS

After an animal is field-dressed, it should be taken to your hunting camp or all the way home as soon as possible. No matter how the carcass is transported, care should be exercised to keep it cool and as clean as possible. Dirt, leaves, animal hair, and other debris won't ruin meat, but they will require cleaning up before meat can be cut and wrapped. In excessively dusty or grimy conditions, it's a good idea to wrap a carcass in a commercial meat bag or tarp before lugging it out of the woods. Some bowhunters simply sew the belly incision back up with cord or a green strip of hide before transporting an animal to keep debris from settling inside the body cavity.

It's always nice when you can drive to your deer after you shoot it, but this is often impossible because of the terrain where your animal drops. A bowhunter who happens to be with a well-equipped outfitter can get deer, elk, moose, caribou, and other large animals out to a vehicle with the help of horses or mules, either by dragging game with a rope or hauling it on a pack animal's back. Quite often a horse or mule is the only feasible way to cart out really big animals that are shot miles from the nearest road.

However, the vast majority of deer and other big-game animals are lugged out of the woods by bowhunters themselves. Different methods of transporting animals work best in different situations. A lone bowhunter with a fairly small deer can usually drag the critter quite a distance, lash it to a backpack frame and haul it out, or simply throw it across his back and head for his rig. It is unwise to carry any big-game animal on your back if other hunters are poking around—one might see antlers and hair floating above the bushes and poke an arrow *at you* as you plod along with your trophy over your shoulders. Adorning your deer with fluorescent tape or another highly visible object is a darn good idea whenever you decide to carry an animal. This precaution can prevent unfortunate scrapes with other hunters. The likelihood of getting shot by another bowman is really quite slim, but there's no point in taking unnecessary risks.

If a bowhunter is stout enough, carrying an animal on his back is much easier and much faster than dragging the carcass across the ground. Big deer can be cut in half with knife and saw, then carried out one piece at a time. The proper place to cut an animal in two is between the fifth and sixth ribs (counting from the back rib). A cut here distributes weight evenly between the halves. Really large animals like elk, moose, and caribou must be quartered before they're backpacked, a step that involves halving an animal as just described and then cutting each of these halves in two lengthwise by splitting the backbone with a meat saw. A bowhunter can always get his meat out if he has the know-how to split an animal in halves or quarters and the gumption to grunt it to the nearest road.

The most worthless method of carrying a deer ever devised is pole carrying, which theoretically allows two bowhunters to dangle a deer by the legs from the middle of a long, stout pole and then carry the animal out by shouldering the pole on each end and heading for the nearest road. Whoever thought up this carrying method deserves a severe beating, a beating he would have received already if he had ever tried out his brainchild. I tried this method once and quickly discovered that the confounded critter swung like a pendulum in a grandfather clock, causing the pole to leap about and dig into my shoulder. When my hunting partner and I finally got to the car we were both worn to a frazzle.

HANGING

Once you get your animal back to camp or to your home, hang it by the head (by looping a rope around its horns or throat) or by the hind legs (by using a two-pronged meat-hanging gambrel which slips into slits cut between an animal's hamstrings and its legs). Whether you hang your animal by the head or the rear legs is up to you—hunters do it both ways with good success. An animal hung by the hind legs cools a little faster because warm air in the chest cavity can rise out of it quickly, but this is a minor consideration. However, if you intend to save the cape and head for mounting, the head-down hanging method lets you cut the head off without ending up with carcass on top of you! If your animal is in halves or quarters, hang these up separately with ropes.

An antlered animal like this big muley buck can be hung by the base of its rack to make skinning quick and easy.

SKINNING

The next step is usually skinning. Jerking the hide off an animal with the help of a sharp hunting knife lets the carcass cool even further (if the carcass is still warm) and prepares it to be butchered for the freezer. It also lets you care for the hide properly if you want to have it tanned or want the trophy head mounted by a taxidermist. In really cold weather, the hide can be left on awhile—cold weather will cool the carcass anyway and preserve the hide for several days.

Skinning is simply a matter of parting the carcass from its hide, stripping the skin off as you'd peel a potato. On young animals, a hide can often be jerked off by hand with a minimum of knife work—simple downward pressure on the hide will strip it off the hips, flanks, and shoulders. Hide clings most tenaciously around an animal's neck, and this area almost always requires some blade work.

Exactly how you should skin your animal depends on what you intend to do with the hide. If you plan to discard the skin

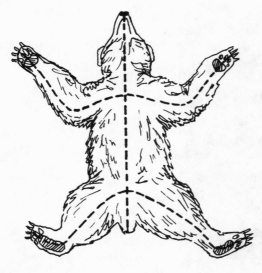

To save the whole hide on a bear or similar animal, make these incisions and carefully remove the skin with the help of a sharp knife.

entirely, any old method of peeling it off will do. However, if you want to save the whole hide for tanning or want to save the cape to mount your animal's head, you should make special incisions in the hide when skinning it to make your taxidermist's life easier (see illustrations). You should also take care not to make too many nicks in the hide with your knife—each of these will enlarge during the tanning process and require a sewing job later on. If you want a head mounted on a rug (like a bear rug) or desire a conventional head-and-shoulder wall mount, don't attempt to skin out the head itself. This complex job is best left to a professional hunting guide or your taxidermist. Simply skin the animal up to the back of the head and cut the head off at the spinal joint that connects with the skull, leaving the whole head attached to the hide.

All exposed flesh on a hide and/or trophy head should be heavily salted, and then the hide should be rolled up tightly with the hair out, double-bagged in plastic garbage bags to prevent freezer burn, and frozen solid. A hide that is left a day or more in fairly warm weather begins to spoil as bacterial action takes place, causing the hair to slip (fall out) and the skin to develop an unpleasant odor. Hides must be frozen quickly to prevent

damage caused by heat. In remote hunting camps without re-
frigeration, skillful guides sometimes skin out an animal's head
as well as the rest of the carcass, salt the hide liberally, stretch
it tightly, and let it dry in the open air. However, as mentioned
before, an average bowhunter should simply freeze the hide and
unskinned head, letting a professional taxidermist worry about
the tricky stuff.

If you decide you only want to keep your animal's horns,
you should skin the carcass, cut off the head where the neck
joins the skull, and then cut off the top of the animal's skull with
a sharp meat saw or ordinary carpenter's saw. This task can be
completed with one straight saw cut that begins at the bridge of
an animal's nose and goes straight through the middle of both
eye sockets to the back of the skull (see illustration). Once this
cut is made, the skull cap should be cleaned of all excess meat
and other tissue, and should then be salted heavily and set in
the open air to dry. Whether or not the hide is left on the skull
cap is up to you—it can be removed with a knife and replaced

*To disconnect antlers or
horns from an animal's
head, make one straight
saw cut from bridge of
nose through both eye
sockets.*

later with leather or velvet if you decide to mount the horns on a plaque, or it can be carefully tucked under the edges of the saw cut and held in place with rubber bands till it dries, resulting in a pleasing, natural skull cover that is also suitable for mounting.

PROTECTING THE MEAT

Once an animal or its parts are skinned, the meat should be loosely covered with lightweight game bags to protect it from grime, blowflies, and carnivorous insects like bees. Flies appear around a carcass by the jillions in fairly warm weather, determined to deposit blows (eggs) on the meat. Fly blows quickly hatch into maggots, which can turn a carcass into a smelly mess. Bees of various sorts are also abundant in some parts of the country, and can devour a lot of meat when left to their own devices. Bagging meat protects it from all these things, ensuring that it reaches the table in tip-top shape. In a pinch, a liberal sprinkling of pepper on a carcass discourages flies and other insects, keeping the meat in good shape till more satisfactory protection can be found.

A skinned animal carcass can be safely hung for a week in warm weather and two weeks or more in cool weather if a bow-hunter follows certain rules. If he's at home, he'll probably take his animal to a professional butcher or cut it up himself within a week, but it's sometimes necessary to keep animals quite a while in backwoods hunting camps. The key words when talking about preserving meat in natural conditions are "cool" and "dry." Flesh-destroying bacteria work best in warm, damp conditions, so an animal carcass must be hung in the shade at all times and should be loosely wrapped so it can glaze over (air-dry) on the outside while it hangs. In really warm weather, a carcass should be hung up at night to cool and dry, and should be carefully wrapped with a heavy sleeping bag or something similar in the daytime to hold in the coolness the carcass has acquired during the night. Covering and uncovering a carcass like this is a nuisance, but it saves meat. I once kept a blacktail buck this way for a whole week when the temperatures were averaging over 90 degrees in the daytime, and the meat turned

A deer can be left hanging in camp for several days if the weather is cold and the carcass is left unskinned to protect it from grime.

out sweet and good. I was bowhunting over 10 miles from the nearest road, and was lucky enough to fill my first deer tag the second day of my ten-day hunt. When I shot my second buck a week later, I packed the animals out on my back one at a time.

Some hunters insist that wild meat must be cured (hung in the open air for a week or more) before it's cut up and packaged. This curing process supposedly improves the flavor and tenderness of wild meat. Other hunters ignore the curing procedure entirely and process their meat at once, claiming that curing is a total waste of time. I've handled meat both ways, and must admit I couldn't tell any difference between the tenderness and flavor of meat packaged at once and meat cured for a week or ten days.

When transporting an animal carcass from your hunting camp or your home to a cold-storage plant or meat locker, you should follow the same meat-handling rules discussed previously. If you keep your meat clean, cool, and dry, it will make top eating.

Properly handling wild meat, hides, and trophy heads takes some time, but the rewards are ample. A little know-how and care result in outstanding meat on the table plus an attractive trophy on the wall.

Chapter 22—SELECTIVE BOWHUNTING— The Ultimate Challenge

Taking any animal or bird with a bow is quite a feat, a feat that seems insurmountable to beginners. I remember when I started deer hunting with a bow, and I remember the first buck I ever shot. I put in almost two weeks of hard hunting before I got that little deer, missed several easy shots in the process, and must admit I was amazed as I finally watched my arrow hit where it was supposed to. Nobody is born full-grown, and a beginner cannot expect to be anything but a beginner. The fine-honed skills and rock-solid confidence required to actually pass up game in hopes that something better will come along do not come overnight—they come after years and years of making blunders and gradually learning to do things right.

However, most dedicated bowhunters eventually get exceedingly good at their sport, so good that they begin hunting selectively. There are several reasons why a top-notch bowhunter goes the selective route, and these are worth considering carefully so you can decide whether or not this route is one you want to take.

The wrong reason for selective bowhunting is ego boost. Anybody who shoots "trophy heads" so he can strut and brag is a detriment to our sport, a screwball with a real problem. Bowhunting is definitely a prideful thing, and a bowhunter who shoots a fine big buck has a right to be happy and a right to share his success with others. One of the most enjoyable parts of bowhunting is swapping hunting tales and looking at other bowhunters' game. However, a few bowhunters push aside good sportsmanship and the experience of bowhunting in an all-consuming drive to shoot big animals and then boast about it. The hunt itself is not the important thing to such people, so they often nail big animals any way they can. This leads to illegal activity and hard feelings with other bowhunters and the general public. There are no more rotten apples in the bowhunting fraternity than in any other sport, so there's no need to belabor my point. It's just unhealthy to hunt selectively for ego-boost reasons alone, and gives all selective bowhunters a bad name.

Many anti-hunters and nonhunters sneer at so-called ''trophy hunters'' because they think that ''stuffing'' an animal's head and hanging it on the wall is a grotesque practice. What these people fail to realize is the intense satisfaction a bowhunter gets when he looks at his mounted trophy and remembers the pleasurable experience he had hunting that animal. A mounted head is far more than a set of antlers or horns glued atop a tanned hide which is wrapped around a mannikin—it is a token of respect for the animal and the challenge it gave the bowhunter, a living monument to an animal taken in fair chase with a primitive hunting tool similar to the tools used for thousands of years by our ancestors.

A ground squirrel is not eligible for the record book, but it's a bonafide trophy if a bowhunter works long and hard to get a shot.

A good bowhunter can hunt selectively for one or more right reasons. For one thing, selective bowhunting is much more challenging than nonselective bowhunting—a selective bowhunter decides he wants to meet a particular challenge and not fill his tag with the first critter that comes strolling by.

It's a mistake to figure that selective bowhunting is always trophy hunting. For example, I once waged a full-blown bowhunting campaign with one cagey old ground squirrel that continually gave me the slip. Ground squirrels seldom weigh over 2 pounds, so they hardly qualify as trophies. However, that grizzled old veteran was smarter than any old buck deer I ever locked horns with—and he won. He lived in a big woodpile in the center of an open pasture, and I hunted him two springs and two summers before he finally disappeared, apparently a victim of old age.

Selective bowhunting is any kind of bowhunting which sets up an extra challenge for a bowhunter. Unless he's after a big-game animal with a monstrous rack of horns or an oversized

A bowhunter can increase his sport by switching from tree-stand hunting to hunting on his feet. He'll have a tougher time scoring on game, and enjoy the fringe benefit of watching animals through binoculars as they move about at long range. The bowhunter in the foreground is Joe Johnston, famous bowhunter and target champion.

skull, this challenge is strictly a personal one. A buddy of mine tried to kill a coyote with his bow for over five years, and when he finally called in a big, well-furred male and skewered it with an arrow, he was tickled pink—a lot happier than when he shot a record-book moose in Alaska. The coyote made no record lists, but gave him twenty times as much bowhunting satisfaction as his moose.

Sometimes selective bowhunting has absolutely nothing to do with the species hunted or the size of the animal taken, either. A bowhunter can simply change his hunting technique to increase his satisfaction, trying for animals by selecting a more difficult hunting method that really taxes his skills. My good friend and bowhunting partner Bob Smith is a challenge-oriented fellow who began this sport over twenty years ago by bowhunting out of tree stands. However, as time went by and Bob developed into a crack shot and a polished hunter, he became bored with waiting motionless in a tree till a deer wandered by, and also became bored with shooting animals at point-blank range. Bob decided to spice up his life by still-hunting deer instead of ambushing them from trees. He hunts on his hind legs exclusively today, still takes his buck every year, and thoroughly enjoys the increased challenge of sneaking and the thrill of taking animals at 30 or 40 yards instead of 10 or 15.

Challenge is one reason people take up bowhunting to begin with, and one reason experienced bowhunters become selective bowhunters. Another equally important reason for taking up bowhunting and eventually going the selective route is the satisfaction gained from spending a lot of time in the woods. A beginning bowhunter can enjoy long bow seasons in most parts of the country, seasons that double or triple his time afield if he loves hunting with a rifle too. An experienced bowhunter often becomes a selective bowhunter for the same basic reason—he can stretch out his time afield if he doesn't shoot the first legal animal he sees. For instance, I have access to some excellent bowhunting land in northern California, land where a good bowhunter could easily fill both his deer tags in a day or two. The only way I can spend a week or more in such a place and really enjoy myself is passing up all bucks that do not meet certain

Trophy hunting gives a bowhunter many extra days afield. The author passed up easy shots at dozens of lesser bucks before shooting this monstrous record blacktail. He hunted this smart old buck for 16 days straight before scoring with one well-placed shot at 35 yards. The animal is his best blacktail, and scored near the top of the record lists.

standards. Most of the trophy bowhunters around the country have a deep, abiding appreciation for their sport, the animals they hunt, and the great outdoors. They would feel cheated of the chance to really enjoy what they love doing most if they filled their game tags in a couple of days.

Selective bowhunting for trophy-sized animals is a thrilling sport, and one of the most challenging things a bowhunter can try. A whitetail buck or bull elk in his prime is a magnificent creature with gorgeous, wide-flung antlers that make any true hunter's pulse shift into high gear. Trophy bowhunting is a special challenge for two reasons: an oversized animal is tougher to find than an ordinary animal—which requires more searching before the actual hunt begins—and is generally warier and more hunter-proof than a younger, less mature specimen. Any deer that's survived five or six years of heavy hunting pressure has habits that helped him survive when other deer didn't, and it's quite likely that he's a bit smarter than younger animals, too. It's true that animals live and die in a few remote areas without ever seeing a hunter, and in these areas the biggest specimens may be just as easy to bump off as the smaller ones. Moose in the heart of British Columbia are a good example. However, a trophy moose hunter in the most remote part of this huge Canadian province still stacks the odds against himself as he looks for a bull with unusually large antlers. The shooting may be fairly easy if he finds his animal, but the looking may be incredibly tough. The bowhunter who sets his sights on a mature animal is doubling the challenge and giving himself many more days afield before he shoots an animal and ends his fun.

Many bowhunters do not hunt for trophy big game, preferring to set up another kind of selection system instead and try for a slippery animal like the coyote or use a more demanding bowhunting technique. And this can be just as difficult and just as satisfying as trying for animals with big horns. However, a great many bowhunters prefer some form of organized competition which lets them meet a special challenge while competing on a friendly basis with other bowhunters. For this reason, various record-keeping clubs have been organized across the country to keep tabs on extra-large big-game animals taken with bows. Most of these clubs honor both the bowhunter and the animal he has taken, which gives credit where credit is due for superior hunting achievement, and also immortalizes a remarkably large animal for posterity.

The king of the record-keeping clubs is the Pope & Young Club, which officially scores and records exceptional animals shot with a bow in North America. The Pope & Young Club was founded in 1958 by a few dedicated men who realized that bowhunters needed a special record-keeping organization to relate to and rally behind. The club has grown by leaps and bounds in recent years, and must be considered a resounding success by any standards. It maintains a continent-wide staff of official trophy measurers who carefully score all trophy antlers, horns, and skulls brought to them by bowhunters. It also upholds a strict set of fair-chase rules. For example, any animal shot with a bow when trapped in deep snow or chased by a motor vehicle cannot be officially recorded as a bow kill. Animals are scored under the same complex measuring system used by the famous Boone & Crockett Club, which records outstanding animals taken fairly by any means. Because of the extreme challenge bowhunting provides, Pope & Young minimum qualifying scores are about 25 to 30 percent below the minimum scores set by the Boone & Crockett Club. Animals that measure up compete for special awards during two-year scoring periods, and

A dedicated trophy bowhunter can spend lots of time afield, and he can also enjoy studying record books and dreaming of days to come. A rack of horns on the wall is a pleasant reminder of good days gone by.

these awards are presented at the Pope & Young Club's Bien-
nial Awards Banquet. In this fashion, bowhunters can compete
according to set scoring rules and greatly increase the challenge
of their sport.

Smaller state and local record-keeping organizations also
keep tabs on outstanding animals taken with a bow. Some of
these record special exotic species found in specific areas in
addition to native game animals. For example, the California
Bowmen Hunters organization records skull sizes of wild boar
taken in this state, and game preserves in Texas usually maintain
their own private record lists. Local tabulations of this kind give
bowhunters a good idea how big a big animal really is, and also
let them compete against themselves and others according to
standard rules.

All record-keeping systems are arbitrary to a certain extent.
For example, the scoring system used by the Boone & Crockett
Club and the Pope & Young Club favors symmetrical horns and
antlers with the same number of points on each side and points
of the same length on each side. Not everyone believes that a
trophy has to be symmetrical to be a fine one, but the conventional Pope & Young scoring system downgrades uneven racks,
anyway. Spread (horn or antler width) is important in scoring
deer by the Pope & Young system, but means very little when
pronghorn antelope are scored—which is both arbitrary and inconsistent. Record clubs are also arbitrary about which kinds
of animals they score. Boone & Crockett and Pope & Young
both ignore the coyote completely, for instance, although this
animal is far more difficult to hunt than most bigger animals.
These clubs measure the skulls of black bear, cougars, and other
hornless species, so it would seem logical to include the wary
coyote too. However, the coyote remains an unsung hero—an
arbitrary decision someone made years ago.

Record-keeping setups must be viewed realistically. They
are not God-given guidelines graven in tablets of stone, so they
are not perfect. However, they do give a bowhunter the option
of accepting the rules and competing on an equal footing with
other hunting bowmen. Every kind of formal competition is an
arbitrary test of skill—from backgammon to baseball to bow-

hunting—and the only decision a bowhunter has to make is whether or not he wants to play the officially recognized game.

I personally derive a great deal of satisfaction from spending days and days after one especially large animal, carefully sizing up his rack according to the rules prescribed by the Pope & Young Club and then doing my darnedest to lay him low with one well-placed arrow. If I win, I'm satisfied, and if the animal wins, I'm also satisfied. Either way, I enjoy practicing and improving my bowhunting skills, watching and learning about the animals, and drinking in the great out-of-doors.

In the final analysis, it really doesn't matter whether you set your sights on a world-record whitetail buck or go after one especially brainy ground squirrel. Either way you've become a selective bowhunter, a bowhunter with an exceptional degree of skill and the desire to become even better by limiting your killing capacity and expanding your time in the woods. When you finally reach this stage of the game, you can consider yourself a *complete bowhunter*.

INDEX

Page references to illustrations are printed in italics.